Accessible Gardening for People with Physical Disabilities

A Guide to Methods, Tools, and Plants

Janeen R. Adil

WOODBINE HOUSE   1994

Published by Woodbine House, 6510 Bells Mill Road, Bethesda, MD 20817. 800/843–7323.

Illustrations by: Carol P. Adil—pp. 5, 33, 109, 110, 112, 136 (bottom), 145, 157
Douglas Howard Adil—pp. 15, 16, 32
Phil Hocking—cover
Wendi Rose M. Kingsbauer—pp. 9, 31, 37, 49, 60, 76, 94, 97, 98, 104, 115, 131, 138, 141, 231, 247
Susan Ready McMath—pp. 55, 69, 72, 82, 238

Photos and slides courtesy of: Thomas S. Adil—pp. 248, 256, 260, 271 (bottom)
All-America Selections®—pp. 181, 183, 188, 189, 191
American Horticultural Therapy Association—pp. 41, 78, 117
Bancroft, Inc., a private non-profit agency with locations in Haddonfield and Mullica Hill, NJ, providing educational, vocational and residential programs to children and adults with developmental disabilities and traumatic brain injuries—pp. 30 (top), 160
Brookstone—pp. 124 (left), 127 (bottom), 148
Bureau of Veterans Affairs Hospital, Long Beach, CA (Jim Bradford)—p. 143
W. Atlee Burpee—pp. 73, 89, 99, 100, 143, 174, 178, 186, 216, 265, 266, 270
Danderyds Sjukhus, Sweden—pp. 7, 31 (bottom), 36, 45, 90, 114, 130 (bottom), 138, 162
The Garden Center of Greater Cleveland—p. 258
Gardener's Supply Company—18, 124 (right), 154, 156, 159 (center), 165
Handform® (H. Yonkers)—p. 125
HearthSong, Inc.—p. 130 (top)
Johnny's Selected Seeds—125 (bottom), 140 (bottom), 141, 176, 268
Kinsman Company—p. 137
Langenbach Tool Co.—pp. 128, 133 (top left & bottom), 147
J.E. Miller Nurseries, Inc.—pp. 224, 225, 226
George W. Park Seed Co., Inc.—p. 140 (top & center)
Garland W. Reedy—pp. 30 (bottom), 116
Rubbermaid®—pp. 46, 159 (top)
Fred Sammons Incorporated—pp. 127, 163
Smith & Hawken—p. 136
Solutions—pp. 133 (top right), 146, 159 (bottom)
Stokes Seeds, Inc.—pp. 262, 263

Library of Congress Cataloging-in-Publication Data

Adil, Janeen R.
    Accessible gardening for people with physical disabilities : a guide to methods, tools, and plants / Janeen R. Adil.
        p.   cm.
    Includes bibliographical references (p.   ) and index.
    ISBN 0–933149–56–5 (pbk.) : $16.95
    1. Gardening for the physically handicapped. I. Title.
SB457.4.H36A35 1994
635'.0240816–dc20   94–3548
                                                          CIP

Manufactured in the United States of America

10 9 8 7 6 5 4 3

TABLE OF CONTENTS

ACKNOWLEDGEMENTS
i

FOREWORD: How This Book Came To Be
iii

INTRODUCTION: The Hows and Whys of Gardening
v

CHAPTER ONE: Ground-Level Gardens, Raised Beds, and Planter Boxes
1

CHAPTER TWO: Gardening in a Variety of Containers
37

CHAPTER THREE: Vertical Gardening
87

CHAPTER FOUR: Tools, and Tips for Using Them
119

CHAPTER FIVE: Choosing Your Plants: Vegetables, Herbs, Flowers, Ornamental
Shrubs and Trees, and Fruit Bushes, Vines, and Trees
169

CHAPTER SIX: Plant Pests and Diseases
229

CHAPTER SEVEN: Children and Gardening
247

APPENDIX: Sources and Resources
287

INDEX
295

ACKNOWLEDGEMENTS

Many people have generously shared with me their time, resources, and knowledge. Among those I particularly want to thank are horticultural therapists Rachelle Malat, Nancy Stevenson, Bibby Moore, Jim Bradford, Diane Relf, and Marianne Soderstrom; Steve Davis, Executive Director of the American Horticultural Therapy Association; Professor Suman Singha at the University of Connecticut, for technical advice; the research staff at *Organic Gardening* magazine; LuAnne Schwarz, librarian at Atlanta Botanical Garden; Michele Addy of Burpee; Kathy Waite of Stark Bro's; Barbara McConnell of Hearth-Song; John Pepper for Rubbermaid; Meg Smith and Helen Rock of Gardener's Supply; Bill Funkhouser of Park; Barbara Kennedy of Johnny's; perennials expert Joanne Walkovic; Janet C. Stever, for artistic advice; gardener and friend Earl Foulkrod; my parents, Bev and Garland Reedy and my in-laws, Carol and Sey Adil for unearthing useful information; and Mary Beth Baker, for getting me started.

My editor, Susan Stokes, and her colleagues at Woodbine House, for their enthusiasm and good advice.

My husband, Tom, for his unflagging support, and my daughter, Rachael, for being my inspiration.

FOREWORD

How This Book Came To Be

In many ways, this book was begun at 2:10 a.m. on September 29, 1988, with the birth of my daughter, Rachael Elizabeth Adil. For it was at the moment of her delivery that my husband, Tom, and I were plunged into a new world, for which we had no preparation and little knowledge: Rachael Elizabeth, with her perfect features and rosebud mouth, also had a hole in her spine.

The following year Tom—knowing my great interest in plants and gardening—gave me for my birthday *The Complete Book of Gardening,* by Michael Wright. In it I found a chapter entitled "Aids for the Elderly and Handicapped," which I promptly read. We had begun to gather all the materials we could on disabilities in general and spina bifida in particular, to find out as much as we could about the "new world" we'd entered.

In search of more information on gardening and disabilities, I went through my own books, checked the selections at the bookstore, and scanned the shelves at the library. The few books I found were old, and British. American gardening books seemed uniformly silent on the subject.

With only a few sources to go on, I put together a short article, which was printed in the spring of 1990 in *The Hartford Courant.* I continued to collect tips, techniques, and suggestions. As my files grew, I decided it was time to make a long-term commitment to this project. The results are now in your hands, and are dedicated to you, the reader and gardener.

Wrote Francis Bacon some 400 years ago, "God Almighty first planted a garden; and, indeed, it is the purest of human pleasures." May this God-given pleasure be yours, to have and to share.

INTRODUCTION: The Hows and Whys of Gardening

Whether you've just purchased this book, are contemplating buying it for yourself or for your child, or have received a copy as a gift, one of two questions has doubtless occurred to you. If you or your child has never gardened before, I suspect you're wondering how someone with a physical disability can manage to maintain a garden. If you're already a gardener, I suspect you're wondering how, after the accident or illness that caused your physical disability, you can return to this activity.

Actually, there's one more question that may be lurking about: *Why* should I garden? It's bound to be too hard—too frustrating—not worth the effort. Other than producing a decent-tasting tomato, how could gardening possibly benefit me? After all, I have arthritis, MS, CP, spina bifida, paralysis. I'm too young. I'm too old.

With regard to the first two concerns, far be it from me to offer a flip or glib answer to the effect that *of course* you can garden! As this book is designed to show, gardening with a physical disability is possible. This holds true whether you use a wheelchair, walker, or cane; whether you have limited upper body strength or use of your arms; whether you have difficulty sitting, kneeling, or stooping; whether you're 5 or 55.

Gardening with a disability, however, also means that some "ordinary" gardening activities taken for granted by other gardeners are going to require adaptations and ingenuity on your part. As Michael Wright, editor of *The Complete Book of Gardening*, puts it, your "particular abilities and disabilities must be taken into account."

Glorya Hale, editor of *Source Book for the Disabled*, offers this observation: "When you have a physical disability gardening can be both immensely satisfying and frustrating." "The greatest satisfaction," she goes on to say, is "achieved by cutting out all work that is too demanding: gardening within your capacity—to the limit if you wish, but never beyond." The goal is to make gardening "as easy and effective as possible."

THE POWER OF PLANTS

Beyond Flowers and Fruit

As for *why* you should garden, I can suggest some rather compelling reasons. Simply put, working with plants satisfies both the body and the soul. Myriad benefits in terms of positive changes and personal growth are possible. For the gardener with a physical disability, four areas in particular—the physical, emotional/psychological, social, and intellectual—are targets for development. Gardening, then, goes beyond producing those good tomatoes: it also becomes a type of therapy, and a most pleasant one at that.

The therapeutic connection between people and plants has long been known. With systematic study and application, this ancient art of healing has become the profession of horticultural therapy. As an established area of study, horticultural therapy is a relative newcomer, established in the United States in 1973 by the American Horticultural Therapy Association. Today a number of schools across the country offer course work in Horticultural Therapy, with Kansas State University offering both undergraduate and graduate degrees.

Horticultural therapists work with people with a variety of needs, including those with all types of physical and mental disabilities; those in hospitals, schools, nursing homes, prisons, and substance abuse centers; and those from disadvantaged backgrounds. In each case the goal is to promote a person's physical and mental well-being through the use of gardens and plants.

From the Therapists Themselves

Many of the suggestions in this book come from horticultural therapists, to whom I am indebted for their ideas, research, and expertise. Following are comments from a few respected therapists, who share their views on the value of gardening for someone, of any age, who has a physical disability. Notice both the unique and the shared perspectives these statements reflect.

Just as the tremendous range of activities offered through the therapeutic medium of gardening is available to the professional horticultural therapist, so too is it directly available to the gardener.

Regardless of ability or disability, the pursuit of gardening can enhance physical condition, can provide relief from tension, and can surround an individual with the sense of accomplishment. There truly is not an individual among us who cannot experience renewal when embraced with the stimulation of the garden setting!

—Steven H. Davis, Executive Director, American Horticultural Therapy Association

Gardening provides us the opportunity and means to eliminate barriers and rewards us by stimulating all of our senses. This is done by growing our favorite vegetable, fruit, or plant. Gardening can be accomplished from either prone, sitting, or standing positions with the use of both hands or only one. Having a visual or hearing impairment does not prevent anyone from gardening. Gardening can be done indoors or outdoors and, best of all, is a year-round activity.

There is much fulfillment when a seed sown by your own hand germinates into a living thing and matures. Perhaps it will result in the harvest of a carrot or the growth of a beautiful flower. Either way, all of our senses and, most importantly, our feelings of accomplishment and self-esteem, are enriched.

Sow a seed and harvest many rewards.

—Rachelle J. Malat, HTM, Horticultural Therapist Bancroft, Inc., Mullica Hill, New Jersey

The essence of horticulture is action. Man as a gardener is active; he is working with plants doing things with them or to them to modify and enhance their growth. This action of man with plants brings about many of the therapeutic benefits of horticultural programs. One explanation for the positive response that man has to working with plants may be because it deals with life cycles, and most people make a ready translation between the life cycle of plants and their own human life cycle.

From being around plants, from observing their growth, man acquires an understanding of life and the rhythms that maintain it. From plants man derives a sense of 'dynamic stability through change.' Without continuous change, plants could not survive. A plant must flower in order to set seed; it must go dormant to survive the winter. There is a natural rhythm, a time and a season for all things, and nothing can be forced out of its natural order and still survive.

—Diane Relf, Ph.D., Extension Specialist Consumer Horticulture, Virginia Polytechnic Institute and State University Blacksburg, Virginia

Gardening is a common ground/denominator among people. The seeds you plant always repay you for giving them the chance to grow and fulfill their destiny. Many elderly patients see planting seeds as a way of extending their mortality. Things they are responsible for planting will live for years, to yield benefits to people who will remember them when they eat the fruits of the tree or vine, or see the beauty in the flowers and shrubs planted by a loved one. Disabled gardening is a beautiful use of time. The seeds you plant have an impact on your surroundings. You can control this aspect of your life, your environment, making it pleasurable for you; and the plants will assist in your recovery.

Plants have a very subtle way of thanking gardeners. They seem to know how to become a silent friend to the receptive. The other benefits include more obvious health aspects, like improving range of motion, strengthening, and endurance of muscles and joints through weeding and trimming or pruning. Any exercise that has dual benefits becomes less work and more fun. People of any age are intrigued by the power of a seed fulfilling its role with Mother Nature: watching life unfold in front of your eyes is heart-warming and reassuring.

—Jim Bradford Horticulture/Vocational Rehab. Therapist, Bureau of Veterans Affairs Hospital, Long Beach, California

Gardening can divert your thoughts about yourself and your situation. Instead, you can concentrate on taking care of the plants, watering and tending them. Very often patients have been taken care of over a long period of time; now they can take care and responsibility for something.

Gardening enables you to be out in the fresh air and at the same time train your muscles. Fine motor movements like planting seeds are developed, as well as larger muscle groups in larger movements, such as digging up a big area of land. Working in the gar-

den enables you to use practically all your muscles in your legs, back, arms, and hands.

Being outside in a garden stimulates all your senses. Your eyes are stimulated by the beauty of colors and shapes, and your ears by the sounds of the wind, bees, birds, and water. Your sense of smell will be stimulated by the different flowers, fruits, herbs, vegetables, and even the soil. Your taste—which is perhaps the most important—is stimulated by tasting your fruits and vegetables.

One of the benefits is intellectual training. You can study about gardening with the help of books all the year through. Gardening suits both male and female, old and young, tall and short.

The gardening can be done on a small scale on the balcony or even a window ledge, or on a larger scale in a garden. You can specialize within one field: herbs, for example, or alpine flowers, or growing seeds for selling or collecting.

Gardening can help you to continue being active and to create a new interest. The activity can consist of simply being out in the garden, enjoying the calmness of it. Gardening helps you use your physical, intellectual, and psychological qualities in a natural way. It can even have social benefits if you work together in a group.

—Marianne Soderstrom,
Chief Occupational Therapist,
Danderyds Hospital,
Rehabilitation Clinic Danderyd, Sweden

WHY GARDEN?: THE BENEFITS

The Physical Benefits

There are many physical benefits to be had from gardening. First, gardening includes such a range of activities that the various muscle groups can be readily exercised. Fine and gross motor skills are developed as the body is involved in movements that stretch and strengthen the muscles and joints. Improvements are also possible in coordination, stamina, and flexibility. Even the eyes can be exercised, as gardening gives the opportunity to practice seeing spatial relationships and hand-eye coordination.

Gardening also gives great pleasure and gratification through the senses. Think of all you can see, smell, touch, taste, and hear as you tend your plants! And as a final benefit, gardening done outdoors lets you enjoy fresh air and sunshine.

The Emotional/ Psychological Benefits

Another benefit possible from gardening is improved self-esteem. You can, for instance, enjoy a sense of pride in your accomplishments after planning and successfully completing a project. Success in the garden is easy to come by, too. It can be measured by as basic an act as planting a seed and having it germinate, to displaying a blue-ribbon plant at the county fair, or at any point in between.

Gardening can also help build your self-image. Because the plants in a garden are largely dependent on the gardener, you can enhance your self-confidence and independence by being responsible for their care. If you've been dependent on someone else for your own care, it can be very freeing to nurture someone—or something—else.

Gardening is a great stress-reducer as well, allowing you to release tensions and anxiety as you work. Physical activities like hoeing or weeding provide a healthy outlet for any feelings of anger or aggression you might have. As you become an active participant in nature through gardening—rather than a passive observer—you'll feel more connected to the natural world around you, which in turn enhances mental health.

Yet another emotional/psychological benefit of gardening is a feeling of enthusiasm, of interest and concern for the future. Planting a garden is really an act of faith, which is renewed daily as you look for the ways your plants have grown and changed. To garden can be to face each new day with eagerness. As the saying goes, "To live in expectation is to live!"

The Social Benefits

The National Gardening Association has estimated that about three-fourths of the households in the United States are involved in some form of gardening. This means that it should be very easy to find someone who shares an interest in this activity! Like the weather, gardening provides a neutral and common topic of conversation. Talking about plants can be a good ice-breaker, or a way to cement a friendship. And, if you don't already know the people who live near you, getting advice and comparing notes with your gardening neighbors is a wonderful way to get acquainted.

Actually, there's no telling where an involvement in gardening could lead you, or how it could benefit you as you interact with other people. You might find yourself taking or teaching an adult education, community college, or university class in some form of horticulture. You might train as a master gardener, or even a horticultural therapist, to share your expertise with others. You might join societies, which exist for enthusiasts of everything from orchids to chili peppers. You might start a community garden or one at the local school, or provide the local soup kitchen with produce. Or, you might write about your experiences!

The Intellectual Benefits

One of the joys of gardening is that you never stop learning. Even if you've been gardening your entire life, there's always something new and different, whether it's an interesting tip, technique, or plant to try. Gardening can sharpen your powers of observation and heighten your sense of curiosity, with the garden as an ideal spot to carry out all types of experiments. Remember that there's a wealth of literature on every aspect of gardening, just waiting to stimulate the intellect. Let your brain enjoy a workout, too!

As you learn and develop new skills, you may even see improvement in your abilities to solve problems and make decisions. Creativity can also be enhanced, through a heightened sense of the aesthetics involved in selecting plants, planning a garden, and using the harvest. And, it's entirely possible that the knowledge and skills gained from what began as a satisfying hobby could eventually lead to a vocation.

These physical, emotional/psychological, social, and intellectual benefits are described with the adult gardener in mind, although some naturally pertain to younger gardeners as well. There are, however, ways that gardening can specifically benefit children; these are discussed at the beginning of Chapter Seven.

BEFORE YOU BEGIN

First Things First

Before you even pick up a trowel, please, *talk with your doctor!* Let him or her know what kind of gardening you're planning to do, and how you intend to go about it. Showing him this book can be helpful, especially if your doctor isn't a gardener himself. Also check to be sure your tetanus vaccination is current, since tetanus can be contracted from any garden soil. (There are even cases on record of people getting tetanus from the soil in a window box.)

If you're taking any medications, you'll also need to talk with your pharmacist. Sunlight can cause adverse reactions with some medicines, and you may well be spending more time outdoors than usual as you begin gardening.

Finally, if you work with physical, occupational, or other types of therapists, get their feedback, too. They should have suggestions on ways that you can integrate gardening with your own particular program of therapies.

Once you're ready to actually start gardening, you'll need to take a few common sense precautions. While they're advisable from a health and safety standpoint, these measures will help ensure that your time spent gardening is pleasurable, too.

- Enlist the aid of a spouse, neighbor, relative, or friend, or hire someone to help with any project in this book that is beyond your abilities.

- Don't work during the heat of the day.

- Be sure to do any warm-up exercises such as muscle stretches that your doctor or therapist suggests.

- Consider sunscreen, a hat, sunglasses, and gloves as essential equipment when you head outdoors.

- If you don't already have one, an umbrella that clamps onto your wheelchair will provide extra shade.

- Bring plenty of drinking water with you.

- Use care when handling tools, fertilizers, and other gardening materials.

- Watch for signs of overexertion, skin breakdown, or pressure sores.

• Be careful with metal mobility aids, tools, and equipment that can get hot to the touch in the sun.

• Do your gardening in short sessions, and stop *before* you get tired!

SOURCES AND RESOURCES

The Catalogues

Have you ever read a magazine or newspaper article that advised you to look for a certain product or a special feature when you went shopping—and then didn't give you any particulars? No brand names mentioned, no stores suggested as places to buy this item, no manufacturers or distributors named. Did you still go searching for the product, or didn't you bother?

If you find this lack of detail as aggravating as I do, you'll understand why this book was designed to provide you with *specific,* accurate information and sources for gardening tools, supplies, seeds, plants, and more. To do this I combed more than 40 catalogues, looking for items that would be helpful to the gardener with a physical disability.

There are two main reasons why I decided to focus on products available through catalogues. The first is convenience. You may not live near a large, well-stocked nursery or garden center, or you may find it difficult to travel. But with a credit card and a telephone, purchasing an item from a catalogue becomes a quick and easy process. And to handle your questions, some companies have fellow gardeners staffing their phone lines, while others have a horticulturalist available to answer consumer queries.

Then there's selection, the sheer variety of items that may only be available through a company's catalogue. For instance, a display stand at the grocery store may feature 50 different kinds of flower and vegetable seeds. You'll have choices, certainly, but look in that same company's catalogue and you'll find *200* varieties!

And because catalogues do typically offer such a wide selection, perusing them can also introduce you to products you didn't know existed—from dibbles and oscillating hoes to soil

millers and worm composters. You can order the item right
from the catalogue, or, picture in hand, you can look for it at
your local store. You might even be inspired to create your
own, similar item.

Throughout this book, then, you'll find these specifics:
products and companies are named, prices are quoted, features are described. Instead of some vague advice suggesting
you "buy a long-handled hand tool," for example, in the chapter on tools you'll discover five different catalogue sources for
individual and sets of tools in many styles, lengths, and prices
(besides tips on making and adapting your own tools).

Many of the names you'll read will be familiar ones; these
companies have been in business for a long time. Others may
be new to you. After you've gathered some product ideas, you
can call or write for catalogues that carry the items that interest you most—addresses and phone numbers are in the Appendix.

Naturally you'll want to check a company's return policy
and any guarantees. While I've no reason to doubt the integ-
rity of any of these businesses, I can only share with you what
I've learned, as suggestions or recommendations.

I found it too cumbersome to list every company that carries each product discussed, along with purchasing options
like sale prices, "two-for" offers, and the various combinations
of sizes, sets, and all their prices. Instead, I've given the name
of one company (or sometimes more than one), plus a single,
rounded-off price that's reasonable for that item.

This information is accurate as of the companies' 1993
catalogues. The costs mentioned don't include shipping and
handling charges, or any taxes that might be applicable. Use
the prices as a general guide. If you can, comparison shop by
checking them against a local store's to be sure of getting the
most for your money.

UP CLOSE AND PERSONAL

One Gardener's Story

In the course of researching this book, I was privileged to have a number of long conversations about gardening with Earl Foulkrod, of South Williamsport, Pennsylvania. In his mid-60s, Earl is a life-long gardener, one who hasn't let cerebral palsy and sight impairments deter him from the activity he loves. A man brimming with good spirits and humor, he in many ways exemplifies the life-affirming attributes that come from caring for plants. During our talks Earl described his gardens, and shared with me his vision for others who garden with a physical disability.

Behind Earl's century-old house is his garden, which consists of a number of boxes of varying dimensions with paths between them. These raised bed boxes yield crops of all sorts, from tomatoes and zucchini to hot peppers and herbs. Vining plants are grown vertically on trellises and posts. Apple and peach trees, thornless blackberries, and very old peony bushes and grapevines round out the garden.

Earl's preferred manner of planting is the square-foot gardening method, as espoused by Mel Bartholemew in *Square Foot Gardening*. Here each type of plant is allotted a square foot of ground, with the size of the plant determining how many can be grown in that space. Sixteen carrots or onions, for example, can be grown in a square foot of ground, or four heads of lettuce, or one eggplant.

When possible, Earl likes to tend his plants from a seated position, using long-handled tools to work the beds. His is a mostly organic garden, with the insecticide Rotenone applied only if necessary. At harvest time Earl cuts as many crops as he can with clippers, then collects them in a handled wooden container that holds a half-dozen berry baskets. Vegetative debris goes in his composter, a plywood-and-hardware cloth bin with a gate. As a boy, he learned the basics of gardening from his grandmother. Now Earl stays up-to-date with gardening practices through catalogues, magazines, and television gardening shows. He loves to experiment, whether it's with plants, seeds, fertilizers, or methods he's devised to improve his garden. With Earl's "I'll try anything once" attitude, it's not surprising that he wishes for a farm, so he could test out all sorts of new plant varieties. Earl's latest idea, which he plans to try in this summer's garden, is to use an agricultural syringe to inject bug killer into a plant.

Not content to keep all his gardening know-how to himself, Earl started a program specifically for people who, like himself, garden with a disability. Naming the fledgling organization "Sod-Busters," he approached national gardening companies for donations of seeds and tools. Volunteers constructed raised beds on borrowed farm land, and in 1992 Sod-Busters was underway.

Despite the setback caused by vandals, which led him to relocate the garden behind his own home, Earl remains optimistic as to the program's success. While always on the lookout for more volunteers, donations, and participants, his vision expands beyond the boundaries of South Williamsport: Earl's dream is to make Sod-Busters a nationwide organization.

If you need a little encouragement to get your garden underway, keep Earl in mind as you read through the rest of this book. As he declares, "If I can garden, anyone can."

CHAPTER ONE

Ground-Level Gardens, Raised Beds, and Planter Boxes

Introduction

A long rectangular bed dug at ground level, planted with vegetables and maybe a few flowers, is probably the first thing most people think of when they hear the word "garden." At least in this country, a basic ground-level bed represents the very essence of a backyard garden.

A ground-level garden, however, presents special challenges for the gardener with a physical disability. For instance, the very soil can be out of reach from a seated or non-bending standing position. Standard garden tools can be too short, too long, too heavy. Mobility can be extremely difficult in and around the garden area. And harvesting inaccessible crops can be impossible. To make this garden more functional than frustrating will require some modifications for accessibility and safety. Depending on your physical capabilities, the changes could be as simple as establishing walking paths throughout the garden. Other modifications might be more complex, requiring the services of a landscape architect who specializes in accessibility design.

Given the extent of adaptations that may be necessary, beginning gardeners who have a physical disability will probably be less inclined to create a ground-level bed as a primary garden. Instead, raised beds, planter boxes, and containers are more likely choices for growing plants. By and large, these three types of gardens are more accommodating of a variety of abilities.

GARDENING IN A GROUND-LEVEL BED

Introduction

The premise of this section is that those most interested in ground-level gardening will be the gardeners who already have an established, flourishing plot, and who—by accident or illness—have had to change the way they tend their plants. The emphasis, then, of the following paragraphs is on adapting an *existing* ground-level bed to suit the gardener with a physical disability: no directions are given to create a new one. Since every situation is unique, focus on the ideas and suggestions that best pertain to your particular needs. (Should you want to dig a new, ground-level garden, read through the specifics on preparing a raised bed for advice.)

Paths and Ramps: Dimensions

The first accessibility requirement is a way to get from the house to the garden site. If mobility is a problem, a paved ramp or path is ideal, providing a firm, smooth surface for a wheelchair or walking aid. Care must be taken that the pathway is level and that the paving material allows for traction. A path that's slippery when wet or that allows rainwater to stand in puddles is an accident waiting to happen!

When there's a slope between the house and the garden, the gradient should be 1:20 or less; i.e., for every 20' of walkway, the path rises no more than 1'. This gradient of 5 percent may still be too steep for some, and if the pathway is long, level areas for resting may be required. A grade of no more than 3 percent (1:33.33) gives an even gentler slope, one that most wheelchair users should have no trouble negotiating. (For very steep slopes, you'll probably need the services of a contractor or landscape architect.)

The width of the ramp or path will depend on the user. Three feet, for example, is considered a minimum width for one-way traffic involving a wheelchair or walker, or for transporting a wheelbarrow. A four-foot width allows a wheelchair user to make a 90–degree turn without reversing. At five feet, the path is wide enough for a wheelchair to make a complete 180–degree turn, again without having to back up.

A few practical adaptations will enhance the safety and efficiency of the path or ramp. Laying out the walkway in a curved design rather than with sharp angles will make it easier to use. Edge guides will keep wheelchairs, crutches, canes, and so on from going off the side of the path. Strategically placed benches or chairs on the way to and in the garden itself make convenient spots for resting.

For the ambulatory gardener, hand rails—either single or double—are a good safety feature. Although it may be tempting to use the rails or supports as a growing spot for climbing plants, it's not advisable. Branches extending onto the path can impede progress or cause tripping. Vines along the railing can make a poor surface to grab onto if the need should suddenly arise.

Paths and Ramps: Surface Materials

What material is chosen for the path's surface is again dependent on who will be using it. Variables include cost of the material, cost of installation, upkeep, and aesthetics, as well as appropriateness for the user. All these factors must be weighed before making a decision, to ensure a choice that's best and safest for you the gardener. If at all possible, see if you can try walking on a surface material before committing time and money to its installation.

The following are some of your options, and include advice from the Chicago Botanic Garden and from the New York State College of Agriculture and Life Sciences at Cornell University.

• Packed soil is cheap and fine for a path—as long as it stays dry.

• Gravel is inexpensive and acceptable for paths as long as you're not trying to push feet or wheels through a thick layer. Loose gravel should be angular in shape instead of round, and contain "fines" so that it packs down. "Screenings," of ¼" size to dust, is a good and inexpensive material, as is decomposed granite of the same size.

• Crushed rock and river rock create a soft and irregular surface that's difficult to negotiate. Cobblestone and flagstone also make unacceptably irregular surfaces for anyone with a problem in mobility.

• Sandstone pavers are a handsome choice.

• Concrete is good but expensive, although maintenance costs are low. It needs to be textured or brushed to create a non-skid surface and reduce glare. The ramp can be laid on site, or precast paving slabs can be used. Interlocking concrete blocks are another option.

• Asphalt is also good but expensive; again, maintenance costs are low. This material absorbs heat, which in a hot climate may prove uncomfortable.

• Brick is attractive and can be a fine choice, but it's expensive and may be difficult to install. The wide joints of sand-laid brick can be a tripping hazard.

• Wood can be acceptable too for a path, although it may be slippery in wet weather. At the Berkshire Garden Center in Stockbridge, Massachusetts, a wooden ramp is covered with chicken wire to provide traction for wheelchair users.

• Woodchips don't make a suitable surface for wheelchairs and walking aids. Wood disks set in sand have wide joints that can be dangerous.

• Epoxy-bonded resin aggregate is yet another appropriate selection.

• Artificial turf and indoor-outdoor carpeting over a gravel base are also feasible.

• Grass paths usually aren't suitable for use with walking aids and wheelchairs.

Some of these surface materials will, of course, need to be installed by a professional contractor or landscaper. Whether you do the work yourself or hire someone else to do it, if your winters are cold, be sure the paths and ramps are installed over the proper foundations. Masonry, for instance, can be laid on a bed of sand instead of mortar to prevent heaving. Surfaces that buckle and crack aren't safe for anyone!

Paths and Ramps in the Garden

Now that you have a path and/or ramp to get *to* the garden site, you'll need a way to get around *in* it. This means more paths within the garden area itself. You may well want

Bordered by 2'-wide planting beds, this handsome and functional garden is laid out as a square-within-a-square. Edging defines and neatens the beds. The plants are easily reached from the wide paved area in the center, while the fence around the perimeter provides vertical growing space.

these to be of the same surface material as the pathway to the garden. Depending on economics or personal choice, however, a different material might be substituted.

Since there are many design possibilities for a garden with paths, explore your options by working out some ideas on a graph paper drawing. Here are just two examples of the way a ground-level garden could be designed to adapt to the needs of a gardener with a physical disability.

Here ground-level plantings combine with raised beds to create a pleasingly diverse gardening arrangement. Plants needing little care can be grown in the ground-level beds, while those requiring closer attention can be grown in the higher raised beds.

PLANTING AND GROWING TECHNIQUES

Garden Design

A ground-level garden is typically composed of long rows of plants. The gardener with a disability, however, will be better able to manage plants grouped in short rows or small blocks. Whether you're seated or standing, the plants will be easier to reach for tending and harvesting. Growing your crops upwards is also very helpful, so be sure to refer to the chapter on vertical gardening for information.

Planning your garden out on paper before you start planting is recommended not only for a ground-level bed, but also for any of the gardens described in the following sections.

Besides showing you how to make the most efficient use of available space, a plan on paper is a useful guide for the following growing season. You'll need to know what was planted where, because crops should never be grown in the same place two years in a row. Soil-borne diseases build up, and the amounts of available nutrients for the plants become unbalanced, unless crops are rotated around the garden from one season to the next. So don't rely on your memory—write it down!

Growing Potatoes

Potatoes merit a special mention. An excellent home-grown vegetable, they nevertheless require a degree of labor, first in the hilling and then in the harvesting. For a ground-level bed you may want to experiment with these methods instead.

• Set out seed potatoes one foot apart on a bed of a few inches of mulch or shredded leaves, or right on the soil. Cover them with 6, 8, or 12" of loose hay. Keep the hay moist, then when the tops die back, pull off the hay to harvest. Unfortunately, slugs can be a problem with this way of growing.

• Place the potato sections one foot apart on the garden soil. Use 18"–wide sturdy black plastic to cover them, securing the edges with dirt or garden staples. Cut an X in the plastic over each potato to let out the growing sprouts. This method was developed in England, where summers are cool, and is best for areas with similar weather—like the Pacific Northwest. In warmer spots the plastic will make the soil too hot for this vegetable.

• Set the potatoes one foot apart in a seaweed-filled trench that's 6" wide and 6" deep. Cover with more seaweed, about 4–6" worth. That's it until the potatoes are full-grown, when the seaweed is simply pulled off. An old-time Down East method, it makes for a clean, easy harvest.

Tools

Chapter Four is full of ideas on appropriate tools and techniques to use when working in a ground-level bed. For example, look for suggestions on low seats such as scoots, trikes, and kneelers. Useful tools include those with long handles and children's tools, and ones that extend your reach: hoes, spades, cultivators, weeders, bulb planters, gatherers, and more.

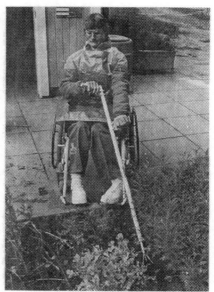

Tips include ways to slide seeds and seedlings down to the ground, and easier methods of watering, using drip irrigation systems of soaker hoses. Naturally, not every idea will be useful to every gardener, so read through this chapter carefully to see what might work for you.

GARDENING IN A RAISED BED

Introduction

The basic idea behind raised beds and other similar structures is that if you can't get down to the soil, make it come up to you! In other words, if you find that ground-level gardening is too difficult or even impossible to manage, *raise up* the level of the soil to a height that makes your garden accessible and thus easier to plant and tend.

In this section we'll look at raised beds and boxes as helpful alternatives to the traditional ground-level garden. You'll also find more alternatives to ground-level growing in the next chapter, Gardening in a Variety of Containers.

A raised bed is typically rectangular in shape, with the soil about 6–12" above ground level and encased in a framework of wood, stone, concrete, or brick. Used by our Colonial ancestors and dating back at least to the Middle Ages, raised beds offer a variety of benefits and advantages, both for the plants and for the gardener.

• Since there are no pathways to take up space, a raised bed can yield up to four times more than a comparably sized ground-level garden.

• Because the ground isn't walked on, it doesn't need to be heavily cultivated every year: the soil stays light and is easily worked and enriched. Drainage is also improved.

• A raised bed can be planted earlier in the spring since the soil thaws and warms more quickly than in a ground-level bed.

• If more than one raised bed is built, each can have a specific soil suitable to the plants grown in it. For instance, some varieties of heath (*Erica carnea*) can't tolerate lime; planting them in a separate bed of rich, peaty soil will let them thrive.

• Having two (or more) raised beds also means that one can be planted with spring and early summer crops, while the other can be for mid-summer to fall ones.

• As long as the plants' requirements for light are met, and yours for accessibility, a raised bed can be put anywhere within your landscaping design.

• Close planting crowds out most weeds and shades the soil, keeping it cooler. Healthy plants and fewer weeds mean less maintenance.

• A trellis can be easily added to a raised bed as an attractive and functional way to grow plants upwards. (See page 114 for details).

• Tending a raised bed can be done from a seated position; from a standing position, little bending is necessary.

• A raised bed can be short or long, low or high—whatever suits *you* best.

• A few hours' work—yours or from someone you hire—can be all that's needed to build a raised bed.

There are admittedly a few disadvantages to a raised bed gardening system: the bed dries out quickly; tall plants can grow out of reach; too much heat can damage plants; the frame may require upkeep. However, as you'll see below, there *are* ways you can offset or counteract these problems.

SITING YOUR RAISED BED

An Accessible Location

Given its structure, a raised bed should be considered at least semi-permanent, so think carefully about where it's to be located. Your first concern is access: where can the bed be sited so that you can reach it without difficulty?

If mobility is a concern, locating a raised bed close to the house will be particularly important. A patio area, with its flat, smooth surface, can be a good spot to build the bed, allowing easy access from your home to the garden. Keep in mind, though, that if your patio is already somewhat sun-baked, your new garden will be too. Note also that the soil in a raised bed can discolor a patio surface like concrete.

When located out in the yard, a framed raised bed can be an attractive addition to your landscaping. Here the only problem is keeping down the long grass along the frame's edge, where the mower can't reach. Besides the bother of frequent hand-trimming of this area, grass roots can grow under the frame and up, to make an unwanted appearance in the garden. Even more importantly, this area needs to be kept clear so you can easily reach the bed, particularly if you use a wheelchair, walker, or other aid.

One solution is to pull up all the grass for several inches (or even several feet) out from the base of the bed. Then either leave the ground bare; cover it with a material like finely crushed rock or peastones; plant a very low-growing groundcover like creeping thyme that can bounce back after being walked on; or lay down strips of indoor-outdoor carpeting or artificial turf.

Sun and Water

Your plants' needs for sunlight will, of course, depend on what types and varieties you choose, but generally speaking, they'll need about 6–8 hours of sun. See if you can plot the bed to run north to south: as the sun moves east to west, the plants will get an equal amount of direct light each day. In the South, though, gardeners who grow herbs will find that these plants do well with a little shade from the hot afternoon sun.

Your raised bed will need about one inch of water a week, whether from rainfall or from the tap. It's important, then, that the bed be near a water source, especially if you'll be watering by hand: you won't want to have to haul cans, buckets, and hoses for any real distance. Installing the hose bib (the fixture into which a hose is screwed) at a higher, more accessible height will help make your watering chores easier.

You can cut down on some of the watering to begin with by locating the bed in a spot with shelter from the wind. Since the prevailing winds will rob a raised bed of the moisture critical to its success, giving the garden some protection from the start can only save you time and effort.

DETERMINING ITS SIZE

Width and Height

Before you head out to the lumberyard to pick up materials, you'll need to do a little measuring. The size most often given for an accessible raised bed is 2' wide if it's worked from one side, or 4' wide if it's approachable from both sides. In *Raised Bed Gardening*, the horticultural therapists at Craig Hospital, Englewood, Colorado recommend the following more customized width measurements for the gardener with a physical disability.

First, extend your arm and measure from the armpit to your fingertips. Use this measurement for the bed's width if you'll be working from one side only. If you'll be working from two or more sides, then double it.

For example, with my reach of 28", a raised bed shouldn't be wider than 2' 4" for me to garden easily in it from one side. My raised bed could be up to 56" (4' 8") wide if it's approachable from both sides. Naturally, a narrower width is in order when fully extending your arms is painful or not possible.

As for the height, a raised bed of 6–12" high is suitable for many—but not all—gardeners. If you use walking aids, a wheelchair, or have difficulty with movements like kneeling and bending, this height can be just right. If, however, you also have difficulties with your arms, or you're tall, you'll probably do better with a bed 18", 24", or 30" high. (These taller structures I classify as planter boxes, and describe later in this chapter. See also ways to garden on a tabletop, pages 256–57 , and A-frame planters, pages 48–49.)

While you don't want your garden to be so close to the ground that it's awkward to work in, it's equally important that the bed not be so high that you're gardening "uphill." Any work done with your arms raised above a comfortable level will soon tire you out. The same work done when your arms are lowered will be much easier.

Seated gardeners can take a tip from the therapists at The Botanical Garden of The University of British Columbia in Vancouver. They suggest determining a garden's height by measuring 12" out from the chair, then letting your arm drop naturally. This "easy hand-drop" will show how high the raised bed (or planter box) should be so that you can work in it without straining to reach up or down, and without leaning precariously from the chair.

Finally, you'll also need to think whether you'll be approaching the raised bed to garden from a facing or sideways position, as this will help determine a comfortable working height. Depending on your physical abilities and limitations, one approach may be better for you than another.

Length and Depth

A maximum length of 10' for a raised bed is often recommended, for the simple reason that going back and forth along the bed, or around and around from one side to another, can quickly tire a person out. Better to conserve some of that energy for the gardening itself!

Actually, a raised bed can be as short or as long as you like—just bear in mind the aesthetics of the site, the type of plants you want to grow, and your own mobility. If you use a wheelchair or walker, allow at least a 3–foot area for clearance around the bed. For turning space between two or more beds, at least a 5–foot area is required.

The final measurement, depth, is of course determined by the raised bed's height. Different plants prefer different soil depths, as discussed below in "Choosing Your Plants."

SELECTING MATERIALS

Wood

Wood is probably the material of choice for most raised beds as it's relatively inexpensive, widely available, and easy to work with. As with all of the materials described here, various woods have definite advantages and disadvantages. You'll have to weigh these pros and cons for yourself before you embark on the project.

Naturally rot-resistant woods like Western red cedar, cypress, and redwood make excellent choices for a raised bed. They weather nicely to an attractive gray and are long-lasting; they are, however, not cheap. Black locust, red mulberry, and Osage orange are three other woods with very high decay resistance, but are only available in limited areas.

Railroad ties are often suggested for raised beds and are often used. Unfortunately, many are treated with creosote, which is harmful to humans and can kill plants. Also beware of wood treated with the toxic chemical pentachlorophenol (penta), another preservative that's damaging to humans. If you use railroad ties, then, be sure they haven't been treated.

Cheaper wood—like basic untreated pine—can be used, but it will need to be replaced in about 3–5 years. Lining the frame with thick black plastic will help extend its life. Applying a water-repellant product, however, won't keep the wood from decaying as long as it's in constant contact with the ground.

Pressure-Treated Wood

A tempting choice and one that's frequently recommended for raised beds is pressure-treated (CCA-treated) lumber: it's less expensive than woods like cedar and redwood, and it's made to last a long time. However, red flags are starting to go up concerning this material, with warnings that it isn't as safe to use as has been assumed.

The three elements that are used to make pressure-treated wood are chromium, copper, and arsenic. All three are very toxic to humans and to plants; the Environmental Protection Agency lists them as "priority pollutants." Even more disturbing is the fact that the EPA classifies arsenic and chromium as "human carcinogens."

It's already been established that plants can take up chromium, copper, and arsenic through their roots. What hasn't been determined, though, is either the rate at which the elements leach from the wood into the soil, or just how much is actually absorbed by the plants. To date, too little research has been done.

One study that has been undertaken, by both U.S. and Canadian government agencies, is a simple "wipe test" performed on playground structures made from pressure-treated wood. Using an ordinary piece of cloth to wipe the wood, researchers found all three elements present on the cloth.

Even those who might argue for the safety of this building material will doubtless agree that gloves and a dust mask should be worn when working with the wood. It's commonly known, moreover, by those familiar with pressure-treated wood, that it's hazardous to dispose of scraps or sawdust by burning since highly toxic fumes are released.

For more information, check out the July/August 1992 issue of *Organic Gardening* magazine, or contact the EPA Hotline at 1–800–424–9346. Until a final safety determination has been made, the wisest course of action seems to be to avoid using pressure-treated wood for any of your gardening projects, whether raised beds, compost bins, or various types of planters and planter boxes.

A Non-Toxic Wood Preservative

There are other alternatives for building a raised bed besides using naturally rot-resistant woods, untreated woods, or woods treated with toxic chemicals. One is making up your own *nontoxic* wood preservative, following a recipe developed by the United States Department of Agriculture's Forest Products Laboratory, and printed in the above-mentioned issue of *Organic Gardening*.

You'll need 3 cups of exterior varnish or 1½ cups of boiled linseed oil; 1 ounce of paraffin wax; and enough solvent (mineral spirits, paint thinner, or turpentine at room temperature) to make 1 full gallon of the mixture. Begin by melting the paraffin over water in a double boiler (never over a direct flame). While it melts, vigorously stir the solvent, then slowly pour in the melted paraffin. Stir in the varnish or linseed oil, and mix thoroughly.

Regular untreated wood can be dipped into this mixture for 3 minutes, or a heavy application applied using a brush. When the wood is thoroughly dry, it can be painted if you like. Tests show that this preservative will protect the wood for 20 years.

Building a Wood Frame

Once you've sorted through your options for a wood-framed raised bed and have decided that a trip to the lumberyard is in order, bring along a sketch of what you want to build (or have built), with the dimensions noted on it.

Your choices in lumber can include 2 x 6, 2 x 8, or 2 x 12 planks; 2 x 4's; plywood; logs; or 6"–wide boards. You might also need 12" strips for cleats; 2 x 4 stakes or 4 x 4 posts for stabilizing; or pieces of re-bar. If you think burrowing animals might be a problem, pick up some fine chicken mesh, too, to nail across the bottom of your frame. Finally, be sure to get a handful of galvanized nails, either 4d, 8d, 16d, or 18d, or some brass screws. And ask if you need advice!

Just two of the many ways possible to build a wooden raised bed frame are shown on pages 15 and 16. Note, though, that the illustrations and descriptions in this book for building your own raised bed, planter box, container, and so on aren't designed to be actual construction plans. They're

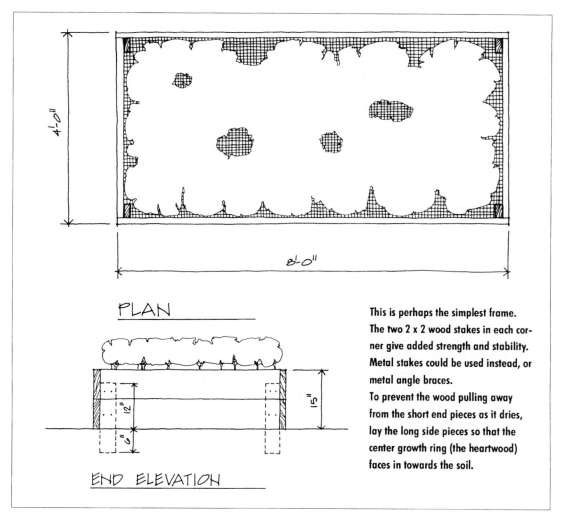

PLAN

END ELEVATION

This is perhaps the simplest frame. The two 2 x 2 wood stakes in each corner give added strength and stability. Metal stakes could be used instead, or metal angle braces.

To prevent the wood pulling away from the short end pieces as it dries, lay the long side pieces so that the center growth ring (the heartwood) faces in towards the soil.

meant to help you visualize some of the possibilities for these structures, and, I hope, give you some ideas for your own garden.

Stone

Stone is another material that, like wood, blends naturally into a landscape setting. Whether it's smooth, weathered rocks, rough-hewn chunks, or professionally cut blocks, stone has enduring good looks.

Since it's unlikely that after a year or two you'll be tearing down and moving a raised bed framed in stone, give a lot of thought to its location. You can do the work yourself, using either mortar or a dry-wall method to construct the frame, but it's a heavy, hard job. If you need to hire a contractor,

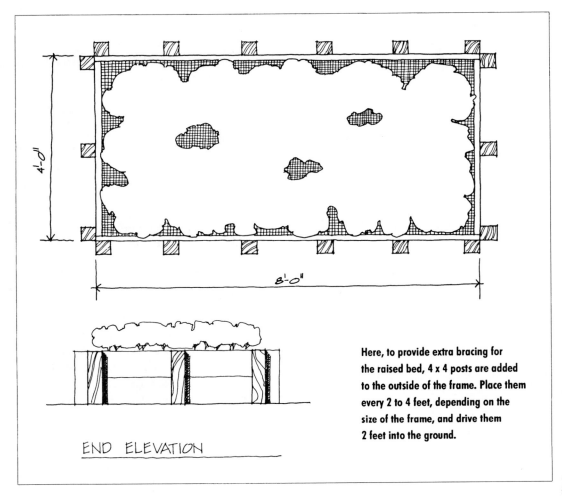

4'-0"

8'-0"

Here, to provide extra bracing for the raised bed, 4 x 4 posts are added to the outside of the frame. Place them every 2 to 4 feet, depending on the size of the frame, and drive them 2 feet into the ground.

END ELEVATION

plus buy the stone, you'll run into some money; on the other hand, if done right, it's a one-time investment.

A final consideration is the possible abrasiveness of the stones. If you have little or no sensation in, say, your lower legs, skin can be abraded by brushing against the rocks. You could choose another building material, or just be watchful of skin-stone contact.

Concrete

Concrete also makes a heavy, durable frame. Large paving slabs (sunk up to one foot into the ground), blocks, and poured concrete are all possibilities, but may well require the skills of a contractor. The surface can be brushed for textural interest; again, you might want to avoid an abrasive finish.

Although of dubious aesthetic quality, cinder blocks can make an acceptable frame for a raised bed. They're relatively

inexpensive, and even though cinder blocks are somewhat
weighty, they aren't too difficult to work with. Cinder blocks
make a fine raised bed for herbs in particular, as they release
lime for the plants and offer good drainage. Note that cracking may be a problem with hard winter frosts.

Brick

Brick in its variety of colors is a handsome choice for a
raised bed. Unless you have some experience yourself, you'll
probably need a brick-layer to properly handle this job. Add
this cost to the price of the bricks, and you'll have something
of an investment—but one that's attractive and very long-lasting. Used bricks, if available, will hold down the cost.
Whether new or used, though, be sure the bricks are suitable
for outdoor use.

Foundations and Footings

Unless your raised bed frame is of wood or cinder blocks,
you may well need some type of concrete foundation or footing that's poured into a trench dug around the perimeter of
the bed. The foundation will support the frame's weight and
prevent it from shifting.

In a cold climate, the footing will have to go below the
frost line. Depending on where you live, this could mean a
rather deep trench. Since the building advice that holds true
in Miami won't apply in Minneapolis, you'll do best talking
with a *local* contractor or builder before you begin the project.

Raised Bed Kits

Another option is to buy a raised bed kit, which you assemble yourself. Here are three different options.

In the Gardener's Supply Company's catalogue is a kit
consisting of brown PVC plastic planks that connect with self-
locking brackets; it's "easy to assemble." The 4' x 4' kit, with
4 planks and 4 corner posts, is $50.00. A 4' x 8' size is avail-
able, too, as well as side and corner extension kits to make
custom-designed shapes and sizes.

Add-ons for this raised bed include a root zone irrigation
kit with Netafim dripper line and connectors. The irrigation
kit for the 4' x 4' sized bed is $15.00. There's also a Season-Ex-
tending Tunnel Kit with hoops, polypropylene fabric, and
hardware, at $25.00 for the 4' x 4' size.

NovaWood products are made from 100 percent recycled
plastics that can be sawed and fastened like wood, but with-

A raised bed kit from Gardener's Supply

out the problems of splitting or rotting. A raised bed/sandbox kit of cedar-colored plastic provides 11 sq. ft. of planting space, and sells for $79.00. Other products include landscape ties, fence posts, and various sizes and shapes of planters. Contact Obex, Inc., Box 1253, Stamford, CT 06904, (203) 975–9094, for more information.

For very sturdy construction, try Allan Blocks. These concrete blocks are stackable—no mortar required—and come in standard, angle, and corner shapes. While designed as a retaining wall system, these blocks can also be used for a raised bed or planter box. More information is available through the Allan Block Corporation, 7400 Metro Boulevard, Suite 102, Edina, MN 55439, (800) 279–5309. You'll be referred to a local representative, who can provide details on pricing.

A Final Bit of Advice

As you decide on a material to use to build a raised bed frame (or planter box), remember that the narrower the frame, the closer you'll be able to get to the soil and plants. The difference between a 2" lumber edging and a foot-wide rock wall is especially important to keep in mind if you're gardening from a wheelchair.

PREPARING THE SITE

Excavating

If the raised bed will be constructed in an existing garden, preparing the site can be done with little difficulty. Begin by digging a 2"-deep trench to match the size and shape of your frame. Mound up the soil in the center of the area, then position the frame in the trench. Add various amendments like compost, peat, fertilizer, decayed leaves, etc. to the mounded soil, mixing well. Finally, rake the bed smooth.

A new raised bed site will require a little more work. First, stake out the area you've chosen, then pick up the phone. As the power companies remind us, call before you dig, to avoid any unpleasant contact between your shovel and a cable. When you have a go-ahead, begin excavating the site.

(If you have the time to wait, however, let black plastic do some of the work for you. Cover the new site with the plastic, anchored securely. In four weeks or less the grass and weeds will be dead, and the soil will be easier to dig.)

First, use a spade to define the bed's borders, slicing straight down to form perpendicular sides. Then pull out all the grass and weeds, along with their roots. You'll want to save the topsoil, though, so shake off as much as you can before tossing the plant material aside. Next, with a spading fork or rototiller, turn over the soil as deeply as you can to a depth of at least 5–6", or preferably 10–12".

Double-Digging

While certainly not required, for the very best results you might want to double-dig the bed. Double-digging, a rigorous method of preparing the ground, involves working two layers of soil, each the depth of a spade's blade, about 10". Widely used in England, this technique has helped the British produce the gardens for which they are so justly famous.

If you're interested in the "proper" way to create a double-dug bed, British author/editor Michael Wright describes and illustrates the technique in *The Complete Book of Gardening*. What follows here is a somewhat easier method.

Begin as above, but remove the top 10–12" of soil from the bed and pile it alongside the excavation. (The soil can be shoveled onto a tarp.) Now loosen the next 10–12" of soil by thrusting a spading fork or spade into the dirt and jiggling or rocking the handle back and forth. Work over the whole bed this way, loosening the soil about every 6" or so, to produce a modified version of the double-dug bed.

PREPARING THE SOIL

Your Soil's PH Level

After you've turned the soil, whether for a single- or double-dug bed, you should test its pH level to see how acid or alkaline the soil is. A scale of 1–14 is used to measure the pH, with 7 being neutral. Thus, if the pH level is below 7, the soil is acid; above 7, the soil is alkaline.

Knowing what type of soil you'll be working with will help you determine the correct fertilizers and soil amendments to use. For example, if the pH level is 7.5 and you want to grow blueberries, you'll need to add organic materials or chemicals to change this alkaline soil to the more acid soil that blueberries need to thrive.

Most garden plants and vegetables prefer a soil that's between slightly acidic and neutral, with a pH level of 6.0–7.0 or 7.5. Potatoes are one exception, preferring a more acidic soil. If your raised bed is to be an herb garden, these plants will do best if lime is added to the soil, for a pH of 7 or a bit above. For other, specific plants, read the seed catalogue; ask before you buy at the garden center; or consult a good general reference book on gardening.

Testing Your Soil

Testing is simple to do, in one of two ways. An inexpensive soil-sample kit can be purchased from the hardware store, nursery, or garden center. Following the directions, strips of treated paper are dipped in a dirt-and-water solution. You then match the resulting color of the paper strip to a color-coded and numbered scale to determine the pH level of your soil.

While a do-it-yourself test kit is reasonably accurate, you might prefer results from a professional laboratory. If so, contact your local Agricultural Extension Service office to find out how to send them a sample of your soil. The Extension Service will provide you with a detailed analysis of your soil for a small cost.

Be advised, though, that if you wait to send them the sample in mid-spring, it may take several weeks to get the results: gardeners keep these folks very busy! Doing it early in the season (say, February) will help ensure that you get the analysis back in time for spring planting.

Once you've tested your soil, decide if you need to raise or lower the pH level. If the soil is acid, add ground limestone to raise the pH. If the soil is alkaline, add aged cow manure, ground sulphur, or iron sulfate to lower the pH level. Follow the specific recommendations from the kit or the Extension Service as to how much of each material to use, and when it should be applied. The testing can be repeated in 6 months, with more soil amendments added if necessary.

Framing the Bed

Finally, after you've dug the bed and taken a soil analysis, you're ready to put the frame into place. If the soil you've turned over is still in the bed, rake it into a mound in the center. Alternately, you can remove the soil to a tarp, which might make it easier to work on the frame. Then proceed as planned with the stone, concrete, or brick frame, which of course will need to be constructed on the site.

If you're using wood to surround the raised bed, first build the frame, then put it into place over the bed. Use a 3' level to check the frame, adding or removing dirt underneath it as needed to make it level.

Making a Good Soil Mix

When the frame is securely in the bed, you can start putting the soil back in. First, mix the topsoil you removed from the bed with aged manure, rotted sawdust or leaves, or compost—and don't skimp on the amounts. Other soil amendments like peat, fertilizer, and moisture "crystals" (see p. 152) can be added too. (Of course, if you left the topsoil in the bed, then dump in the manure or compost and mix it right there.)

Next shovel this new mixture into the bed, which will raise the soil level by several inches. To raise it higher, to about 8–10", additional topsoil—purchased in bags or dug from another site—can be mixed in too.

Now use an iron-pronged garden rake to smooth and level the soil, breaking up any clods and removing large stones. For a 5' x 10' bed, sprinkle 1 pound (2 cups) of a general fertilizer like 8–8–8, 10–10–10, or 5–10–10 over the bed. Rake it into the soil down to a depth of about 2", and give the bed a good soaking.

If you have enough patience, now let your new raised bed "rest" for 2 weeks. The soil will have time to settle, and the bacteria in the dirt can begin working on the organic materi-

als that were added to the soil, converting them into food for
your plants.

All this digging, shoveling, and mixing can be a challenge; for the gardener with a physical disability, it may be too
much. Here's where it can make perfect sense to hire someone, a person who can get the laborious part of the job out of
the way so you can begin planting—and enjoying—your
raised bed.

CHOOSING YOUR PLANTS

Preferred Soil Depths

A large range of annual flowers, bulbs, and herbs (except-
ing mint) can be grown in a raised bed at a soil depth of 6–8".
The following vegetables are also appropriate for this depth:
lettuce, shorter carrots, onions, leeks, beets, spinach, garlic,
radishes, peas, kohlrabi, turnips, parsley, okra, strawberries,
mustard greens, Swiss chard, cucumbers, and watermelon.

An 8–10" depth is good for corn, squash, peppers, pole
and bush beans, broccoli, kale, Brussels sprouts, cabbage, melons, longer carrots, pumpkins, eggplant, Chinese cabbage,
mint, and cauliflower. At 10–12" you can plant parsnips, tomatoes, and peanuts. For deeper-rooted vegetables like salsify,
sweet potatoes, and Irish potatoes, you'll need a soil depth of
1–2'.

Perennial flowers can be grown too in a raised bed if they
have a rich soil of about a 10" depth. Because the soil in a
raised bed—and thus the roots of the perennials—are more
exposed to cold winter temperatures, however, there is the
risk of damage or loss of these plants. And, without the blan-
keting protection of surrounding ground-level soil, perennials
can also be damaged by alternate periods of freezing and thaw-
ing. Selecting cold-tolerant plants, using thick mulches, and
sheltering the bed from the north wind will all help protect
these flowers.

These recommended soil depths, by the way, shouldn't be considered hard-and-fast rules, but rather general guidelines. Use them to help you distinguish between shorter-rooted and longer-rooted types of plants. And remember that experimentation can bring unexpected rewards in the garden!

When and What to Plant

If yours will be a spring garden, you can begin planting it 8 weeks or so before the last expected frost for your area. A summer garden can be planted about a week after your last expected frost, and a fall garden can be put in about 10 weeks before your first expected frost.

For specific varieties of plants to grow, see Chapter Five, Choosing Your Plants. There I discuss a wealth of vegetables, herbs, and flowers that are especially recommended for the gardener with a physical disability. These plants include both compact growers that are easier to reach from a seated position, and taller plants that are good for growing vertically, to reach from a standing position. I'm sure you'll find plants described here that are ideal for what you envision growing in your new raised bed.

PLANTING A RAISED BED

Wide-Row Planting

The preferred technique for planting a raised bed is called wide-row planting. Equally effective for a ground-level bed, wide-row planting involves sowing seeds or setting out transplants in broad bands (small blocks), as opposed to a straight, narrow row. Because the plants are spaced more closely together, weeds are crowded out and the soil is shaded, thus reducing water loss through evaporation. More abundant crops are yet another advantage to planting in wide rows instead of single ones.

Plants in a wide row will ideally be equidistant from each other. When mature, their leaves will touch but the plants won't be so close as to be crowded. If your garden plants must compete for available space, soil nutrients, water, and sun, they'll show their unhappiness with poor growth, susceptibility to disease, and fewer crops. Certainly no gardener sets out with *that* as a goal!

Spacing Your Plants

To make the best use of space, and to save you from making mistakes in planting, first sit down with a pencil and some graph paper. Using the information provided on the seed packet, pot label, or in a gardening reference book, see what measurement is given as the recommended distance to allow between plants. Peppers, for instance, are usually planted 18–24" apart.

Use the smaller of the 2 numbers (18") as your guide to planting the peppers closely but without crowding. Then plot out on paper how you'll arrange the wide rows to make maximum use of your gardening area. Since each section will probably be in the shape of a rectangle or square, your final garden plan may form a neat geometric pattern.

If you want to put in more than two rows of those peppers—or any other plants—you'll most efficiently use the available space by staggering the rows. The peppers in every other row, then, will be between the peppers in the row next to it.

Visualize dropping cookie dough on a baking sheet. You probably don't put three spoonfuls of dough in each row, but instead make a row of three, then a row of two, then a row of three, and so on. This way you can fit more of the cookies—or peppers—in the same space.

Sowing Seeds

Once you've decided where each plant is to grow, it's time to get your garden underway. Sowing seeds in a wide row can be done in one of two ways. The first is to carefully plant individual seeds at equal distances from each other. A rake, drawn both vertically and horizontally across the bed, can be used to create a type of grid for sowing the seeds. A multi-dibble or planting board can be used instead, as described on page 138.

Although it's more time-consuming initially to place the seeds precisely, you'll be compensated later when the job of thinning has been eliminated. When you want to make certain that a seed will sprout in a particular spot, you can plant 2 seeds together, about ½" apart. Then, if both germinate, either gently pull one out or snip it off at ground level. If this sounds wasteful, remember that seeds, after all, are the cheapest part of gardening.

The alternate method to sowing seeds in a wide row is to scatter them over a square or rectangle of soil that has been raked smooth. Then either rake a little more dirt over them or broadcast it by the handful. Pat the seeds into their bed with your hand or the back of a tool, then water carefully. Thinning is a must with this technique since the seed has been sown thickly.

Besides pulling and snipping, thinning can also be accomplished by pulling a rake across the bed. Some seeds and seedlings will be wasted in the sowing and thinning, but again, the loss is negligible.

Setting Out Plants

If you're starting with transplants, spacing them at an equal distance from each other is easily done: just use a grid design or a ruler to measure off the distances. Set the individual plants—either knocked out of their containers or still in their original pots—on the soil to make sure you have the proper spacing, then plant them according to your pattern.

INTENSIVE PLANTING TECHNIQUES

Your raised bed, planted by the wide-row method, has just become an intensive garden (sometimes referred to as planted by the French intensive method); that is, the plants are closely spaced for high yield and high production.

Now you may want to investigate the methods of interplanting, succession planting, companion planting, and vertical growing to increase your yields and keep your garden fully productive. Careful planning will be the key to success with these various planting techniques. For a good resource book on growing a lot of vegetables in a small space, consult *Square Foot Gardening* by Mel Bartholomew.

Interplanting

Interplanting is an ancient technique for growing more than one crop at a time in the same garden space. A classic example is the Native American arrangement of the Three Sisters: corn, beans, and squash. Winter squash (or pumpkins) are planted in the corn patch between the rows of corn, while pole beans climb up the stalks. Three crops are then produced from just one planting area.

Other examples of interplanting involve radishes and lettuce. Quick-maturing radishes are often planted in the same row as a slower-maturing vegetable like parsnips. The radishes are ready to harvest before the parsnips need the space to expand, and as a benefit, this early crop has helped loosen the ground for the steadily growing, later one.

Lettuce, which prefers cooler weather, is also frequently interplanted. During the hot summer months when lettuce benefits from some shade, the greens can be planted below a tall grower like broccoli, corn, or tomatoes.

Succession Planting

Succession planting is another way to keep your garden productive. Here a new crop is planted as soon as an old one is ready to be pulled up and put in the composter. After the harvest of spring peas is over, for instance, don't leave that spot of earth unfilled: plant something in it—zucchini, perhaps—for summer and fall harvests.

As a variation, a crop can even be planted before the old one is done. The zucchini seeds can be planted right between the rows of still-producing peas, thus gaining several weeks' growing time. In areas where growing seasons are short, this technique is particularly handy for crops that are slower to mature, like peppers and tomatoes.

Companion Planting

Adherents of companion planting say that when grown together, certain combinations of plants benefit from their mutual association. Herbs are often used with vegetables both to enhance growth and flavor, and to repel specific insect pests: tomatoes, basil, and marigolds are one such grouping.

While there isn't complete agreement on the effectiveness of companion planting, researching the topic and experimenting in your own garden may well bring positive results. A few suggested combinations are described in the section on pests and pest controls in Chapter Six.

Vertical Growing

A final technique, vertical growing, is another way to save gardening space while producing high crop yields. It is described more fully in Chapter Three.

CARING FOR A RAISED BED

Water

Your first concern for maintaining a successful raised bed is making sure the plants get adequate water. Your garden needs about one inch of water a week to grow and thrive. If you don't get that amount from regular rainfalls, give the bed a thorough but gentle soaking with a hose or watering can.

Be sure to feel the soil with your hand to check for dryness and dampness, since judging by appearance alone can be deceptive. Moreover, the leaves of the closely spaced, mature plants can act like umbrellas, keeping moisture away from the ground. This means that even after a rainfall, parts of the bed could still be under-watered, so use your hands to check.

Mulching, as described on pages 149–51, is a good way to reduce the need for frequent waterings. Besides helping to keep moisture in the soil, mulches cool the soil and deter weeds, too. An organic mulch will also feed the soil, and thus your plants, as it breaks down.

Fertilizing

Fertilizing can be done throughout the spring and summer with a general fertilizer like 10–10–5. A granular type is easy to use: simply sprinkle it on the soil every other week and water it in. Check the package directions for the proper amount to use.

Maintenance

A raised bed garden tends to require less maintenance than a ground-level garden, giving you more time to enjoy the fruits of your labors. Do, however, keep any weeds pulled, spent flowers removed, and any wayward branches pruned back, not just for appearance's sake, but for the health of your garden.

To conserve warmth and so extend the growing season, polyethylene can be stretched over the frame in the fall. (Spread it over metal or plastic hoops, or tack it to side boards you've added to the frame.) Once the season is over, remove the dead stalks, leaves, etc. to the composter. Mulch any perennials, protect any trees against winter damage (talk to a horticulturalist at the local garden center or nursery, or check a gardening reference book for specifics), and dig some compost into the soil.

Next spring, remove the mulches after the danger of frost has passed. The soil in the raised bed will have settled over the winter, so top it off with some fresh dirt. As you turn over the soil—notice how easy this job is now!—work in a good portion of compost. If you then continue to supply the bed with compost over this second growing season, you probably won't need to add fertilizer.

Finally, rake the bed smooth. Consult your graph paper planting chart from the previous year to help you plan out your new garden, and you'll be ready to begin again.

Special Tips for Perennials

Joanne Walkovic, past president and co-founder of The Hardy Plant Society, Mid-Atlantic Group, gave me these suggestions for growing and caring for perennials in a raised bed or planter box. First, she recommends selecting only "reasonable-care" plants, and matching them carefully with your microclimate (that is, the climate in your particular spot, as opposed to that of a whole area).

"Put the right plant in the right place to begin with," she told me, to increase your chances for success. Focusing on native varieties, varieties derived from native plants, and varieties from places with a similar climate will help ensure that your perennial garden gets off to a good start.

Note that there's always room for experimentation, however. Joanne has a thriving passionflower vine growing outside her Pennsylvania home. Normally hardy only in warm climates, this vine gets winter protection and warmth from a kitchen wall, and heat from the nearby blacktopped driveway. Tender perennials, of course, can be overwintered in a greenhouse or other protected spot if you don't want to try them outdoors on a year-round basis.

Joanne grows her perennials in 9' x 12', 10" high raised beds. Every year she tops the beds off with compost, and every spring she literally lifts up her plants and adds more soil around them. The raised beds save the perennials from the wet conditions that can do them in. "Winter wet," she points out, causes more plant losses than any other problem.

When cold weather hits, covering the plants with evergreen branches to protect them is often recommended. Not all of Joanne's perennials receive a winter mulch, however.

She reserves her Christmas tree boughs for the newer and smaller plants only.

To protect the roots from excessive cold, Joanne passed along a tip she came across in her reading: line the sides of a raised bed or planter box with styrofoam. Styrofoam's insulating properties are, of course, widely used in a variety of ways, to guard materials from extremes of cold or heat. It should come as no surprise then that gardeners are taking advantage of this material, too!

GARDENING IN A PLANTER BOX

Introduction

A raised bed, at 6–12" high, won't be the answer for every gardener with a physical disability. To make the garden accessible, a height of 18–30" may be required instead. While still a raised bed in every respect, for the sake of distinction I term this taller structure a planter box.

The advice given above for siting a raised bed also applies to a planter box. Since it's even more likely that this bigger structure will be fairly permanent, its location must be very carefully considered.

Although a rectangular shape is perhaps the most common, a planter box can be constructed in a square, a circle, a triangle, an oval, an "L," or a "T" shape. When more than one box is built, pleasing arrangements of various designs can be incorporated into the landscape. Also, if the shape permits it, a cap or border for sitting is especially nice on a planter box and can be quite helpful to the gardener.

DETERMINING ITS SIZE

A Personal Fit

The size of a planter box, as of a raised bed, depends on your personal situation. Again, the width shouldn't be more than 2' if the garden is worked from one side only, or 4' if it can be approached from both sides. For a more customized

width, follow the directions on page 11 for measuring your reach.

The height of a planter box, as suggested by the Craig Hospital horticultural therapists, is determined by the degree of your physical involvement. Heights of 18", 24", and 30" are all possible for a gardener with either temporary or permanent lower body involvement, or with temporary upper body involvement. The gardener with permanent lower and upper body involvement will have greater success with boxes that are 24" and 30" high, or with table-top gardens.

BUILDING A PLANTER BOX

Building Basics

The materials used for framing a raised bed—wood, stone, concrete, and brick—are equally suitable for building a planter box. Foundations and footings will be especially important for these larger structures. Also, if the planter box is built on a paved area like a patio, weep holes to carry off excess water will need to be installed at the base of the planter box. While still possible for the do-it-yourselfer, constructing a planter box may well require the services of a professional carpenter, mason, or contractor.

Special Modifications

Various modifications of the basic planter box will help make the garden as accessible and manageable as possible for the gardener with a physical disability. As with a raised bed, for instance, the hose bib should be installed at a greater height to make it easier to reach. Likewise, to cut down on watering chores, perforated pipes can be installed in the planter box. Watering is then easily accomplished via a basic on/off valve. This will of course add to the construction costs, but save you time and labor for as long as you continue gardening.

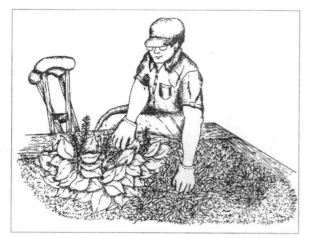

An edge for sitting can be another helpful feature that's easily added to a planter box. Use it for resting, as a place to lay down tools, or, if you're able to comfortably turn your torso, you can work from a sideways position. A 1 x 4 section of deck lumber—with edges rounded and nailed across the top edge of a wood box—makes a functional seat. Flagstones can also be used for a shelf/seat on boxes with a broader edge to the frame.

Yet another useful design modification is to create a toe space around the planter box. Having this extra room for your feet will allow you to more easily and comfortably reach the bed for gardening, and is especially advantageous for the gardener working from a wheelchair.

One way to make a toe space is to angle the planter box's sides inwards, instead of building them at a 90–degree angle to the ground, i.e., straight up and down. Or, as the University of British Columbia therapists suggest, a planter box can be constructed to have a recessed space of 8" in and 8–12" high along the bottom. For safety's sake, the help of a professional is recommended for both of these designs.

A planter box with toe space.

The gardening experts at the University of Bath, England, have devised two more ways to make gardening in a planter box even easier. D-shaped handles from the hardware store can be affixed to the top edge or along the sides of a wood or brick box. A gardener can grasp the handle with one hand for support while working with the other hand. The researchers also suggest installing "leaning posts" along the front edge of the planter box. By leaning into the corner made by the post and the box, the gardener has both hands free to work.

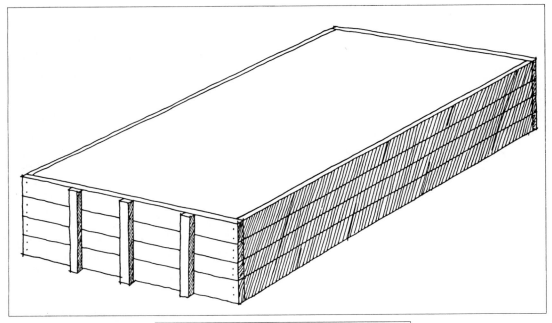

Cleats strengthen this frame. A planter box longer than 4′ should have the additional support provided by buttressing, as spaced at 4′ intervals.

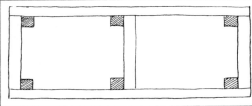

Left, a 2 x 4 placed horizontally will prevent the sides of the box from bending outwards.

Creative Designs

Creative designs are possible with the planter boxes, for both practical and aesthetic reasons. These are but three of the many ways to change the look of a basic planter box.

• An attractive variation on a brick planter box is to include planting holes here and there throughout the pattern, every two or three courses down. These small holes are the size of a header, or end, of a brick, and not only break up a solid expanse of brick, but also allow more room for planting.

• A stone planter box can be similarly designed, with a soil mix used instead of mortar. Occasional planting holes are created in the wall, with the opening bridged by the stone in the course above it.

• For growing plants vertically, a trellis can be easily added to a planter box, as described on page 114.

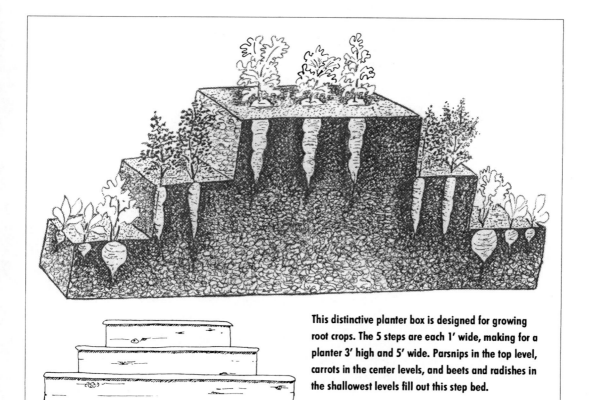

This distinctive planter box is designed for growing root crops. The 5 steps are each 1' wide, making for a planter 3' high and 5' wide. Parsnips in the top level, carrots in the center levels, and beets and radishes in the shallowest levels fill out this step bed.

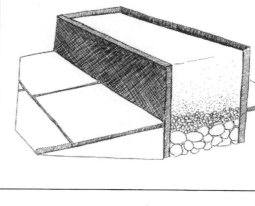

Here a two-step bed—ideal against a south wall—is designed for growing heat-loving vegetables. Eggplants and peppers are in the front row, with tomatoes in the back on a supporting trellis. The bottom step is 1' high, the top one is 2' high, and each bed is 15" wide.

Concrete or stone paving slabs are braced against the end of a paved area such as a patio. Hardcore is packed behind the slab to hold it in place vertically; smaller stones and soil then fill the bed.

On pages 32–33 are a few designs for planter boxes, in both basic and innovative shapes.

FILLING A PLANTER BOX

Drainage

To improve drainage, a planter box that's 2' high or taller can be one-third filled with gravel, crushed rock, broken bricks, or a mix of broken concrete and stones. This drainage layer has the added benefit of reducing the ultimate amount of soil you'll need to fill the planter box.

British gardening writers at this point make a very good suggestion that I have yet to come across elsewhere. After putting in the drainage material, these writers advise adding a layer on top of it made of sections of sod, laid upside down—that is, grass downwards. The drainage layer and sod layer together can account for about half the depth of the planter box, which is then filled up with soil.

These reversed sods (or turves, as the British call them, which is a plural form of "turf") have three important functions. They do an excellent job of retaining water, let the excess water drip through slowly, and prevent the top layer of soil from sifting into the drainage material and then clogging it. As you excavate the site for your new planter box, consider cutting out the blocks of turf and laying them aside for just this use.

Soil

The soil used to fill a planter box can be as basic as two parts good, well-draining garden soil mixed with one part composted leaves, peat, or compost. This soil is suitable for perennials, small shrubs, and most bedding plants. Another "formula" is to mix equal parts garden soil, peat moss, or compost to lighten the soil, and clean builder's sand to improve drainage. A cup of 5–10–5 fertilizer can be mixed in for each 5 gallons of mixture, or a slow-release fertilizer can be added instead.

If making up a batch of amended soil for your planter box will pose difficulties, you can use any commercial brand of soil labelled "planter mix." While not an inexpensive way to fill up the box—especially if it's a large one—remember that the soil is only topped off each year, not replaced completely.

Finally, be sure to test your soil's pH level to determine how alkaline or acid it is, as outlined above. Doing so, and then following the recommendations for specific soil amendments, will help get your new garden off to a good start.

PLANTING AND CARING FOR A PLANTER BOX

Selecting Plants

Whereas the depth of a raised bed will determine what plants can be successfully grown in it, the deeper planter box garden affords more options in vegetables, flowers, herbs, and other plants. One class of plants in particular—the alpines—is ideally suited to planter box growing, since the boxes provide the excellent drainage these special plants demand.

From an aesthetic standpoint consider including some of the various trailing plants, especially if your planter box is made of concrete slabs. Plants cascading over the edge are useful for breaking up the somewhat stark lines of this type of bed.

Note that the taller the planter box, the more important it will be to select smaller and shorter plants, to keep them within an easy and accessible reach. Again, be sure to read over Chapter Five for ideas on suitable plants, including dwarf and miniature varieties.

Maintenance

The recommendations for first planning your garden out on paper also apply to planter boxes. Then follow the suggestions in the section on raised bed gardening for wide-row intensive planting, and the various techniques to further increase crop yields.

Water, fertilize, groom, prune, and harvest throughout the growing season as weather conditions and plant growth indicate. Later, when frosts dictate an end to blossoms and fruit, remove dead vegetation and apply mulch, if needed. Work

some compost into the soil now, and again next spring as you make ready to start your next gardening season.

CHAPTER TWO

Gardening in a Variety of Containers

Introduction

Gardening in containers is an old idea that continues to increase in popularity with both novice and experienced gardeners alike. Growing plants in pots, barrels, baskets, and boxes has a wide appeal among a diverse population, for container gardening has much to recommend it.

• This method of growing plants is as appropriate for urban residents with no land of their own as for those in rural areas, who can use containers either instead of or in addition to a backyard garden.

• Since you either buy a commercially prepared planting mix or make up your own preparation, the various problems of no soil, poor soil, and soil-borne diseases are all eliminated.

• Containers of plants can be readily moved from one spot to another, to take advantage of the changing patterns of sun and shade. They can also go with you if you move to a new home.

• From a preschooler with one potted marigold to an octogenarian with a full range of vegetable plants, container gardening is possible and fun for all ages.

• Almost any flower, herb, or vegetable can be grown—or at least attempted—in a container. Many fruits, shrubs, and trees can also be grown in pots, to expand your choices even further.

• Seeing how different plants can be combined for the best practical and aesthetic results encourages a gardener to be creative. A carefully planted container can truly be a work of art!

• Experimentation is encouraged too, as a gardener may be more likely to try out a new crop in a small pot rather than devote a section of the regular garden to the experiment. A gardener who's never grown radicchio, for example, might plant a few seeds in a container to see what happens.

• Experimenting with a crop or flowering plant that normally isn't suited to your area is another possibility. A far-Northern gardener might be able to muster enough warmth for a heat-loving plant like okra, say, if it's planted in a container. The pot can be moved close to the house, where reflected heat from the walls could spell the difference between a gardening success and a failure.

• Since virtually anything that holds soil can be used as a container for planting, start-up costs are kept to a minimum. While an elegant $200 terracotta urn from Italy might set off your plants to perfection, a 5–gallon olive oil can brimming with herbs has its own, vastly cheaper, charm. Shopping for containers in various sizes and shapes can be an interesting activity, but suitable pots are probably already around your house and garage, just waiting to be "discovered."

• Because they're usually located close to the house, container gardens invite everyone to "stop and smell the roses." These gardens encourage sensory contacts of touch, feel, and sight, and simple puttering. They also tend to require less maintenance—and *far* less weeding—than a ground-level garden.

• The wide array of pots, boxes, and so on that can be used for growing plants can help create exciting and attractive focal points around your home, and greatly enhance its landscape design.

• Finally, for the gardener with a physical disability, growing plants in containers has special advantages in addition to the ones described above. Because there is great flexibility in the size, shape, and placement of a container, this type of gardening is quite adjustable to an individual's needs. Whether you garden from a standing or seated position, you can arrange the containers at a height and in a grouping that makes them totally accessible for *you*.

SITING YOUR CONTAINER GARDEN

Adaptable Locations

When it comes to locating your garden, you'll find that container gardening is wonderfully adaptable to just about any situation you have to offer. The various types of containers can be placed on patios and porches, on rooftops and balconies, along a drive or walkway, next to the front door or out on the deck, on a windowsill or under it, hung in the air, or sunk into the ground.

Sunlight

You'll need to think about how much sunlight these different locations receive. Generally speaking, your plants will need either full sun, or at least 6 hours a day. If you're growing vegetables, they'll prefer 8 to 10 hours of sunlight daily. Areas that are in part or full shade don't have to be neglected, however, as there are many plants that would thrive in just such spots.

Keep in mind that you can have some control over the amount of sunlight your plants will receive. If you can put the containers on casters, dollies, or group them in a child's wagon or a cart, they can be moved to follow the sun or shade. If this isn't feasible or is too difficult physically, just be sure to match the plants' light requirements with your particular environment as you make your selections of what to grow.

If you do place your containers near a wall and in full sun, keep them about 1½' away from the wall. Air needs to move around the plants, plus the reflected heat from the wall must be able to dissipate or else your plants could end up "cooked."

Water

Water is an equally important requirement for your container garden, which will probably need frequent waterings. You'll want to locate your container garden near a water source since you'll likely be doing at least some if not all of the watering by hand. Wrestling with hoses and heavy watering cans can be difficult, to say the least, so remember that you'll be responsible for somehow supplying that all-important moisture.

It's for the same reason, then, that a few large planters are preferable to 25 smaller ones: they won't dry out as fast. Watering lots of small pots may not seem like such a chore at first, but as the season wears on and your plants are demanding daily—or more—waterings, you may well regret the decision to put each plant in its own container. You'll save yourself both time and energy if you're watering a few containers as opposed to many.

Sizes

In terms of accessibility, the Horticultural Therapy Department of the Chicago Botanic Garden recommends a container height of around 2' (or 20–28") if you'll be gardening from a wheelchair or other seat, or if bending over is a problem. Two feet is also an average reach from a seated position, so a container shouldn't be more than 4' in either width or diameter. If your planter is backed up to a wall, or if you'll be gardening from just one side of it, keep the width at 2'.

CHOOSING YOUR CONTAINERS

A Variety of Materials and Styles

Let's begin by looking at your choices of materials for homemade or purchased containers: clay, plastic, wood, metal, concrete, stone—there's something for every taste and budget! Each material has its special advantages and uses, so you can match your container with the planting project you have in mind. And even if a container isn't itself suitable for planting, it can always be used as a cachepot for a separately potted plant.

Clay

Clay, first off, is a classic choice for containers. Good-looking pots are available in every range from thumb-sized to one big enough to hold a small tree. Styles include something as basic as a standard pot with a rolled lip, to an ornate urn, to a strawberry jar that's both functional and pretty when potted up with either berries or herbs.

Clay containers can be purchased either unadorned, with decorative details added, or glazed. Their heavier weight means they're less likely to tip over or be blown over in a high wind. The term terra cotta, by the way, is often used interchangeably with clay in referring to a planting container. Technically, however, it describes a pot made in Italy of terra cotta clay, as opposed to one made of American clay. Look for words like "Italian Clay" or "Da Roma" on the bottom of the pot if you're searching for a true terra cotta. These containers are thicker than clay pots made in this country and can be more durable, as well as a little more expensive. For most purposes, however, a standard clay pot is fine.

Like any material, clay has its disadvantages too. The main problem is that because of its porous nature, containers made of unglazed clay dry out quickly, especially the smaller-sized pots. Daily watering can be necessary; watering twice a day is not unheard of. Also, clay pots can chip and crack, and need to be put away in a sheltered spot during cold winter weather.

Larger Clay Containers

For a different look in clay, try flue tiles or drainage pipes. Available from construction suppliers, these containers come in many sizes at generally reasonable prices. They're durable, long-lasting, attractive, and can withstand winter exposure. Tiles and pipes not only make good above-ground planters, but the smaller sizes are also useful sunk into the ground to contain rampant growers like mint.

Note that flue tiles and drainage pipes are very heavy. When filled with soil, a weight in the hundreds of pounds is possible. Their very sturdiness can be a boon for the gardener with a physical disability. You can lean against a container as you work, or use it as a prop should you lose your balance and begin to fall. If the garden will be on a balcony or roof top, however, be quite sure that the structure will be able to support this weight.

Unusual things can happen when a plant is given more than a minimum depth for growth in a container. As recorded on a PBS "Victory Garden" segment, some British gardeners found that a parsnip planted in a flue-tile pot rather exceeded their expectations for length. After a few hours of maneuvering to gently wrest this giant from the soil, the men were finally able to record the parsnip's size—just under 4' long!

Plastic

Plastic containers are often a good alternative to clay. They can be bought inexpensively and come in a wide range of colors, sizes, and shapes. Handsome plastic pots made to *look* like clay can be a fine compromise between these two materials. A discarded tree container from the local nursery will also provide sturdy support for your plants, as will 3–gallon containers from restaurants and ice cream shops. And, although they're rather less than glamorous, plastic items like laundry baskets, garbage cans, pails, dishpans, foam ice chests, wastebaskets, and buckets can be pressed into service as planting containers, too. Just be sure to make drainage holes in them, as described later in this chapter.

A Chicago gardener has an unusual use for another type of plastic container. For winter growing in her basement, she fills a child's wading pool with rich soil and puts it in a spot where the flowers and vegetables that fill this container garden get sun all day long. The yields, she reports, are "surprising."

Plastic containers of any type have both advantages and disadvantages. Because they're lightweight, larger plastic containers can be moved more easily than similar pots made of heavier materials. They won't, however, offer the same stability and durability. Since plastic isn't a porous material, plants in these containers don't need watering as often as those in clay ones, which is certainly an advantage. Because the pots *aren't* porous, though, care must be taken not to overwater the plants.

Wood

Containers made of wood blend nicely and naturally into the landscape. Half whiskey barrels are widely available at garden centers for under $20.00 and make good, sturdy planters.

Whole barrels, with planting holes cut into the sides, are useful too. Or, for a nice rustic look, try using a hollowed-out log as a planting container.

Large planters popular for use on a deck include square, rectangular, and octagon shapes; some have matching benches and other furniture pieces. Planters to suspend on or over a deck railing, and window boxes, are also commonly made of wood. Cedar, cypress, pine, redwood, and imported hardwoods are most frequently used for these various types of containers because they hold up well to exposure from all kinds of weather.

Less expensive choices in wooden containers include bushel baskets, crates, and boxes from the grocery store, and cheese boxes from a gourmet shop. These containers won't last too long, but since they're usually readily available, replacing them shouldn't pose much of a problem.

Homemade planters and containers are most often made of wood, in a great array of designs and shapes. Some ideas for building your own are described on page 47.

Metal

The most commonly used metal containers are wire hanging baskets and frame-type planters to hang on a house. A construction of welded steel with a heavy plastic coating gives these containers durability and an attractive appearance. Naturally, the best-built pieces will give the greatest service, but lighter, cheaper ones are also functional.

Other types of metal containers include aluminum window boxes, and even metal buckets and washtubs. And, as mentioned above, a large, decorative can like one holding olive oil can be cleaned out and used to plant a few herbs, flowers, or a single small vegetable. Fifty-five-gallon drums are sometimes suggested too for planters, but since they so often store potentially harmful materials I can only urge caution with their use.

Concrete

Besides the ubiquitous clay pot, many garden centers also carry various urns and containers made of concrete. Preformed concrete objects such as sewer pipe from a construction supplier are another possibility. While obviously sturdy, the weight of concrete containers can be either a plus or a minus. Common cinder blocks and builder's bricks can also be used as small planters, with the hollow center filled with herbs, alpine flowers, or sempervivums.

Stone

British gardening books often mention old stone sinks as being excellent containers for planting alpines, conifers, rock plants, and so on. Should you happen upon one, or have access to one, be advised of its gardening potential! Stoneware crocks, on the other hand, are more easily found. They make good-looking containers but lack drainage holes, making a bottom drainage layer a necessity.

Wicker

Wicker baskets make graceful containers, but need to have a liner of tin or plastic in which drainage holes have been punched. Since excess water seeping through the holes will eventually rot the wicker, choose an expendable basket to plant up, not an antique one.

Cardboard

The cardboard box has the obvious advantage of being easily procured at no cost, and the obvious disadvantage of a short lifespan. Line it with sturdy plastic before adding the soil.

Tires and Wheels

Using old tires for a container garden may not appeal to everyone's aesthetic sense, but they have produced some successful results. The tires—painted with latex paint if desired—can be stacked at whatever height is most accessible for the child or adult gardener. By placing three or more columns of tires in a curved formation, with the center column being the tallest, a crescent-shaped garden can be created for an interesting effect.

Even discarded car wheels, painted or plain, can be recycled for use as a container garden. Fill the bottom half of the wheel with gravel, and then add soil.

An unusual way to plant potatoes is to set them in at ground level, each plant surrounded by an old tire. Then, as the potato plants grow, they are "hilled" by stacking more tires atop the first and shoveling in soil, to about a four-tire height. Results are said to be quite good.

There's a special benefit to growing potatoes in any type of container, by the way. Whether you're using tires, a plastic or burlap bag of soil, a bucket, bushel basket, or tub, the potatoes are harvested by upending the container rather than digging them out of the ground. This way the spuds remain undamaged, with nary a stab mark from your garden fork.

Planting Bags

Planting bags, or pillow packs, are a way to grow flowers, vegetables, and herbs right in a bag. The easiest method is to simply use an unopened bag of soilless planting mix. Alternately, you can fill a heavy plastic garbage bag with planting mix and close it securely with a twist-tie. Lay the bag on its side for use with smaller plants, or prop it upright for larger ones. Then cut X's into it for the plants or seeds, and a few slits on the bottom for drainage.

The bags can be laid out on a table or other firm surface at any suitable height, and can also be squashed a bit if needed to conform to an oddly shaped area. If small, the planting bags can also be portable, as demonstrated by the use a clever Arizona gardener found for them. She plants flowers in gallon-size bags, then occasionally brings them indoors— with the bag hidden in a bowl or basket—for a pretty, living centerpiece.

Smaller-sized vegetables, herbs, and flowers are good candidates for this type of container gardening, although tomatoes will also do well if provided some sort of stake or trellis as support. Then, when the harvest is done, the used soil mixture makes a fine mulch.

Natural Fibers

Natural fiber containers have been used in the nursery trade for a number of years. Made of recycled paper fiber, with wax and resins added for waterproofing, the containers are light and strong. Unlike plastic, the fiber "breathes," so roots grow well and have some insulation from heat and cold. These containers last for several seasons, and are then completely biodegradable. Shepherd's Garden Seeds carries the containers in sets of various shapes and sizes, including hanging baskets. Prices range from $15.00–35.00 per set of 3 to 10 containers.

Self-Watering Containers

A self-watering planter can be very helpful in reducing the need for the frequent waterings typically required in container growing. Gardener's Supply says their model will keep your plants watered for a month, or even more. The plastic hanging pot has a reservoir holding 2½ cups of water, and costs $13.00.

Solutions also carries self-watering hanging baskets. Plants draw up water by capillary action from the reservoir at the bottom of the pot. This plastic planter, selling for $10.00, comes with a hanging chain.

For a large container garden to set on a porch, patio, or indoors, try Rubbermaid's Anywhere Garden™ Container. Wicking material in the bottom of the one-gallon reservoir draws water up to the plants' roots. Suitable for vegetables, flowers, and herbs, this container has a detachable saucer. A trellis kit is also available, to expand your gardening options. The trellis retails for $9.00, and the container for $18.00.

The Anywhere Garden™ Container from Rubbermaid.

CONTAINERS AND PLANTING BOXES TO BUILD

Woodworking Projects

Many designs are available for homemade planting containers, which you can either make yourself or have someone make for you. Look for ideas in the Sunset and Ortho book series, or in woodworking books from the library. Remember that the dimensions given in the plans are suggested sizes only. Adapt the boxes and containers to suit your space requirements, and, especially, your own range of motion, to keep them entirely accessible.

Refer back to page 43 for suggestions on choosing the wood for your projects.Then, once you've selected the wood, you'll need rustproof hardware to go with it. Look for items in stainless steel, brass, and aluminum alloy to help you create a more durable product. Since nails can work loose over time, use wood screws to hold the boards together, which can be countersunk and plugged if you want a more finished look.

A FEW OPTIONS IN CONTAINER GARDEN DESIGN

Usual and Unusual Options

As stated at the beginning of this chapter, your container garden can be set up in just about any accessible location. If you want to expand your options, however, consider the following different garden designs. Since the proportions of each garden are quite flexible, they're adaptable to each gardener's particular needs for sitting, standing, and reaching. Of course, there's probably no end to the interesting designs a creative gardener can devise!

A Garden on Shelves

Take a few cement blocks (or stacks of bricks, or sawhorses) and some 2 x 4's, and you have the makings for a simple shelving system for your container garden. The blocks can be upright or on their sides; used singly or in multiples; in whole-block or half-block forms, with a pair of boards laid across them to form shelves or benches. Containers of all sorts, and planting bags, rest right on the shelves. Any number of configurations and shapes are possible, as are a variety of lengths and heights. While not particularly elegant, a shelf garden is inexpensive and easy to put together, to rearrange, and to disassemble. A smaller version might be just right for putting a child's container garden within an accessible reach. Whether for you or a child, however, be sure the blocks are level and stable, to prevent any tipping accidents.

Pole-and-Post Gardens

Jack Kramer, author of *Easy Gardening,* calls pole-and-post gardens a "no-bend kind of gardening." Indeed, these special arrangements of plants are meant to be built at eye or waist level, both for looks and for ease in care.

To create a pole-and-post garden, sink a 4 x 4 post into the ground, with a concrete footing for stability, or else anchor it to a wooden deck with L-shaped brackets. Then bolt a pot with a bottom drainage hole on top of the post. An arrangement of three to five posts of varying heights makes a dramatic "floating garden." The pots can be planted with annual or perennial flowers, herbs, and/or vegetables; cascading and trailing plants are particularly effective.

Tiered Gardens

A variation on this pole-and-post garden is a tiered garden. Clip-on pot hangers will let you hang standard clay pots on the sides of the pole—just don't overload the post. Or, you can make or buy a similar sturdy post but with four wooden feet firmly attached. (Imagine a coat rack without the hangers.) Again, suspend pots up and down the post. Note that this type of garden will dry out quickly, and should have some protection from the wind.

A-Frame Planter Stand

The A-frame planter stand is a wonderful design for either an adult or a child with a physical disability. If you'll be sitting while gardening, the frame can be built low enough to allow a few inches' clearance over the knees so a wheelchair or other seat can be brought right up to the planting box. If you'll be standing, a higher frame will offer you some support to hold onto while you work.

The planting box, which should be about 8" deep, offers a nice-sized growing area for a variety of flowers, vegetables,

and herbs. Attaching hanging baskets to the top of the stand is an attractive way to increase your growing space. Vining plants can be added too, in containers set on the ground on either side of the A-frame. Let them climb up the frame, or string a trellis to the top support bar.

Suggested materials for constructing this planter stand are pine 2 x 4's for the frame, and construction-grade plywood for the planting box. Phillips wood screws and metal sawhorse clamps will securely hold the stand together. Be sure to drill ¼" drainage holes in the planting box, which can be lined with heavy plastic in which holes have been punched. If you don't want to plant right in the box, you could instead use it to hold a variety of plants growing in their own containers.

Just as with any other form or type of gardening, however, the A-frame planter stand—like a table-top garden—isn't right for everyone. When gardening from a seated position, for instance, the box (or table) must be high enough for you to get your knees underneath it. This in turn means that you'll be working with your hands and arms raised. If you have limited upper body strength and mobility, this position may well be too difficult and tiring.

CHOOSING YOUR CONTAINERS: SIZES AND SHAPES

Containers for Vegetables

To help make growing vegetables in containers a successful venture, use the chart below to determine what size pot you will need for each variety. The information comes from the Burpee and Park seed companies, who were referring to standard-sized plants. If you select from the miniature and dwarf varieties discussed in Chapter Six, you can adjust the size of container needed. The one basic guideline is to choose a pot that will allow for good, sturdy root development.

Although the capacity of different pots varies with their thickness and style, these measurements in diameter and depth will help you determine their size. A 1–gallon container measures about 7" in diameter x 6" in depth; a 2–gallon is 8" x 8"; a 3–gallon is 10" x 10"; a 4–gallon is 12" x 11"; a 5–gallon is 12" x 12"; and a 6–gallon is 13" x 13".

For some of the following vegetables, alternative numbers and sizes are indicated within brackets; this additional information has been gathered from various other sources. I offer these other size suggestions not to confuse the potential container gardener, but rather to show the flexibility inherent in this type of gardening. Experiment, experiment!

number of plants per size of container

artichokes	1 plant per 3–gallon container
beans, bush	5–6 / 3 gal. [minimum 2 gal.]
beans, pole	NA [min. 10 gal.]
beets	4–5 / 8–10" diameter container [up to 24 / 10 gal.]
broccoli	1 / 1 gal. [min. 10" deep]
Brussels sprouts	1 / 3 gal. [min. 10" deep]
cabbage	1 / 1 gal. [3 / 10 gal.; any container at least 8–10" deep]
cabbage, Chinese	[8–10" deep]
carrots	5–6 / 1½ gal. [min. 6" deep for short carrots or min. 12" deep for long ones]
cauliflower	1 / 1 gal. [min. 10" deep]
celery	NA
collards	4–5 / 3 gal.

corn	6 / 15 gal.
	[min. 10 gal., but 15–20 gal. better; at least 5 plants per container for pollination]
cucumbers	2–3 / 3 gal.
	[1 / 3–5 gal.]
eggplant	1 / 3 gal.
	[1 / 4–5 gal.]
escarole	8–10 / 3 gal.
garlic	6–8 / 1½ gal.
kale	1–2 / 1½ gal.
	[8–10" deep]
kohlrabi	2 / 3 gal.
	[min. 6" deep]
leeks	5–6 / 3 gal.
lettuce, head	1 / 4" dia. container
	[1 / 2 gal., or 3 / 10 gal.; min. 4" deep]
lettuce, leaf	6–8 / 1½ gal.
	[min. 4" deep; use as edging for containers holding other crops]
melons	1–2 / 5 gal.
mustard greens	8–10 / 3 gal.
	[6–10" deep]
okra	3 / 3 gal.
onions (plants)	5–6 / 3 gal.
onions (sets)	10–12 / 1½ gal.
	[any size container if it's large enough for mature bulbs]
onions, spring	[6–8" deep; ½ gal.]
parsnips	6–8 / 1 ½ gal.
	[min. 12" deep]
peanuts	3–4 / 3 gal.
peas	15 / 15 gal.
	[min. 10 gal.]
peppers	1 / 3 gal.
	[min. 8" deep]

potatoes, Irish	4–5 / 1½ gal. [2 seed pieces / 5 gal. or larger]
potatoes, sweet	3–4 / 3 gal. [min. 12" deep and 15" wide with center 4' stake]
pumpkins	2 / 3 gal.
radishes	10–12 / 8" dia. container [up to 36 / 10 gal.; min. 4" deep for small radishes, or 6–10" deep for long ones]
romaine	8–10 / 2–3 gal.
salsify	[min. 12" deep]
spinach	6–8 / 3 gal. [3 / 2 gal.; at least 7 / 10 gal.]
squash, summer	3–4 / 5 gal. [1 / 5 gal.]
squash, winter	3–4 / 3 gal.
strawberries	4 / 3 gal.
"summer" spinach	4–6 / 3 gal.
Swiss chard	6–8 / 2–3 gal. [min. 6–8" deep]
tomatoes	1 / 3 gal. [1 / 1–5 gal. for smaller plants; 10–20 gal. for larger ones; 10" container for TINY TIM-type]
turnips	2–3 / 8–10" dia. container [min. 4" deep for "baby" turnips]

Plants in Boxes

From *Gardening in Containers* come some size suggestions for planting vegetables in boxes. A 2' x 3' box that's 8" deep is suitable for a variety of plants: beets, carrots, onions, lettuce, leeks, turnips, kohlrabi, corn, and zucchini. Plants that can be trained up a trellis—like peas, pole beans, and cucumbers—will do well in a box that's 1' x 4' and 8" deep, as will kale, broccoli, and lettuce.

Trellises, strings, and stakes are advisable for vegetables planted in boxes, and for those in pots, too. Growing these plants vertically is a great space-saver, and can be even more successful than ground-level planting, as a larger leaf area is exposed to the sun. Look to the next chapter for specifics on vertical gardening.

Containers for Herbs, Flowers, and Vines

Herb and flower plants, of course, make equally wonderful choices for containers; flowering vines are also good candidates for vertical growing. The proper size container can be selected by considering the plants' overall size at maturity. If you know whether the plant is shallow- or deep-rooted, that information is helpful, too. Again, for specific suggested varieties, see Chapter Five.

Containers for Bulbs

Flowering bulbs offer brilliant color not only in the spring garden, but at other seasons as well. When grown in containers, their beautiful display can be enjoyed indoors as well as out. For cold winter areas, learning how to "force" bulbs—as discussed later in this chapter—will provide you with color and fragrance even when the garden is blanketed with snow.

Any container can be used for bulbs as long as it has a drainage hole and is deep enough to allow a minimum of 2" of soil below the bulb, so roots can develop properly. Bonsai pots can be especially effective with miniature flowering bulbs.

Containers for Bushes, Shrubs, and Trees

While a potted geranium might come more quickly to mind as an example of a container plant, shrubs and trees can be as equally qualified for this type of culture as their smaller relatives. Slow-growing or dwarf varieties are clearly the best candidates. With some careful pruning, however, other large plants are worth trying as well. To get you started, 25 shrubs and trees appropriate for container growing are described in Chapter Five, plus a wide variety of bush and tree fruits.

Suitable containers need to be strongly built and appropriately sized to accommodate a mature specimen. Half whiskey barrels are one good choice and are widely used for the larger trees and shrubs. Miller Nurseries carries a light-but-strong polystyrene tub for big plants that's 18" deep and just shy of 24" across ($14.50). A more formal choice is a square wood planter, like the white-painted pine ones offered by Jackson &

Perkins ($60.00 for the 15" size, and $70.00 for the 20" one).
For a less expensive planter, try wood-look white plastic.

Dwarf fruit trees will also need big, sturdy containers. Redwood tubs, half whiskey barrels, and wooden planter boxes
are among the popular containers for these trees. Whatever
your selection, the container should be at least 2' wide and
about 18–20" tall. Grapes and berries can be planted in a container about half this size.

CHOOSING YOUR PLANTS

Plants for Pots

Suggested vegetables, herbs, fruits, flowers, shrubs, and
trees for growing in all types of containers include dwarf and
miniature types, and varieties that have been especially bred
for container gardening. Use the information in this book to
help you match an appropriate plant for your garden with a
suitable container. While a single plant in a single pot is sometimes desirable—or even necessary—there are other options,
as discussed below.

Mixed Plantings

Combining herbs, flowers, and vegetables in a container
opens up a realm of gardening possibilities. While usually discussed in reference to a ground-level garden, the concepts of
interplanting and companion planting are also quite useful for
containers, boxes, and baskets. Here compatible plants are
grown together for both aesthetic and practical reasons.

Leaf lettuce, for instance, can be interplanted with flowers, herbs, or other vegetables along the rim or edge of a container. It makes an attractive addition with its smooth or
ruffled leaves in red and light and dark green. On the practical side, if taller plants are grown in the middle of the container, they'll provide needed shade for the lettuce during the
hot days of summer.

Other times, plants are grown together for their mutual
benefit. Marigolds and basil, for example, are considered helpful companions to plant with tomatoes. They're thought to enhance the tomatoes' flavor and growth, plus the marigolds
have been shown to deter nematodes in the soil. Planted to-

gether in a large pot, these three make an attractive grouping, as well.

Many of the theme and specialty gardens for children described in Chapter Seven are also good suggestions for container plantings. Fill a 10–gallon container with a tomato plant, a pepper, a few onions, some garlic, oregano, and basil, and you have a pizza garden! Or try edible flowers like chives, calendulas, nasturtiums, Johnny-jump-ups, borage, and signet marigold massed together in a planter.

Sometimes the opportunity for creative combinations simply presents itself. I once visited a local nursery in mid-summer and found its selection of herbs marked down to half-price. Unable to resist that kind of a bargain, I ended up filling a big clay pot with a lime geranium, lemon balm, coconut cascading geranium, lemon verbena, pineapple mint, and ALTAR OF ROSES geranium, for a refreshing summer mix.

Combining Sizes and Shapes

To maintain a visual sense of balance, it's often suggested that three or more different types of plants be combined in a container or planter: a short, bushy plant, a tall one, and a trailing one. Put the upright plants in the center of the pot, surround them with the bushy, mounding ones, and let the trailing plants cascade over the edge. If annuals and perennials will be sharing a container, planting the perennials in the middle will let you pull out frost-killed annuals without disturbing the other plants.

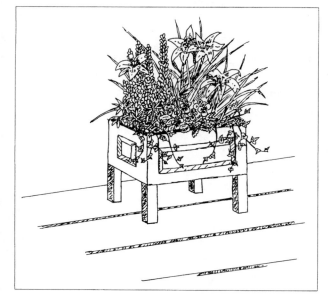

For a full, lush look, most annuals and herbs can be planted closely together, ignoring the usual spacing requirements. As long as the roots have room for healthy growth, many plants can be spaced as tightly as 1½ plants per inch of pot diameter. This means that in a 12" container, for example, you could conceivably plant 18 flowers. Or, try this rule of thumb: 4 small plants, or 1 big one, per 6" pot.

Vegetables, though, must have enough room for their crops to develop; tomatoes, in particular, need space for sunlight to reach the fruit.

The possibilities are practically endless for plants that can be grown together, so do try out a variety of combinations!

PLANTING A CONTAINER GARDEN

Soil for Containers

Along with sunlight and water, your container plants must have a good soil in which to grow and thrive. Before you run out to the backyard with a shovel, however, heed this rule: *don't use garden soil or ordinary dirt for a container garden!* Even if your garden boasts a lovely loam, the soil will be too heavy and won't drain properly in a pot, plus you risk introducing your plants to weed seeds, insects, and/or soil-borne diseases.

Opt instead for special container soils called soilless mixes, found at the local garden center under several brand names, including Jiffy Mix, Pro-Mix, and Redi-Earth. These all-natural preparations allow good drainage, yet hold enough water in the soil to adequately supply the plants. They also permit air to circulate around the roots, for if roots become waterlogged, a plant will die.

These soilless mixes are composed of two parts: an organic (either peat moss, fir or pine bark, redwood sawdust, etc.) and a mineral (either vermiculite, perlite, builder's sand, etc.). While the proportions and ingredients vary with the brand, the mixes offer the advantages of being clean, easy to use, lightweight, properly water-retentive, and disease-free. They make good all-purpose soils for use in containers and planters.

Note that a soilless mix containing perlite will dry out faster than one containing vermiculite. If you're apt to get frequent rains, choose the mix with the perlite. Fertilizers, however, will leach out more quickly and thus need to be replaced more often when the soilless mix has perlite in it.

Make-Your-Own Soil

Several "recipes" are available should you wish to make up your own soilless container mix, using items available from most gardening centers, or hardware or home-supply stores. This version is from the U.S. Department of Agriculture:

> 1 bushel shredded peat moss
> 1 bushel vermiculite
> 1¼ cup ground limestone (preferably dolomitic)
> ½ cup 20% superphosphate
> 1 cup 5–10–5 fertilizer
>
> * Mix thoroughly, adding a little water if needed to keep the dust down.

For a large quantity of mix, this basic recipe from *Gardening in Containers* makes one cubic yard:

> 14 cubic feet peat moss, nitrogen-stabilized fir bark, or pine bark
> 14 cubic feet vermiculite or perlite

Pour the ingredients out on a tarp and mix with a shovel, dampening the mix with warm (or hot) water. Spread over the pile:

> 5 pounds ground limestone
> 5 pounds 5–10–10 fertilizer
>
> * Turn the pile several times to mix it thoroughly. Store any excess in plastic bags or plastic garbage cans. Reduce the amount of ingredients proportionately if you want to make a smaller amount.

In *Crockett's Victory Garden*, Jim Crockett explains that he generally uses the commercial soilless mixes for planting his smaller containers. For the larger ones he makes a home-made soil mix.

> one part peat moss
> one part garden loam
> one part sand (not from the beach—too salty)
> slow-release fertilizer (14–14–14)

You may be wondering why this master gardener seems to be disregarding the advice about not using garden soil in containers. The rule still stands but, as with most, there is an exception.

It is possible to use good garden soil *if* it's first mixed with organic matter—compost, manure, peat moss, molding leaves, ground-up bark. This mixture will lighten a heavy soil and help a sandy one hold onto water. It can be used when a sterile soil isn't absolutely required—as with most shrubs and trees—and for planting very large containers.

Special Additives

When using a commercial soilless mix, check to see whether fertilizer is already one of the ingredients. If not, a fertilizer like 5–10–5, 5–10–10, or 20–20–20 can be mixed into your soil before planting, or try adding a slow-release fertilizer like Osmocote. Follow package directions carefully for the correct amounts to use.

Another additive well worth considering for your container garden soil is one that will reduce the need for the constant waterings that this type of gardening demands. "Moisture crystals" are sold in garden centers and catalogues, as described on page 152. A water-absorbing polymer, the "crystals" expand to absorb water, which is then time-released into the soil as the soaked chunks dry out.

PREPARING THE CONTAINER

A Clean Pot

First, be sure that your container is clean. Since a dirty pot can harbor disease, you'll need to disinfect the container if it's been used before. Scrub the container well with a rag or old toothbrush; sandpaper will help clean surface deposits off of a clay pot. Then soak the container for 10 minutes in a solution of 1 part household bleach to 9 parts water, and rinse well. Alternately, you can run the pot through the dishwasher.

Once an unglazed clay pot is clean, soak it in water prior to planting. Otherwise, the clay will draw moisture away from the potting soil when the container is filled.

Drainage

Before filling your clean container with the soilless mix, check to be sure it has one or more drainage holes. If none exist, or if more are needed, ask the nursery staff where you bought the container to make the holes.

To do the job yourself, use a hand or electric drill for wood and solid plastic; a nail and hammer will punch holes in a metal container. Space them evenly either in the bottom of the pot or on the bottom rim. Four holes might be a good number for a small container, while a large one, of course, will require more. Most clay pots will have a single hole in the bottom.

Whether your container has one drainage hole or many, cover the opening(s) with a piece of mesh screening or a shard (a small piece from a broken clay pot), to keep the soil from washing out. Then, to help drainage, put a layer of coarse gravel in the bottom of your container. Some gardeners like to add sphagnum moss and charcoal, too.

For large pots you might want to try this tip from a Massachusetts gardener. She first fills the container ⅓–½ full with empty aluminum cans, and then adds the potting soil and plants. This makes her container garden lighter and thus easier to move.

Providing for drainage in a strawberry jar requires a special trick. Roll some mesh screening into a cylinder the height of the jar. Position the cylinder in the center of the jar and fill it with rocks, then proceed with the potting soil and plants. This way the cylinder will act as a conduit when you water the strawberry jar, ensuring that each plant gets the water it needs.

Sometimes, given the material, it's impossible to make a hole in a container. While it's best to have drainage holes, you can get by with a one-inch layer of stones, pebbles, or broken bits of clay pot in the bottom of the container.

Planting containers like open-sided laundry baskets, cardboard boxes, wicker baskets, and, possibly, wooden boxes will need to have a liner, one in which drainage holes have been punched. Use any type of heavy plastic (scout around the house for a piece), or a pre-made tin form for the liner.

Air Circulation

Large tubs, barrels, and containers will need to be put into their chosen sites prior to being filled with soil and plants; otherwise, some very heavy moving will be required. Since wood will rot from prolonged contact with the ground, raise up a wooden container like a whiskey barrel by putting three or four bricks under its edges, or small blocks of wood under a tub or box.

Big containers can also have casters attached to the bottom edge. This will help make moving them easier, provide air circulation by getting them up off the ground, and foil some earth-dwelling pests, like slugs.

A caddy, dolly, or drainage saucer with casters is another possibility for large pots. Shepherd's has a set of 12" square wooden caddies with casters (3 for $36.00). Terra cotta-colored plastic plant dollies on casters come in three sizes in the Gardeners Eden catalogue. The smallest is 10" in diameter and holds 150 lbs. ($16.00).

Large clay pots benefit too from the air circulation provided by raising them up. For a look that's decorative as well as practical, try pot feet: concrete or clay "feet" to slip under the edge of a container. In the Kinsman Company catalogue, 4 styles in 2 sizes, starting at 3 for $4.50, are available.

PLANTING THE CONTAINER

Preparing the Soil

Now that your container is ready, it's time to prepare the soil. Before pouring your commercial or homemade soilless mix into the container, wet it first with warm or hot water. Either pour the mix into a big tub, add water, and stir it all up, or else simply slit the top of the mix's plastic bag, add water, and work it in by kneading the bag. Letting the soilless mix sit for several hours or overnight will ensure that it's evenly moistened.

Sowing Seeds

To start your plants from seed, fill the container with the dampened soilless mix, to within about an inch of the rim. Sow the seeds right in the pot, following the directions on the packet for proper spacing and planting depth, then water well.

Adding Plants

If you're starting with potted plants, fill the container to within about 5" of the top, then remove the plants from their containers. For plastic cell packs, squeeze the bottom of a cell—or push up with your thumb—to make the plant "pop" out. A putty knife is handy for cutting blocks of soil to remove plants from flats.

For those growing in plastic pots, give the pot a brisk, sideways rap and ease the plant out. Plants in biodegradable containers like peat pots can be planted in their entirety if you first tear off the upper edge of the pot, and punch holes in the bottom. Just be sure, though, that you don't *pull* any plant out of a container!

Now examine the rootball. Does it look overgrown, a tight mass of roots? A plant that grows in a small container for too long will become pot-bound, which often happens with plants purchased mid- or late-season. You'll need to release the roots so the plant can grow properly. Try to loosen the mass with your fingers, but if this doesn't work, more drastic measures are called for. With a sharp knife make a few cuts along the sides of the rootball, from top to bottom.

Next, arrange the plants in the container, taking into consideration the planting suggestions described above. (If all your plants are in small plastic pots, you can leave them in the pots while you move them about.)

When you're pleased with the arrangement, remove the plants from their pots if you haven't already, and start filling in around them with more of the soilless mix, to within an inch or two of the rim. Be careful to keep the plants at the same depth as they were when growing in their pots at the nursery.

Finally, give the plants a good drink of water. If the weather is hot and sunny, let the container rest in the shade for a day or two as the plants adjust to their new environment.

Techniques for Extra Help

These two suggestions from horticultural therapist Bibby Moore will make the job easier if you're potting up plants with just one hand. First, if the pot tends to slide around on your work surface, attach a furring strip or similar piece of 1" x 2" wood to the front edge of the table. The container can then be steadied against the furring strip as you work to fill it. Then, if additional support is needed, set a felt-covered brick on each side of the pot.

Even greater stability can be achieved through the use of a special wooden potting box that you or a handy friend can make. Holes to fit different sizes of pots are cut into the top of it, with the box itself weighted to stay in place.

As helpful as this potting box can be, however, there is a potential drawback. Unless you're using lightweight plastic pots and soilless mix, the containers could be too heavy for weak hands to lift up and out of the box. If the top of the potting box is made to lift off, or cut in half and hinged to swing apart, the pots will be easier to remove after planting.

CARING FOR YOUR CONTAINER GARDEN

Watering

Your container garden will require watering and fertilizing more often than a ground-level garden. With limited soil and space, plants dry out more quickly, and with the extra watering, nutrients are leached out of the soil along with the overflow. Check your plants every day and water whenever the soil surface is dry, preferably in the early morning or late afternoon. Avoid watering in the evening, for if the plants' leaves stay wet overnight, they're more at risk for disease.

Notice as you water that the leaves of your closely spaced plants can have an umbrella-like effect, making for wet leaves but dry soil. Reach in through the growth with the spout of your watering can or watering wand, to make sure the soil is getting a thorough soaking. Likewise, don't assume the plants have gotten a good drink just because it rained. The leaves may have deflected the water, so *feel* for dryness with your hand.

When you water a container, don't be in a hurry: you could end up washing the top layer of soil right out of the pot. Fill the container and wait for the water to be absorbed.

If you've kept the soil to ½–1" below the pot's rim, one watering may be enough to get the entire rootball wet, with the excess moisture draining out. If not, then repeat the application until water runs out through the drainage holes. With a thorough watering, moisture will be available to the whole root system, plus fertilizer and mineral salts won't have a chance to build up in the soil and damage the plant.

After watering your container garden, empty the saucers so that the plants aren't sitting around with wet feet. For big, heavy containers, try removing the excess water with a baster or siphon tube. Since it can be difficult to do this with a hanging basket, you may want to eliminate the saucer altogether.

To lessen the need for frequent waterings, mulch your container garden, just as you would a ground-level garden. Choose from any mulching material (see pages 150–51), and apply it thickly. Besides being very practical, mulch can create an attractive base around the plants—with the added benefit of keeping your cat from digging around in the dirt. Of course, if you added the "moisture crystals" to the soil when you first potted your plants, you've already saved yourself a lot of water, time, and effort.

If you live in a hard-water area, there's one extra step you can take to help ensure healthy plants. Damaging mineral salts have a way of building up in the soil, but they can be removed with a simple process called leaching. This involves nothing more than giving your plants a thorough soaking about once a month, by letting the garden hose run slowly for 20 minutes in each container.

For helpful tools to aid in the whole watering process, see the section beginning on page 152.

Tips and Techniques for Watering

One almost work-free way to water is by osmosis. As you pot your plants, insert a length of cotton wicking, rope, or cord through the bottom drainage hole, so that one end is buried in the soil and the other end extends out of the hole. Set the pot in a gravel-filled saucer and let the wick rest among the stones. Keep the saucer filled with just enough water so that the bottom of the pot stays dry. The wick will pull water from the saucer to the plant for a steady supply of moisture.

For another easy-care method, group small pots together in a wooden box, with ground bark or peat moss filling in the spaces between the containers. The pots will be both insulated and mulched, while evaporation is lessened. Peat moss is also useful for protecting a plant in a clay pot from too much heat. Set the pot within a larger pot, adding the peat moss as an insulation layer at the bottom and sides of the bigger container.

If you have a large container garden, a length of galvanized roof gutter, capped at both ends, can be helpful for watering many plants at once. Line up the containers and lay the gutter across the rims. Punch a hole in the bottom of the gutter to correspond with each plant. To water the garden, simply fill the trough with water. Liquid fertilizer is also easily applied in the same way.

Vacation Care

When you're away for a weekend or on vacation, there are several things you can do to help your plants survive until you return. For instance, even if you choose not to water on a permanent basis with the roof gutter method just described, it's a good way for a friend or neighbor to take care of your garden. Another arrangement—either for permanent or vacation use—involves a drip-irrigation system. Water flows through a plastic pipe that has spaghetti tubes spaced along its length. At the end of each tube is a drip spitter, which rests in the container and provides the plant with a small but steady amount of moisture.

Giving the containers extra shade will also help reduce water loss. To shade the pots (clay, in particular) from the sun, set them up in a row, then lean a long board horizontally against the pots. Or, keep the pots and thus the plants cool by sinking the containers into garden soil.

Fertilizing

Your container garden will continue to grow and thrive with periodic light applications of fertilizer. Suggestions as to amounts and frequency of feeding seem to differ with each container gardening expert. The size and depth of your container and the number of plants in it, the type of soil used, the nutrient requirements of various plants (some are "hungrier" than others), and how often you water are all factors that come into play.

Perhaps it's best to say that there are no hard and fast rules, except that too little fertilizer is safer for your plants than too much. Experiment with these recommendations:

• If you mixed fertilizer in with the soilless mix, the garden can be fed once a month.

• Timed- or slow-release fertilizers are another option. Granular kinds can be sprinkled on and mixed in with the soil; stick kinds can be pushed into the soil.

• Every 3 weeks, a teaspoon of 5–10–5 per square foot of soil can be mixed into the top half-inch of soil and watered thoroughly. Or, use water-soluble fertilizer, diluted to $\frac{1}{4}$ strength, again watered in thoroughly.

• If your plants seem to need an extra boost, diluted fertilizer can be applied every 2 weeks.

• Fish emulsion can be used weekly.

• Be sure to read the package directions for the manufacturer's recommendations, too.

On-Going Care

You probably won't need encouragement to keep your container garden groomed: one of the joys of this type of gardening is having the plants literally right at your fingertips. The plants will doubtless enjoy a bit of fussing as you keep stragglers pruned back, dead flowers and leaves picked off, the odd weed pulled out, and any crops harvested. If you groom your plants once a week, rotate the container at the same time to let the light evenly reach every side.

Gardeners in a warm climate can enjoy their container gardens year round. In colder areas the containers of plants can be brought indoors, provided there is sufficient light for continued growth.

Otherwise, before winter cold settles in, you'll need to empty your pots of annuals and store them in a sheltered place to prevent cracking. Containers of perennials can be wrapped with a protective blanket of burlap or a thick layer of straw, or moved to an unheated shed or garage. Every so often, check the containers to be sure they haven't dried out. Some potted perennials, though, can handle winter exposure without special treatment.

For large wooden tubs and barrels, remove the frost-killed plants to the composter but leave the soil in place. The dirt will act as an insulating layer to keep the wood from shrinking and splitting.

SPECIAL TIPS FOR PLANTING BULBS

Forcing Bulbs

Start with a clean container and cover the drainage hole with a pot shard or piece of window screen. Add soil to a level deep enough so that the bulbs' tops are one inch below the container's rim. (Here any soil is fine, as its only real function is to support the bulbs.)

Set the bulbs in the pot with the flat end down and the pointed end up. Space them closely, with just ¼–½" of room between them, and gently settle them into the soil. Don't let them touch each other or the edge of the pot, however. For tulips, which have a curved and a flat side, try this method. Place the bulb so that the *flat* side is towards the *inside* of the pot. A large leaf will grow from the flat side and curve over the container's edge, for an attractive effect.

Cover the bulbs with more soil so that their tips are at the soil line. Finally, water thoroughly. Let the pot soak in a bucket of water. When the soil surface is moistened, remove the pot and let the excess water drain from the bottom.

Cold Treatment

Now put the container in a box and cover it with peat moss, shredded polystyrene, sawdust, or other mulch. Keep it in a cold, dark spot where the temperature will stay between 35° and 50° F.—an unheated garage or basement should be fine. The bulbs will need 8–14 weeks of this cold treatment for the roots to develop their strength. Keep the soil moist, but not wet. If your winter climate is too warm to give the bulbs this chilling, refrigerate them for 6 weeks before planting them in a container.

For an optional but pretty addition, sprinkle grass seed (such as bent grass, *Agrostis tenuis*) in the container as soon as it's removed from cold storage. By the time the bulbs bloom, the surface of the container will sport a carpet of fresh green grass.

When the bulbs have sprouted, bring them into a cool (60° F.), dim room for about 2 weeks, or until the new growth is 2" tall. Begin watering more often now, and never let the container dry out completely. As the leaves appear and grow, move the container to a cool, bright room until the flowers appear. Then the potted bulbs can be displayed wherever you like.

Another Way to Force Bulbs

While this is the standard way of forcing bulbs, it isn't the *only* way. Jim Crockett relates that he used to put his newly sprouted bulbs in a dark spot, as described above. However, after seeing the results of an experiment his daughter, Mary, conducted, he opted instead to grow them in full light on a sunny but cool windowsill. The results, he says, are much superior, and easier to boot. Why not try both ways and see which you prefer?

Double-Decker Bulb Plantings

For a wonderful show of blooms, try this professional trick with daffodil bulbs. Plant the bulbs in a double layer: five, say, for the bottom layer, arranged as a circle of four with one in the center, then above it a circle of four, in the alternating spaces. The shoots from both layers will appear at the same time, for twice the bloom in one pot.

The Dutch—who know a thing or two about flowers—have recently been using a similar method at The Netherlands' showplace for the flower industry, Keukenhof Gardens. To try it, first plant tall-growing bulbs about 8" deep in a container, then cover them with 3" of soil. Next, plant a layer of low-growing bulbs on top of that, with 5" of additional soil and 1" of mulch to finish off the pot; water well.

One suggested combination is yellow or peach tulips, and bluish-purple grape hyacinths. The two-tone, double-decker effect will be dramatic and beautiful!

Bulbs in Water and Pebbles

Hyacinth bulbs are a popular choice for forcing in water. The flowers are lovely and very fragrant, the bulbs are widely available, and both grownups and children enjoy watching the roots grow to fill the glass jar. You might have an appropriate container already around the house, with an opening just big enough to cradle the bulb. Special hyacinth glasses, though, are shaped just for this purpose and aren't expensive. Fashioned in both clear glass and in colored, the jars can be used as flower vases, too.

Also popular for forcing are narcissus bulbs, particularly the paperwhites. For these you'll need a shallow bowl or other container that's about twice as deep as the bulbs. Fill the bowl

⅔ full with pebbles, then place several bulbs on top of them. Pour in water until it reaches the base of the bulbs. Surround the bulbs with more pebbles to hold them in place, but don't cover their tips. Store the container in a cool, dark place to let the roots develop. Then, after about 2 weeks, bring them to a cool, sunny area. Add water as needed throughout the forcing time.

Both the hyacinth and the narcissus bulbs will need a cold treatment, so store them in the refrigerator for about 6–8 weeks before you want to start forcing them. The only drawback to this method of forcing is that it rather thoroughly depletes the bulbs. Even when they're later planted outdoors, the bulbs seldom recover. There is, however, certainly no harm in trying.

Caring for Your Bulb Garden

After the bulbs have bloomed, keep the container in a cool (50–55° F.) spot if you're planning to later plant the bulbs outdoors. Since the leaves are busy making food for the bulb to store until growing time next season, let them grow on for as long as they can. It's tempting to pull off the withered leaves, but resist the urge to remove them until they're brown and crisp. The same bulbs can't be forced again next year, but they can be planted in an outdoor garden. Either set them out after their indoor stay, or else let them remain in the pots until fall and then plant them.

SPECIAL TIPS FOR PLANTING TREES AND SHRUBS

A Choice of Two Methods

First, make sure your clean container has drainage holes, then add a drainage layer in the bottom of the pot. A few inches of gravel, clay pot shards, marble chips, or other similar materials will help keep roots from becoming waterlogged.

Now decide which of the following two ways of planting best suits your needs. The easiest is to simply plant the young tree or shrub in the prepared container. For soil use a mix of good garden loam, compost or peat, and coarse sand, adding

moisture "crystals" and/or slow-release fertilizer if you like. Although the pot will initially be too large for the plant, the shrub or tree will grow to fill the container at maturity.

This method eliminates the need for repotting, and is the advice given by more than one reputable nursery for planting their fruit trees, vines, and bushes.

Alternately, bare-root and dwarf trees can be grown for one season in a 5–gallon pot or can. The following spring, when the tree has established a good root system, repot the tree into a larger container. Continue repotting over two or three seasons into increasingly larger containers, until the tree is in its permanent tub, box, or planter.

The advantages to this method are that the plants are easier to handle when they're young, plus a plant grown in an appropriately sized container can easily get the nutrients and water it needs. Regardless of which method you choose, be very careful to plant your tree or shrub at the same level at which it was growing in its nursery pot. For bare-root trees, follow the nursery's directions—many catalogue sources will send a booklet or page on planting and care when you order. Special care must be taken when planting most dwarf fruit trees, namely that the graft union (where the tree was grafted onto the rootstock) is kept *above* the soil line.

CARING FOR SHRUBS AND TREES IN CONTAINERS

Watering

Water your plants regularly to keep the soil slightly damp, but never waterlogged. As described earlier, leaves can have an umbrella-like effect, so be sure to feel the soil with your hand to determine dryness. If your plant needs a drink, give it a thorough watering by filling the pot until water runs from the drain holes. Since frequent or even daily waterings can be necessary, having well-drained soil is vitally important. Leaching will need to be done about once a month in hard-water areas.

Whether your tree or shrub is in its temporary or permanent container, remember that mulching will help to conserve water in the soil, eliminate weed growth, and keep the soil cool. A thick layer of an organic material like bark chips is both practical and attractive. Even a layer of small, smooth stones, marble chips, or pea gravel can be used.

Another mulching alternative is to plant a ground cover in the container. An evergreen like vinca is a good-looking choice, or you could select a flowering ground cover like alyssum. A Northwest gardener decided to mulch his dwarf apple with white clover, to create a handsome base around the tree and to take advantage of clover's ability to fix the nitrogen in the soil.

Note, however, that a living mulch will compete with the tree or shrub for available moisture in the container. If you find yourself having to water more often because of the ground cover, you'll be defeating one of the purposes of adding a mulch in the first place!

Fertilizing

To help your shrub or tree grow and thrive, periodically give it light applications of fertilizer, letting its general health and appearance be your guide. Fish emulsion can be watered in monthly, or a complete fertilizer in liquid form applied at half strength every 2 or 3 weeks. Pelleted slow-release fertilizers, which will slowly dissolve over time, are another option. Citrus trees may like their own special "mix," which can be purchased at a nursery.

If your tree will be staying outdoors during the winter, fertilize it until about the middle of July, and then stop. If the plant makes new growth too late into the season, the sprouts won't be able to harden off before winter cold damages or kills them. If the tree will be spending the winter indoors, it can be fed through the whole growing season.

On-Going Care

While you enjoy your potted shrub or tree, keep an eye out for any signs of trouble, such as insect damage, broken limbs, etc. Prune as necessary to keep the plant within bounds of its container. For fruit trees and bushes, follow the nursery's advice for encouraging a crop, which may involve a spraying schedule, branch spreading, and judicious pruning. Citrus trees will enjoy a monthly shower with tepid water.

After 2 or 3 years, you'll want to prune the roots on your container-grown tree. Remove the tree from its pot and examine the rootball. If roots are growing outside the rootball along its sides and bottom, use a sharp knife to make a few cuts along the sides of the rootball, from top to bottom. Then re-plant the tree at the same level, firming in some fresh soil and watering thoroughly. This pruning will encourage new root growth, and will also counteract the plant's tendency to bunch its feeder roots along the walls of the pot, which can cause the tree to go into decline.

If the rootball doesn't appear to be overgrown, simply remove about one inch of root when you repot the shrub or tree. Be sure to prune a bit off the top of the plant too, to keep it in balance. Both new roots and new top growth will be the healthy result.

Winter Care

Since a container-grown plant's root system is more exposed to cold temperatures, even a hardy shrub or tree will need winter protection. If you can move the container, relocate it to a cool but protected area such as a garage, porch, or basement. If you can't move the container, and your winters are severe, blanket it to ensure survival. Wrap the container and the plant in a cylinder of chicken wire, then fill it with "insulation": dried leaves, straw, hay, or other similar materials. Finally, drape a waterproof cover over the whole affair to keep everything dry.

Stark Bro's Nursery recommends that in Zones 4–7, dwarf and miniature fruit trees grown in containers be protected from the cold. After temperatures drop below 20° F., the potted tree should be moved to an unheated garage, shed, or other sheltered spot. Don't bring the tree inside, however. Cold is required for the tree to go into dormancy, so that normal growth and blooming will resume the following spring.

Dwarf citrus trees, however, can spend a Northern winter indoors.

PLANTS IN A HANGING BASKET

A Suspended Garden

Hanging baskets in all shapes and sizes are a wonderful way to create planting space where none exists. They also combine nicely with a container garden, giving you in effect a double-decker area for growing plants. These suspended gardens add a lot of visual interest to a patio or deck, while many can be very effective indoors.

Keeping Baskets Accessible

For the gardener with a physical disability, hanging baskets offer either an option or an addition to growing plants in boxes, containers, and planters. The baskets can be hung wherever you'll get the most enjoyment from them: if you use a wheelchair, for instance, hang the basket low enough for you to see its beauty.

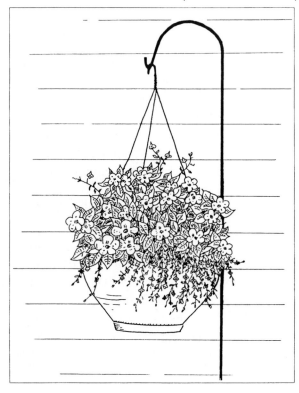

Hanging baskets, however, do require access for watering, fertilizing, and grooming. To avoid aching, tired muscles from trying to work with your arms above your head, suspend the basket with a homemade pulley system, or buy a ratchet pulley designed for easy raising and lowering of a hanging basket; long-reach watering wands are also very helpful. (See page 154 for more information on catalogue sources for buying pulleys and wands.)

Another possibility is to hang the basket—at a lower level—from a sturdy post so that it's permanently accessible from either a seated or standing position. Look in your local stores for the hardware, or else consult a catalogue. Plow & Hearth sells a long steel hook to clamp on a deck railing. It features a thumbscrew to adjust the hanger up or down ($22.00 for a single hanger, $25.00 for a double). Alsto's long steel hook can be mounted anywhere with its 3" x 3" bracket ($22.00).

PLANTS FOR HANGING BASKETS

Flowers, Vegetables, and Herbs

A number of plants suggested for use in outdoor hanging baskets are outlined in Chapter Five, in the section on Flowers for Hanging Baskets. Some of the most popular choices include cascading or trailing plants like nasturtiums and ivy geraniums; mounded plants like the Dahlberg daisy; and showy flowers like tuberous begonias and fuchsias.

The Tumbler Hybrid Tomato from Burpee.

Also in Chapter Five are some vegetable varieties that are suitable for hanging baskets. These include cherry tomatoes like WHIPPERSNAPPER and TUMBLER HYBRID; SALAD BUSH HYBRID cucumber; POT HYBRID sweet pepper; and THAI HOT hot pepper. You'll find descriptions of these plants under Vegetables for Containers.

Many herbs, of course, are attractive choices for hanging baskets. Some, like rosemary, are available in both upright and trailing, or prostrate, forms. Just as with flowers, foliage plants, and vegetables, herbs can be used either alone or in various combinations. See the discussion above for some ideas on creating successful mixed plantings.

It's also worth experimenting with plants not typically used in hanging baskets, for some interesting results are possible. When suspended in the air, an upright growing plant, for instance, may begin with drooping branches; new growth, however, can take a lateral turn.

As with any plant you select for your garden—whatever type or form it may be—be sure that the ones chosen for a hanging basket match your environmental conditions. A shade-loving plant can't be expected to thrive in the sun, for instance, so don't set yourself up for a gardening disaster by failing to take an individual plant's needs into consideration.

TYPES OF HANGING BASKETS

Choices in Materials

Clay, plastic, wood, and wire are the materials most often used for hanging baskets. Typical forms include various standard flower pots, bowls in assorted sizes, and baskets of heavy wire which typically range from 1–2' in diameter. (For a huge 30" wire basket, try the Kinsman Company catalogue; they offer a good selection of hooks, too.)

Another option in materials is natural fiber. Used for many years by the nursery trade, these containers are made from recycled paper fiber with wax and res:.is added for waterproofing. They last several seasons and are then biodegradable. Shepherd's carries sets of 3 hanging pots in graduated sizes; with hardware, they're $15.00.

If planted carefully and kept watered, any of these choices has the potential to make a beautiful hanging basket, one blanketed with leaves and flowers.

Pot Hangers

Clay and plastic pots can be purchased with hangers already attached; pot hangers are also available separately, or you can make your own. These suspend the pot either by clamping onto the rim—as with a clay pot—or are hooked into three holes in the rim, as with a plastic pot.

A container with a single hole in the bottom can be hung by means of a threaded metal rod and a nut-and-washer assembly. The top of the rod is either bent into a hook shape or else screwed into a flange for hanging from the ceiling or a beam. You can make one yourself with little difficulty. For a ready-made hanger, Kinsman carries a 24" aluminum hook with a screw-and-nut assembly. It can be used with any pot with a bottom drainage hole ($6.00).

Hanging baskets usually need to be turned to receive adequate light on all sides: this promotes even growth and a rounded, handsome appearance. A hanger with a built-in swivel is a very useful feature, so look for it when you go shopping. For a homemade pot hanger, use a fisherman's swivel from the sporting goods store or your tackle box.

WALL-MOUNTED BASKETS

A Hanging Basket Variation

Something of a variation on the classic hanging basket, a pot mounted on a wall or on a wall trellis has the obvious advantage of precise placement: it can be hung at any height the gardener chooses. Whether you work from a seated or standing position, the garden is kept right at your level. A staggered display of pots in clay, plastic, or wire can be especially effective.

Or, try half-round baskets on a wall. Walt Nicke carries two types: a plastic one with attached saucer and hanging wire included for $5.25, and an attractive English wall basket of vinyl-coated wire for $9.00. Kinsman sells a similar wall basket, in two larger sizes ($14.00 and $16.00). This company even has baskets for corners. An in-the-corner hayrack is $35.00, and an around-the-corner one is $42.00. Both are of plastic-coated steel.

While a southern exposure is usually wonderful for plants, a south wall in the midday summer sun may be too much even for heat- and sun-loving plants. If the heat builds up, try another spot. Whatever the exposure, though, be sure to check wall-mounted containers often, as they dry out quickly.

More Pot Hangers

To hang standard 8" clay pots on a wall, check the Plow & Hearth catalogue for plant hangers. Of black iron, they feature a loop to hold the pot, and three different brackets to attach right to a fence or wall ($17.00 for a single bracket and loop combination). Black iron rings in five diameters to screw to a wall can also be found in the Kinsman catalogue ($3.00–4.50). Kinsman also has fancier Victorian style cast iron pot holders in two sizes ($12.00 and $27.00).

Another way to hang a pot on a wall—or fence, post, stake, or trellis—is with a pot clamp. Kinsman's clever English-made steel clamping device hangs from a nail or screw. It will hold a clay or plastic pot up to 7" in diameter and 20 lbs. in weight (2 for $7.00). Walt Nicke's version adjusts to hold a 5–8" pot and its saucer by supporting them from the bottom of the pot ($4.00). Yet another type is a steel French hanger to either hook over a fence or mount on a wall. The pot sits on a saucer at the base of the bracket and is held by a sliding clamp, adjusting to fit pots from 5–7½" high (Gardeners Eden, $10.00).

PLANTING A HANGING BASKET

Preparing the Basket

Before planting a hanging basket, be sure the chains and hook that will support the basket are strong and of the length you want. Then follow the advice given above for container gardening: use a clean pot, drill drainage holes if necessary, and partially fill it with damp container soil, pre-mixed with the water-absorbing polymer "crystals" and/or slow-release fertilizer if you're using them.

Filling the Basket

Placing the basket on an upturned bucket while you work is helpful, especially when your plants include trailers. Arrange the plants as you like, then fill in around them with more soilless mix and firm them into place. Water the basket thoroughly. For a mixed grouping, place cascading plants around the edges, and a bushy plant (or plants) in the center.

To insert plants into a hanging basket that has planting holes in its sides, or sides made of slats or wire, try this trick to make the job easier. Cut a piece of strong plastic—as from a garbage bag—about 3" square, poke a hole in the center, and cut from one corner to the hole.

Slip this plastic collar around the plant's stem, then gently push the plastic and the rootball into the planting opening. Now you can fill up the basket with soilless mix without worrying about it spilling out the holes. Alternately, try wrapping a little sphagnum moss around the stem instead of using the plastic collar.

Filling a Wire Basket

Wire baskets need some sort of a liner, which is usually sphagnum moss. Begin by soaking some sphagnum moss in water. Next take a chunk of moss and wring out most of the water, then press it into place between the wires around the top rim of the basket. Fill in the rest of the basket with big pieces of moss; overlapping them will help keep the soilless mix in place. To help conserve moisture, a saucer can be positioned at the bottom of the basket.

Add a few inches of soilless mix, then poke some holes through the moss at the soil level and begin inserting your plants. Lay the plants sideways so the roots rest on the soil, and cover them with container mix. Work your way up the sides of the basket, continuing to add soil and evenly spaced plants as you go. After you put in your final plants at the top, fill the basket to within one inch of the rim and water well.

Basket Liners

Alternatives to a sphagnum moss liner include plastic and coco-fiber. Although not the most attractive choice, a heavy green or black plastic liner is serviceable, if a few holes are first poked in the sides to release excess water.

One source for premade coco-fiber liners is the Kinsman catalogue ($1.75 for one fitting a 12" hanging basket). They're a natural brown, last longer than moss liners, and can be trimmed with scissors to fit a particular basket or to insert plants. These liners can be a boon if you think working with the sphagnum moss will aggravate sore or weak hands.

CARING FOR YOUR HANGING BASKET

Watering

Especially if they're lined with sphagnum moss, hanging baskets dry out quickly; exposure to bright sun and wind will of course hasten the process. A basket will probably need to be watered thoroughly every day, or even twice daily.

Fertilizing

All this watering means that fertilizer is going to be washed out of the soil at a steady rate. Rather than being subjected to massive doses of nutrients offered at irregular intervals, your plants will appreciate instead a continuous light feeding. Timed-release fertilizers can be mixed with the soil, or fertilizer can be given at every other watering. If you opt for this second method, be sure to use just one-fifth the amount of fertilizer as indicated on the package directions.

Grooming and On-Going Care

Remove dead leaves and flowers, and prune as needed to keep your hanging basket looking its best. Later in the season, winter weather will likely do the basket in, since the roots are so exposed to the cold air. Unless you live in a perennially warm clime, then, or can bring it indoors, consider your hanging basket to be seasonal.

When cold weather ends its beauty, put the plants and soil in the composter. If you had a liner of sphagnum moss or coco-fiber, it can be saved and used again.

PLANTS IN A WINDOW BOX

Another Type of Hanging Garden

Window boxes are another lovely way to add interest to your home's exterior. They can brighten up an otherwise plain house front, or lend additional decoration to an already attractive facade.

If the area below your windows is accessible, by all means install your window boxes in their traditional location—and remember that window boxes can be tended from either outside or inside the house. There are alternatives, however, if this would put them out of reach. With the proper supporting bolts and brackets, a window box can be hung on just about any wall or fence.

Alternatives to Hanging

Actually, there's no real reason why a box would have to be hung at all: it could rest on the ground, on a bench, on a table, or anywhere that makes enjoying and caring for the plants easy for you. If the window box isn't suspended, raise the box up a few inches with pieces of brick or board underneath the bottom to allow air to circulate and water to drain properly from the holes.

TYPES OF WINDOW BOXES

Materials and Sizes

Materials commonly used for window boxes include wood, plastic, and wire. Wood is perhaps the most popular choice, and can be painted to match or contrast with the plants and the house color. To downplay the planter, paint it forest green; against a red brick wall, try white; against white, try blue; or paint the box to match the house trim. Also consider adding decorative detail with paint or wood trim to the box itself. Supporting brackets can be either ornate or simple, to harmonize with both the window box's and your home's decor.

As with the planting containers described above, choose a wood that can stand up to the elements, for a soft wood will quickly rot. Restrict paint to the outside of the window box. The inside can be coated with a non-poisonous wood preservative, if desired.

The size of a window box is up to you, but remember that a soil-filled box is a very weighty container. Instead of one long box, opt instead for two shorter ones. A workable size might be 10" wide, 12" deep, and 28–36" long.

Wire frame window boxes are another popular choice. Even when not filled with plants, many are handsome enough to stand on their own. Check out the ones offered by Kinsman: ranging in price from $29.00 to $55.00, the English-made hayrack-style planters are of welded steel coated with black plastic. For other sizes, try the Walt Nicke Company catalogue.

Liners

Some window boxes come with detachable plastic or metal liners, or the liners can be purchased separately. These can be quite handy to have. For instance, if there's no one to water your window box daily while you're on vacation, remove the liner to a shady place in your yard to lessen evaporation.

Or, with multiple liners you can make quick seasonal changes. One liner might have summer annuals growing in it, say, ready to pop into the window box when the liner planted with spring bulbs begins to peter out.

Anchoring the Box

Even if you choose a lighter-weight material like plastic, a window box is going to be heavy when filled with soil and plants. It's very important then that the box be anchored securely. Bolt it firmly in place with lag screws or carriage bolts (Kinsman recommends a 3½" x ⅜" diameter bolt). For brick or masonry, you'll need to first put in a bolt anchor.

To provide extra support, attach the box to wall studs if you can. Adding two or three brackets underneath the box is also a good supporting idea. These can either be of wood to match the box, or sturdy L-shaped iron brackets.

Another option is to mount the window box on pinned door hinges. Then, to remove the box for planting or storage, simply pull out the pin. A hinged box is also convenient if you expect to be painting the house in the near future: just lift the box up to paint underneath it.

Other Boxes and Containers to Hang

The rectangular box hung underneath a window is a classic design, but it's possible to hang other types of containers as well. A wooden box, for example, can be attached to the wall with hinges, with the rest of the weight carried by chains running from the outside corners of the box to the wall.

Rain gutters, with their ends capped and drainage holes drilled in the bottom, can be fastened in place on a wall with standard roofing clips. Several of these can be staggered on the wall at an accessible height. Alone or mixed with wall-hung pots, the gutters can make a practical and eye-catching garden.

Railing Planters

Railing planters have that typical window box rectangular shape, but are meant to straddle a deck rail instead of being hung and bolted in place. Gardeners Eden carries wooden slatted planters in many sizes and widths; there are even planters designed to fit the corners of the railings. They can either be filled with potted plants, or, with the addition of a liner, planted themselves ($49.00–89.00).

Alsto's offers a comparable size selection for their slatted deck planters, but with three choices in wood: cypress, stained poplar, and redwood (from managed farms—not old growth). Prices range from $45.00 to $85.00. The deck planters in the Plow & Hearth catalogue are of cedar slats. They come in three sizes plus a corner planter ($35.00–50.00).

A less expensive option is a French vinyl-coated wire frame in two sizes that hooks over a fence or balcony rail. The frame holds potted plants, or a rectangular planter can be added (Gardeners Eden, $14.00 and $18.00).

Finally, although these polypropylene resin planters probably won't last as long as ones made from wood, they're very reasonably priced. Burpee sells the deck planters, which have a mount to screw onto the deck rail, as a set of 2 planters with 4 brackets, for $13.00.

PLANTS FOR WINDOW BOXES

Flowers, Vegetables, and Herbs

Flowers and foliage plants undoubtedly come first to mind for growing in a window box, and you'll find a nice variety of them discussed in Chapter Five. However, while these plants make wonderful choices, they aren't your only options.

Also try any of the smaller herbs such as parsley or thyme in your window box, or petite and pretty SPICY GLOBE basil, with some sun-loving flowers. Or how about planting salad ingredients, like red and green leaf lettuces, little round and "baby" carrots, GREEN CURLED endive, arugula, and mixed windowsill greens (the last available from the Shepherd's Garden Seeds catalogue)? Another attractive and edible choice is

alpine strawberries, with their tidy, mounded shapes and succulent berries.

Besides aesthetic considerations, plants for window boxes
must be chosen from a practical standpoint, too. As with any
container plants, your environment and the plants' requirements will need to correspond. Is your window box in full sun,
part shade, or full shade? Will it receive any rainfall, or do the
eaves block the rain? Is the plant you're considering fairly
small and neat in habit (perhaps with a bit of pruning), or will
it quickly grow beyond the size of the box?

Mixed Plantings

Whereas a hanging basket might feature one spectacular
fuchsia, for instance, a window box almost begs for mixed

plantings. Stick to one
color, various shades
of one color, or com-
bine two or three com-
patible colors. Look at
the leaf colors and
forms, too, and the
plants' overall shapes
to get the most inter-
esting and effective
mix. Remember that
scented plants in a
box beneath an open
window offer beauty
and fragrance.

Put taller, bushier
plants to the back of the window box, with mounded forms
next, and trailing plants along the edge. Arranging them in
staggered rather than straight rows, and crowding the plants a
little to set them about 4–6" apart, will give your window box
a fuller, more lush look. While it's entirely possible to plant a
window box without using any trailing flower or foliage plants,
it's almost a shame not to: cascading plants tumbling out of a
window box are a fine sight!

PLANTING A WINDOW BOX

Preparing and Filling the Box

While not every gardening expert considers drainage holes to be essential in a window box, most do as the holes will prevent overwatering and the risk of suffocated roots. If your box doesn't already have drain holes, drill several in the bottom and lay pieces of window screening over the holes to keep soil from washing away. Drips from watering won't be a problem if there is a groundcover or some bushes below the box to absorb and diffuse any overflow.

Whether or not your window box has holes, it's a good idea to add a 1 to 2"–layer of materials—stones, pieces of brick, or clay pot shards—in the bottom of the box to help ensure adequate drainage. This layer is then covered with partially decomposed leaves, hay, straw, coarse peat moss, or upside-down grass sods to prevent the soil from sifting downwards and clogging the drainage layer.

Now the window box can be filled to within a few inches of the top with dampened soilless mix, i.e., commercial all-purpose potting soil or container mix. If you wish, add slow-release fertilizer and/or the water-absorbing polymer "crystals." Following the directions above for planting a container garden, arrange your plants, fill in with more soil, firm, and water well.

Alternately, you can forego the soil and simply use potted plants in the window box, adding sphagnum or peat moss to fill in around the pots. This is a convenient way to create changing, seasonal displays. Where summers are short, it's also an easy way to move the plants indoors when the growing season is over.

CARING FOR YOUR WINDOW BOX

Watering

Window boxes need frequent watering since they dry out quickly, especially if they're in a hot, sunny area. Even a good rain won't help if the eaves are blocking the moisture. Check your window box daily, and if the soil surface feels dry, water the box carefully and thoroughly. When water begins to drip through the drainage holes, you'll know that the soil has gotten a good soaking.

Fertilizing

Feeding options include mixing a granular fertilizer with the soil, inserting fertilizer spikes near the roots, or using a complete soluble fertilizer every two weeks (like Miracle-Gro or Peter's). And, to keep the soil aerated and aid in the absorption of water and fertilizer, prick some holes in the surface every so often.

Grooming and On-Going Care

To encourage blooming and keep up a tidy appearance, regularly remove dead flowers and leaves. When necessary, prune back any plants that are looking leggy to encourage bushy, mounded growth. Before frost threatens, you might want to take cuttings for growing indoors and for a headstart on spring planting. Then, when your window box is done for the season, don't resign yourself to an empty container for the next few months. Small evergreen shrubs like boxwood, Japanese holly, false cypress, juniper, English ivy, and yew can provide winter greenery.

Watch out for dehydration and loss of these plants, however, in areas where the soil is frozen for a long time. Sun and wind can cause the shrubs to lose moisture faster than it can be replaced by the roots.

For care-free decoration, gather materials like pine boughs, bittersweet, and winterberry holly to fill the box. They'll stay fresh-looking in the snow and frozen soil, to provide you with additional natural beauty. Come spring, fill your window box with new soil and begin again.

UNUSUAL CONTAINERS

Beyong the Standard Clay Pot

In the category of interesting or odd containers for plants—depending on your perspective—are the following: An old bathtub. A wheelbarrow. Fishing boots. A toilet. A hollowed-out stump. The remains of a vintage Cadillac.

Perhaps most unusual of all, though, is a grouping of cast-off boots and shoes—each sporting a cache of bright flowers—that adorned a wall in Falkland, Scotland. Every year the villages in County Fife vie for the title of Best-Decorated town as local gardeners show off their skills. The woman who created the display of footwear as part of the competition followed it up the next year with articles of children's clothing as her planting containers. No one ever said gardening had to be serious business!

CHAPTER THREE

Vertical Gardening

Introduction

Climbing and trellised plants have a great many uses in the garden. Whether you're growing a natural climber or a plant that needs to be trained to a trellis or stake, form and function combine when a plant is grown upwards. The following are some of the advantages to including vertical growers in your garden.

- These plants can be an attractive feature in and of themselves.
- They can disguise an unpleasant structure or view.
- They can provide visual interest in winter when other plants are gone.
- They can soften a stark surface.
- They are appropriate in any size garden.
- They can create a natural architecture.
- They can provide shade in summer.
- Vertical growing provides good air circulation all around the plant, helping it grow better.
- Since many insects don't like to crawl, a plant grown upwards can avoid certain pests.
- Tender plants out of their usual environment can be trained to grow up against a south wall, as with an espalier fruit tree. Benefitting from the wall's heat, these plants can thrive, whereas in other parts of the garden they would probably fail.

Special Advantages

For the gardener with a physical disability, there are three additional and important advantages to vertical growing.

- First, this method greatly increases the number of crops and plants that can be grown, using a minimum of space.
- Second, training plants to grow upwards can make them accessible to the gardener, putting them within easy reach.
- And third, the stakes, trellises, and other systems used for upward growth can be used in raised beds, planter boxes, and containers, as well as in ground-level gardens.

A Number of Methods

Vertical growing can be accomplished in several different ways. The classic crisscross trellis of wood or plastic might come first to mind, as a fan, rectangle, or arbor. There are also cages, stakes, and towers, and thin poles affixed in a tepee design. String trellises and pulley systems are used as well. Special vine eyes and soft lead nails hold plants against a brick wall, as will simple twine on a fence. A gardener can make a handsome planter from wood, with a support for vertical growing built right in, or a trellis can be added to a container, planter box, or raised bed.

A Note of Warning

If you're at all unsteady on your feet, plant stakes for vertical growing are a potential hazard should you stumble and fall. To help avoid a nasty accident, do not use stakes with pointed ends, or use only circular supports instead.

GROWING VEGETABLES VERTICALLY

A Variety of Benefits

There are a number of vegetables that can be grown vertically, with multiple benefits for the gardener as well as for the plants. Vertical growing, first off, saves a lot of space. A tomato or squash, for instance, if left to sprawl in the garden, can take up 6 square feet of ground. Grown vertically, however, the same plant occupies just 2 square feet.

Moreover, the crops of plants grown upwards (tomatoes, especially) are more likely to ripen sooner and are less likely

to rot or suffer damage from pests like slugs. And, because the plants are better exposed to sun and air, the chances of a mildew or fungus infection are reduced.

These crops are also cleaner than those that ripen on the ground, while vertically grown cucumbers will produce attractive, straight fruits. From an aesthetic standpoint, plants grown on a trellis can be an attractive feature of your garden. Finally, trellised crops are easier to harvest, which is perhaps their greatest boon to the gardener with a disability.

Disadvantages

The few disadvantages to this system are easily offset or balanced. Plants grown upwards require more frequent waterings, but a good thick mulch will help keep moisture in the soil. More time and labor is needed at first to set up the cage, stake, or trellis, but vertical growing can save both time and labor later on, particularly when crops are ready for harvesting.

Special Considerations

I hope that after reading this chapter on vertical growing, you'll decide to include some trellised plants in your garden. When gardening with a physical disability, however, there are several factors that must be taken into consideration before you select your seeds, plants, and vertical support systems.

- Will your plants be grown in a ground-level garden, a raised bed, a planter box, a tabletop planter, or in a container?

- If the plants won't be at ground level, how high from the ground will they be planted?

- How tall will the plants be at maturity?

- How high will their supports need to be?

• And, finally, will you be gardening from a seated or standing position, and how high can you comfortably reach?

If you want to keep your plants accessible, you'll need to answer these questions and take the necessary measurements. Without some pre-planting mathematics, the results could be quite frustrating if your plants grow out of reach. Moreover, it's exhausting to work with arms raised for any length of time. A combination of planting methods may in fact be necessary. If your garden is a 30" high planter box, for example, a crop like pole beans may need to be planted at ground level.

Although it's possible that you'll still require some help in erecting supports and in harvesting—depending on where and what the crops are—advance planning will certainly help you towards the goal of a successful garden.

Planning on Paper

Probably the easiest way to figure out these combinations of measurements is to plot your vertical garden out on paper. This way you can make sure that you'll be able to tend to the plants, harvest the crops, and enjoy the flowers, right from where you're sitting or standing.

Another advantage to first setting up your garden on paper is that you can also make sure any tall structures are going to be on the *north* side of the bed. Sun-loving vegetables won't appreciate the shade if a trellis is located anywhere else. Also make a note to put the stakes or trellises on the *downwind* side of the plants. This way the prevailing winds will push the plants against their support. If the plants are instead blown against their ties, the stems may be broken.

Yet another advantage to planning on paper is that you'll have a record of where things are planted. This information will be especially important if you plan to leave some of the larger vertical supports in place in the garden. It can be hard work erecting a strong trellis or a sturdy fence, and it makes sense to not pull up stakes as it were at the end of the growing season. However, remember that you're asking for gardening trouble the following year if you put the same type of plants in the same spots.

Although it might be tempting to keep growing peas on that nice fence you put in, as discussed on page 96, crops shouldn't be planted in the same spot two years in a row. Your plants can suffer unless crops are rotated each season, so use your records to help you plan out the garden. This time, why not grow cukes on that fence, instead?

CHOOSING YOUR PLANTS: VEGETABLES

Catalogue Sources

Specific varieties of vegetables suitable for trellising are described in Chapter Five, Choosing Your Plants. Refer to this section for more information and the sources for the vegetables mentioned below. Several catalogue sources for trellises, cages, stakes, and so on are also included. As noted in the Introduction, study these catalogues if you're interested in learning more about a company's products.

TOMATOES

Tomatoes are often grown with some sort of caging or staking system to keep them upright, particularly if they are classified as indeterminate plants. This type of tomato plant is large and vining, and continues to grow after the fruits have set. If planted inside a cage, indeterminate tomatoes won't need pruning; if trained to a stake, they will.

Because determinate tomato plants are shorter and bushier, they don't need pruning. Staking can be difficult, but other kinds of support can be used if desired. Unlike the indeterminate types, their growth slows down after the fruits have formed. Tomatoes are produced over a shorter period of time, about 3–4 weeks. Most early tomatoes are determinate, while late varieties are usually indeterminate. For a combination of the best qualities of each type, try the new BETTER BUSH and HUSKY varieties.

Cages

Indeterminate tomatoes are often grown in circular wire cages. Although the fruits will mature a little later than if the plant had been trained to a stake, a big crop will be produced, and the plants will keep bearing until frost.

Tomato cages can be made from a 5' length of concrete reinforcing wire, by bending the cut wires and hooking them to the other end of the mesh to form a cylinder. The 6" openings in the mesh will let you get your hand in for harvesting. To support the tomato cage, some of the cross wires can be cut out of the bottom of the cage and the cylinder then pushed into the ground.

Alternately, the cage can be tied or wired to a 4' stake that is firmly driven into the ground next to the cage. Long stakes can also be inserted horizontally through several wire cages in a row, to help hold them in place. Later, when the season is over, either dismantle the cages and store them flat, or, if you have the space, put them away as is.

Tomato cages are available commercially too, in cylinder, square, triangular, cone, and rectangular forms. Some of these shapes easily fold flat for winter storage. While these ready-made cages will cost a little more than the home-made variety, they will save you labor and, possibly, scratched hands from working with the wire.

A few catalogue sources for tomato cages include a 14½" x 30" galvanized wire cage from Park (4 for $20.00); a 14½" x 40" one from Burpee (4 for $25.00); a 14⅜" x 32" one from Gardener's Supply (4 for $25.00); a 47" tall, PVC-coated steel cone from Smith & Hawken (2 for $24.00); and an 18" x 40", enamel-coated galvanized wire triangle cage, also from Smith & Hawken ($24.00). Your local garden center will have tomato cages, too.

Stakes

Indeterminate tomatoes can also be trained to a stake. While caged tomatoes need to be spaced 3' apart, staked tomatoes can be planted closer together, with 2' between plants. Pruning to a single stem by removing all the suckers will give you early tomatoes; the fruits will, however, be more subject to sunscald since there isn't as much foliage left to protect them. The yield, moreover, won't be heavy.

Cutting out the suckers and tying up the plant as it grows are chores that will need to be done weekly. There are advantages to single-stem pruning, but it isn't considered the best way to handle the plants for an all-season crop.

As a variation on growing to a staked, single stem, remove suckers just on the bottom 18" of the stem. The top will bush out to provide sun protection for the fruits, which will still be early.

Training the plants to two, three, or four stems is another option. You'll get more tomatoes, with better foliage protection, than with the single-stem method. Removing suckers and tying up the stems will still be necessary.

Staking can be done either just before or right after setting out the transplants. (If you wait to do this job later, you'll run the risk of damaging the root systems as they grow and spread.) Drive a 6–7' wooden stake into the ground next to the plant, far enough down so that the stake is anchored securely, about 1–1 ½'. Soaking the ground thoroughly beforehand can make this rather difficult job easier, as will using stakes with an angled or sharpened tip.

Metal or plastic stakes can be used instead of wooden ones, with the obvious advantage that they won't rot over time. Metal fence posts, in particular, are useful for large plants with heavy crops that need the extra support. A post-hole digger will help you get the posts into place without undue effort.

Tying up Tomatoes

Foot-long plastic-coated twist ties, garden twine, and strips of pantyhose or soft rags can all be used to tie the tomato plant—carefully—to the stake. Making a rather loose figure-eight loop around the stake and the stem will prevent the tomato vine from being damaged as it grows.

If you want to buy ties for your tomatoes and other plants, one choice is from Gardener's Supply. Their cushioned plant ties are made of foam-coated stainless steel wire and won't damage the plants' stems. A 30' roll, to cut as desired, is $7.00. Jung carries Twist-Ems® ties in a ¼" x 150' continuous roll. The roll is in a dispenser with a steel cutter and costs $5.50. Self-grip tape is offered in the Dig This catalogue at 3 meters (9' 10") for $8.00; elasticized strips with Velcro tabs are $1.25 for 36 cm (14"). These products are especially useful as they eliminate the need for tying, which can be a difficult job if your hands are weak.

Towers

A variation on the stake is the tomato tower, which eliminates the need for tying altogether. The tower is made of 3 sturdy galvanized rods, with a 3–prong base to securely anchor the structure in the ground. The tomato's main stem is guided between the rods as it grows and is held in place by the branches. Park's tower is 5' tall overall and sells for 6 for $22.50.

Trellises

This technique for indeterminate tomatoes is popular with many commercial growers. Drive 2 sturdy 6' fence posts into the ground 6' apart. Plant the tomatoes in a line between the posts, at 1 ½' intervals. Stretch a wire across the tops of the posts and nail or staple it in place; then attach another wire across the posts 6" from the bottom. Finally, run string between the two wires at each spot where a tomato is planted, and train the tomato vine to grow up it.

Keep the plant pruned to a single stem as it grows. Twisting the string around the tomato, by the way—instead of the other way around—will help prevent the plant from breaking.

The system requires continual attention to keep the suck-

ers removed and the vines trained to the strings. The fruit, though, is clean, easy to pick, and often earlier than with other methods. If windy weather and heavy fruit set cause the structure to sway, guy wires can be attached to the posts to help anchor them.

Another system, called the "Florida weave," involves running two strings, one beneath the other, horizontally between two posts. The tomatoes are planted in a line between the posts and then woven in and out through the strings, which provide the support to keep the plants growing vertically. No tying is necessary.

Various Other Options for Tomatoes

There are several variations as well on these caging and staking methods for tomatoes. For instance, some gardeners construct rectangular wooden cages for their plants, with evenly spaced crosspieces to hold the structure together. Others use double wood stakes, one on either side of the plant, with three crosspieces for support. Still others prefer a wooden A-frame or tent design built of 1 x 2 stakes.

Linda Tilgner, in *Tips for the Lazy Gardener*, describes another way to keep tomatoes upright. Begin by nailing or stapling a 5' high length of hog wire to strong stakes. Make two of these fences, then set them up parallel to each other at 1½ –2' apart and drive the stakes into the ground. Set out the tomato transplants between the fences. As the plants grow, slide cross-sticks through the fences to provide further support.

Finally, for shorter tomatoes, you can make a platform of cinder blocks and boards. Plant the tomatoes in the spaces between the boards so the platform will support them as they grow.

PEAS, BEANS, AND CUCUMBERS

Peas are another vegetable that is often grown upwards on a fence or trellis. The following peas grow 4–6' high, making them good choices for the gardener who can stand but not bend: TALL TELEPHONE (or ALDERMAN) and MULTISTAR for "regular" green peas; SUGAR SNAP and MAMMOTH MELTING SUGAR for snap peas; and NORLI and CAROUBY DE MAUSSANE for snow peas.

As their name implies, pole beans are at their best when allowed to grow vertically. Choices in these climbing vines include a large selection of yellow, green, shell, and lima beans; the Vermont Bean Seed catalogue alone carries 20 varieties. Several pole beans are as decorative as they are productive. Be sure to note heights, however, if you need to keep the plants within an accessible reach. SCARLET RUNNER and WHITE DUTCH RUNNER beans, for example, with their beautiful, hummingbird-attracting blossoms, both grow over 10' tall!

Cucumbers also do well when grown vertically. Off the ground, the fruits stay clean and away from bugs and rodents, plus they will be nice and straight, a shape many people prefer. Even the bush-type cucumbers like SALAD BUSH HYBRID that are so good for containers can have a small trellis added to their pot.

Fences

Stretching chicken wire between two stakes or posts, with seeds planted along the bottom in a single row, is a popular way of growing peas. For a larger crop, a double row can be planted instead, with the seeds 6" apart on either side of the fence. Even a single section of split-rail or chain-link fencing can be used for growing a variety of vegetables. Or try a section of lattice from the lumberyard.

For a ready-made pea fence, try the Park catalogue. The connected panels of galvanized wire have 6" spikes to secure them in the ground. Each panel measures $14\frac{1}{2}$" x 30"; the 7 panels together are 16' long ($19.00).

Taller peas, and cucumbers too, can be grown on Burpee's pea fence. The galvanized wire fence is 8' x 40" and folds flat for storage. A package of 2 fences is $23.00.

Tepees with Poles

Yet another option is the tepee, or tripod. This design is easy both to construct and to erect, since the ends are only pushed a short way into the soil. Three or more long bamboo poles are the "classic" choice, but stakes or poles of wood, metal, or plastic, or saplings, are also possibilities. Tie the poles together, one-fourth of the way down from the top, with sturdy string or wire. Then spread the poles apart, set up the structure in the garden, and plant around the base of it.

Use the tepee as is for pole beans; for peas, cover it with trellis netting (see below) first. Children, by the way, love to hide and play inside the vine-covered tepee!

For quick and easy assembly, try the bamboo tepee kit from Gardener's Supply. The six 6' foot poles are inserted through the openings of a special plastic disk, so there's no tying required ($10.00).

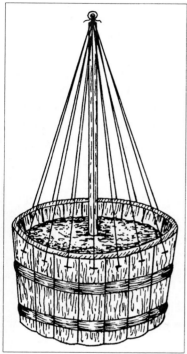

Tepees with Stakes and Strings

Instead of using poles, a tepee can be created from stakes and string. Drive an 8' wooden post, with a screw eye at the top, 2' into the ground. Next, circle the post with 6 short stakes at a distance of 2–3' from the bottom of the pole. Then run strong strings or garden twine through the screw eye and tie them to the stakes to make a tripod shape (rather like a Maypole). Plant peas, beans, or ornamental vines around the base of the pole and let them climb up.

The same design helps you turn a half or whole whiskey barrel planter into a tepee for your climbers. Again, use a stake topped with a screw eye, and affix it in the middle of the barrel. Add more screw eyes around the barrel's perimeter, then run strings up and down to make a tripod.

Poles

A single stake is the most basic support for pole beans; it does, however, need to be driven in about 2' for it to withstand a summer storm. A homemade pole can come from a dead cedar tree on your property, or from a discarded Christmas tree. Trim off the branches—with a few short, stubby ones left on—and drive the tree into the ground. For extra support, add a metal post next to it and lash the two together.

Just as Native Americans trained pole beans to climb up cornstalks, you can use sunflowers as supports. Choose the 10–12' giant varieties and let them get established, then plant your pole beans around the base of the stalks.

For shorter vines, drill evenly spaced holes on an angle up and down an old wooden fence post. Insert short pieces of dowel rod and let the plant use these to twine about as it climbs.

Trellises

A simple trellis such as a piece of lattice can be tacked to a compost bin and cucumber seeds planted at the base. The plants will be well fed from the compost and should produce a fine crop.

For tall peas, try a fence-like trellis, as described by Kathleen Yeomans in *The Able Gardener*. Drive 8' metal fence posts into the ground, no further than 10' apart. Next, firmly

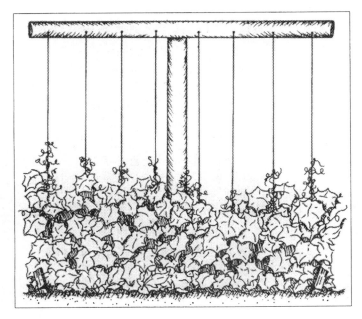

stretch plastic-covered wire (clothesline) between the posts and either tie, staple, or nail it in place. String another length of line along the bottom. Then weave strong twine at 4" intervals back and forth between the wires. After the peas are harvested, cut down the twine and vines for composting, and leave the rest of the structure standing.

If you want to use a tall vertical support structure but can't reach the top sections, a little Yankee ingenuity can help you create a harvesting method for trellised peas and pole beans. Instead of anchoring the top support in place, rig it up as a pulley system so that the bar—with vines attached—can be lowered for harvesting. This method is particularly useful for the gardener working from a seated position.

For pole beans, try a crisscross design trellis. Place tall poles 3' apart and run twine or string from the top of each pole to the bottom of the neighboring one. Plant the beans at the base of each pole and train the vines to climb up the twine, forming an "X" pattern.

The T-shaped frame from an old clothesline brace, or an abandoned child's swing set frame, can form the basis of yet another trellis support system. Two short stakes on the outside of the frame, with a length of twine strung between them, will give you a horizontal line so that more twine can be stretched vertically, from the top of the frame to the bottom string. Again, plant seeds under each vertical string and train them upwards. This method is just as effective with peas or cucumbers.

Trellis Netting

Nylon or plastic trellis netting can be purchased at garden stores or from many catalogues, including Gardener's Eden, Gurney's, Burpee, Park, Mellinger's, Johnny's, and Jung. The netting can be used with stakes or posts, lasts for years, is inexpensive, and comes in a variety of sizes. A 6' x 8' length of Ross netting, for instance, is $3.50 and a 5' x 15' length of Trellis Plus™ is $4.00, both in the Mellinger's catalogue.

Towers

Although often referred to as bean towers, these structures are equally good for snap peas, cucumbers, and annual vines, as well as pole beans. To build your own tower, set up a tall 3 x 3 post with 2 pieces of 1 x 3 nailed to the top in an "X" shape. Two more 1 x 3's are nailed to the bottom of the post at right angles to each other. Add screw eyes at the end of each 1 x 3, top and bottom. Then run strings between the screw eyes, one to another, up and down in a crisscross pattern.

Bean towers are available commercially, too. Burpee's tower features a 6' galvanized pole with hoops at the top and bottom. Nylon monofilament is included to string between the hoops ($23.00). The tower offered by Park is similar in design, but has a 5' galvanized pole and biodegradable cotton cord (70' provided). Its cost is $20.00.

Strawberry Towers

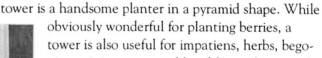

A *strawberry* tower is a handsome planter in a pyramid shape. While

obviously wonderful for planting berries, a tower is also useful for impatiens, herbs, begonias, miniature vegetables, foliage plants, and more.

Typically made of redwood, a tower is thus rather expensive. Given redwood's weather-resistant qualities, however, a strawberry tower will last for years. They are usually available in two sizes: 2' high and 2' square at the base, for 26' of planting row, and 4' high and 2' square at the base, for 46' of row.

Among half a dozen catalogues, Park has the lowest prices on both the smaller tower, at $55.00, and the larger, at $75.00. Prices run from about $5–20.00 higher with other companies. If you can, you might want to comparison shop at your local garden center.

A-Frames

To build an A-frame, nail four pieces of wood together to make a frame, either rectangular or square in shape. Attach nylon trellis netting or hog wire to the frame, build another just like it, then join the two at the top with a hinge. Set the A-frame up in the garden and plant cucumber seeds along each bottom edge. Tie up the vines as they climb. This design can also be used with melons, squash, peas, pole beans, tomatoes, and annual vines.

Gardener's Supply offers an easy-to-build kit for a bamboo A-frame. It includes 11 six-foot poles, plastic ridge clips, nylon netting, and special staples to secure the bottom edge of the netting ($19.00).

A metal A-frame kit is carried by Smith & Hawken. This kit has five zinc-plated steel poles and nylon netting to make a 5' x 8' trellis ($23.00). A bit smaller is the galvanized steel A-frame from Park. Measuring 5' x 5', it too comes with nylon netting ($24.00).

Cages

The cylindrical wire cages you bought or made for tomatoes can also be used for peas, beans, and cucumbers. Plant the seeds around the *outside* of the cage, then let the peas or beans climb; tie up the cukes. Add some manure and compost inside the cage, and you've just fed the plants as well.

Short Supports

If dwarf peas, which grow about 1½' high, are planted thickly, they'll provide their own support as they hold each other up. NOVELLA, a new type of pea, has strong tendrils that provide built-in support by interlacing. Or use pea brush, an old-time method to get the vines up off the ground. Simply push dead tree or shrub branches into the soil in the middle of a wide row of peas, to give the vines a natural brush trellis on which to climb.

MELONS AND SQUASH

The long, vining plants of cantaloupe, watermelon, winter squash, gourds, and pumpkins are usually left to sprawl about the garden, taking up large amounts of space and making themselves rather inaccessible to the gardener with a disability. There are a few varieties of melons and squash that are bush-like in habit, which makes them candidates for container growing. If instead you want your plants to grow vertically, try the following types and techniques.

Since the melons, squash, and so on will need support to keep them from breaking off the vine as it climbs (more on that in a moment), varieties with smaller fruits are a good choice. MINNESOTA MIDGET cantaloupe, for instance, is a compact grower producing 4" melons. For a watermelon to train upwards, try YELLOW DOLL HYBRID, with its shorter vines and "icebox size" fruits.

Likewise, winter squash with shorter vines and smaller fruits—like BUTTERBUSH—are possibilities for growing on a trellis. There are even some special varieties of summer squash that can be grown vertically: LONG GREEN STRIPED, ZUCCETTA RAMPICANTE, and TROMBONCINO.

Gourds, whose vines can run 12' long, can also be trained on a trellis or fence. Choose the smaller-fruited varieties, which are often sold as a mixture of shapes and colors. Miniature pumpkins in orange and white will also grow up a pole or fence; JACK BE LITTLE and BABY BOO are among the names to look for.

Various Vertical Supports

Many of the methods described above for vertical growing are also suitable for melons, squashes, and similar plants. Be sure the trellis or other support is strong and anchored firmly in the ground. If not, the added weight of the fruits could cause the whole structure to collapse or blow over.

The vines, which are ramblers by nature and not climbers, will need to be tied up periodically. Any of the ties used for tomatoes can be used for these plants as well, to securely but loosely train the vine to its support. The fruits themselves will also have to be supported as they become heavier. A sling made of a section of old pantyhose and tied to the trellis will hold up the squash or melon and keep it from breaking off its stem.

The A-frame design, covered with trellis netting or hog wire, is often used with shorter-vined melons and squashes. The angled frame provides both good sun exposure and a surface on which the fruits can partially rest as they grow. Similarly, a tepee of poles covered with netting also works well.

Other possibilities include fences of various sorts, with strategically located wooden shelves to hold individual melons or squashes. A short wooden step ladder might also be used as a support for vine crops, as can a sturdy trellis. Gourds can climb up a discarded, trimmed Christmas tree or cedar, or up the post-and-dowel structure described above.

Depending on your ability to bend and reach, even partially elevating these heavier crops might make all the difference in accessibility. Three small boards nailed together to make the simplest of benches can bring a squash, melon, or other crop up off the ground. A piece of lattice laid across cinder blocks will also support heavier fruits. Arrange it over the bed, then carefully train the growing stems to come up through the openings in the lattice.

CHOOSING YOUR PLANTS: FLOWERING AND ORNAMENTAL VINES

Factors to Consider

Flowering and ornamental vines offer a wide variety of decorative choices. Before you make a selection, though, you'll need to consider several factors.

First, do you want to grow an annual or perennial vine, or both types? Annual vines are good for quick, bright color and rapid growth, but since they die off each year they'll need to be replaced. Perennial vines, which feature pretty flowers, berries, and/or foliage, will grow on each year. Some perennials are fast growers; others, however, will require patience as they mature at a slower rate.

Next, how much maintenance will the vine need, and will it grow out of reach? For example, can that 30–footer be left alone to grow and ramble, or will it need pruning? Will the vine climb and twine on its own, or will it have to be tied up? If pruning and tying are required, are these chores physically possible for you?

Consider what features you want in a vine. Does it bear flowers, and are they fragrant? (This feature can be especially nice if the vine will grow near a window.) Is the vine evergreen or deciduous, and if the latter, how will it look once the leaves have dropped? Will it bear fruit?

Think about where you want the vine to grow. Will you need to provide support, or is there an appropriate existing structure on which it can climb? Will the vine be in the sun or shade, in a dry area or wet? Is it possible the vine will outgrow its support, or cause it to topple?

Also find out *how* a particular vine climbs. Ivy, for instance, is a handsome, useful vine that clings by means of tendrils. If it's climbing on a painted surface and you should need to pull off the vine, however, know that the paint will come away too. Moreover, it's next to impossible to remove the fibrous material that an ivy vine leaves behind.

Finally, is the vine compatible with your climate? Check to see how it's labelled for hardiness, then compare its rating with the USDA Zone Map in the Appendix. Don't set yourself up for failure by trying to grow a bougainvillea outdoors in Maine!

ANNUAL VINES

Some Popular Choices

Seeds for these popular annual vines are readily available in catalogues or at the garden center. All prefer full sun.

climbing sweet peas (*Lathyrus odoratus*): annual; the old-fashioned fragrant types are especially nice; flowers come in brights and pastels; 3'

black-eyed-Susan vine (*Thunbergia alata*): perennial; simple white, orange, and yellow flowers, some with dark eyes; very easy to grow; 5'

climbing nasturtium (*Tropaeolum majus*): annual; easy to grow with orange, red, and yellow fragrant flowers; leaves and flowers edible; 6'

morning glory (*Ipomoea purpurea*): annual; a quick grower in pastels and brights; prefers poor soils; 8'

scarlet runner bean: red flowers attract hummingbirds; use whole beans when young or harvest bean seeds later on; large green leaves provide shade; over 10'

moonflower (*Ipomoea alba*): perennial; huge, white, fragrant flowers open in evening and close the next morning; perennial in mild areas; easy to grow; 15'

PERENNIAL VINES

Some Popular Choices

Perennial vines are usually sold as plants. They may need to be established before flowers appear.

clematis (*Clematis*): sun, part shade/ these very popular vines prefer their roots in the shade and tops in the sun; hybrids have huge flowers; let them climb on a fence or train up a trellis; 2–50', depending on cultivated variety

wisteria (*Wisteria floribunda*): sun/ big, showy clusters of lavender flowers in May; a vigorous twiner; needs training and support; height depends on variety but can reach 30–50'; can be grown in a container and trained as a small tree

trumpet vine (*Campsis radicans*): sun, part shade/ vines attach themselves; flowers beloved by humming-birds; 15–20' or more

silver lace (or fleece) vine (*Polygonum Aubertii*): sun/ a twining climber, it clings without damaging its support; sprays of white flowers; can grow 15' in a year to 30–50'

climbing hydrangea (*Hydrangea anamola*): sun, part shade, or shade/ clings to trees or masonry; showy white flowers; woody vine; deciduous; can climb 50' or more

honeysuckle (*Lonicera*): sun, part shade, or shade/ support this twining climber; both evergreen and de-ciduous varieties, some with fragrant flowers; will smother shrubs and trees if left to run rampant; 2–30'

jasmine (*Jasminum officinale*): sun/ wonderfully scented flowers; semi-evergreen twining shrub; for warmer climates; can reach 40' with support

perennial sweet pea (*Lathyrus latifolius*): sun/ white or rose flowers; 10' with support

bougainvillea (*Bougainvillea*): sun/ brightly colored flowers; for warm climates

passion vine (*Passiflorax alatocaerulea*): sun/ fast-growing evergreen vine; not fully hardy; interesting purplish flowers; needs support to cling by its tendrils; grows to 20–30'

Dutchman's pipe (pipe-vine) (*Aristolochia macro-phylla* or *A. durior*): sun, part shade/ a large-leaved rampant vine useful for covering areas with foliage; yellowish-brown flowers; deciduous and hardy; 10–30'

bittersweet (*Celastrus scandens*): sun/ decorative or-ange berries in fall; a deciduous twining climber; bet-ter in cold climates; grows to 10–20'

Virginia creeper (*Parthenocissus quinquefolia*): sun, shade/ clings to walls; leaves bright red and orange in fall; grows to 30'

Boston ivy (*Parthenocissus tricuspidata*): part shade/ climbs without support by means of sticky discs on the tendril ends; leaves turn a beautiful red in fall; usually deciduous in the north; high-climbing

English ivy (*Hedera helix*): sun, part shade/ comes in several green and variegated forms and various leaf sizes and shapes; will climb and stick to stone and brick walls; evergreen; 10' to more than 50' for ivies in general

rose (*Rosa*): sun/ types include climbers and ramblers; red BLAZE is extremely popular; some shrub roses can be trained against a wall; easy to grow; less than 2'–30', depending on variety

glory vine (*Vitis Coignetiae*): sun, part shade/ rich crimson leaves and small grape-like berries in fall; deciduous; climbs to 60' or more

common grape (*Vitis vinifera*) and **fox grape (*V. Labrusca*):** sun, part shade/ large handsome leaves; edible fruit; deciduous; climbs by tendrils and can reach great heights

VERTICAL SUPPORTS

Existing and Purchased

There are many choices in vertical supports for flowering and ornamental vines. A support might already be on your property: a living or dead tree; a split-rail, wire link, or other kind of fence; a post like that for a mailbox or carriage light; the wall or roof of a building; a porch railing.

Alternately, you might choose to provide your vines with a special support you've built or purchased. Trellises are a handsome choice, and are available in a variety of materials, sizes, shapes, and price ranges. Redwood and other woods, vinyl, fiberglass, and so on are used to make trellises in square, rectangular, fan, dip, and arch shapes. Another alternative, steel pillar frames, create an architectural effect.

Arbors and arches are classically beautiful when planted with roses, wisteria, or grapes. They can run into the hundreds of dollars but provide many years of enjoyment. Arbors and arches are particularly pleasant when a sitting area is included, to fully appreciate the flowers and fruits of your labor.

Training and Tying Vines

To tie up your vines, any soft material can be used, although you'll probably want something unobtrusive. Strips of old pantyhose are fine for tying up tomatoes, but less than lovely when holding up a wisteria! Green, of course, will blend in naturally, and is the color of many types of commercial tying materials; brown garden twine is another possibility. Refer back to page 93 for some suggested sources.

For training a vine up a wall, special wall nails can be used. These have steel heads to drive into masonry or wood, and a bendable lead strip attached to the head to wrap around the plant's stem or branch. Walt Nicke sells a 25–count package of wall nails for $5.50.

The company also carries wall plant trainers, which are flattened nails with an eye in one end. They can be hammered into wood or masonry, then threaded through the eye with wire to help support and train the plant. These come in a package of 10 nails for $4.50, and can also be used with espalier or cordon fruit tree training.

CHOOSING YOUR PLANTS: FRUIT TREES AND VINES

Training Fruit Trees

Before the development of dwarf and miniature fruit trees, gardeners discovered other ways to control a tree's growth. If you've ever seen fruit trees trained as cordons, espaliers, dwarf pyramids, or fans, you'll know how very attractive and ornamental this growth style can be. Trained fruit trees are popular with gardeners for practical reasons, as well. The tree and the fruit are kept right within reach, particularly if the gardener is working from a wheelchair, plus the fruit is borne early and tends to be of excellent quality.

While the trees do require a certain amount of attention and care, it's pleasant work with rewarding results. Training fruit trees into shapes, in fact, may well become a fascinating hobby. Moreover, working with the trees can be an enjoyable family activity; alternately, an older child may want to take on the training as a special project.

Giving explicit directions for training fruit trees in the various shapes is beyond the scope of this book. What follows are general descriptions of the methods involved, in hopes that they will spark your interest to explore the potential of this kind of fruit growing.

If you're interested in pursuing the subject, I urge you to contact your local Agricultural Extension Service for advice. Your public library may also have reference books on fruit tree training; one excellent work to look for is *Dwarfed Fruit Trees* by Harold Bradford Tukey. You may also find information through a local horticultural society, and through a state college of agriculture.

TRAINING AS CORDONS, ESPALIERS, FANS, AND DWARF PYRAMIDS

Training Basics

One-year-old trees ("whips" or "maidens") with a single main stem are commonly used for forming cordons, espaliers, fans, and dwarf pyramids. Regardless of the type of tree or the shape desired, however, the young tree must have been grafted or budded onto a dwarfing type of rootstock: this is essential for success. While these trees are most often grown at ground level, large planter boxes can also be used, with good results. Instead of wire trellises, a strong wooden frame can be secured to the box and the tree trained to it. In the early years of growth, the fruit tree will require consistent pruning; once trained, however, subsequent care is rather simple.

One source for an appropriate tree might be as close as your local garden center or nursery. Be sure to look for that dwarf rootstock; getting advice from the staff horticulturalist will help ensure that you'll be beginning with the right plant material. Also check to see that the tree is hardy for your area, and find out whether it's self-pollinating or will need another tree as a pollinator. The nursery may carry trees that have already been started as espaliers, in 5–gallon containers.

Fruit trees can also be purchased through catalogues. Again, check with the company if you have any questions about suitability. Several catalogue sources for small-size fruit trees are outlined in Chapter Five, Choosing Your Plants. Two companies in particular are highlighted, Stark Bro's and Miller Nursery. A representative of Stark suggests any of their dwarf apple or pear varieties for training, while a spokesman for Miller recommends their Compspur apple trees for espaliers. Your Agricultural Extension Agent can suggest varieties, too.

Fruit trees are probably the most popular plants for training since they are not only beautiful, but produce wonderful fruit as well. They are not the *only* choices, however. Certain shrubby plants can be trained too, to produce a decorative effect. Pyracantha (firethorn) is one such plant. Easily espaliered against a wall, its quantities of red, orange, or yellow berries make a very ornamental show.

A cordon fruit tree.

Cordons

A fruit tree trained as a cordon has a single stem that grows at a 45–degree angle, with the fruits forming close to the trunk or stem. Because cordon trees are space-saving and thin, many of them can be grown in a rather small area. Apples and pears are the most popular choices for cordons, but gooseberries can be trained this way, too. (Note: there are horizontal and double cordon styles as well, but the single oblique method is what is generally referred to simply as "a cordon.")

The basic planting method involves setting the whips 2–3' apart at the 45–degree angle. Each tree is tied to a 6–8' cane; the canes, set in the ground at the same 45–degree angle, are tied to wires stretching between posts. Over the span of several seasons, new lateral branches are cut back to just a few buds. When the main stem reaches the desired height, its growth too is stopped.

Cordon trees can also be grown against a brick or masonry wall. Vine eyes (small metal loops) are driven into the mortar, then lines of plastic-covered wire are stretched out between them. The whips are planted about one foot away from the wall, to allow easy access for pruning and harvesting. Training is handled in the same manner described above.

Espaliers

Espaliers are trees whose branches grow in single-plane, horizontal tiers. These selected vertical branches are trained to wires to grow against a wall or fence. Again, apples and pears are the best candidates for this type of growth training.

Horizontal wires are strung at one-foot intervals between strong posts or between vine eyes affixed in a wall. One or two tiers are suggested for the gardener who uses a wheelchair, while three or four tiers are suitable for the gardener who stands but has difficulty reaching.

The whip is allowed to grow vertically for a while, with two side shoots tied in to the lowest wire. As new side shoots appear, these are tied in to the next wire, and so on through several growing seasons, until the final tier is formed.

Espalier fruit trees.

Fans

As the name suggests, fruit trees can also be trained in the shape of a fan. As for an espalier, the tree is formed to grow in one plane, either against a wall or a post-and-wire fence. It is started in the same way; then, after the first pair of branches has been tied in horizontally, each subsequent pair is trained at ever-steeper angles to achieve the fan shape.

Apples and pears are again good choices for fans, but other fruits can be trained too. Peaches, nectarines, apricots, figs, plums, cherries, red and white currants, blackberries, and loganberries can all be grown as fans, with a sunny, sheltered spot required by the first four.

Dwarf Pyramids

Dwarf pyramid fruit trees—like fans and espaliers—are shaped by cutting back the whip to encourage side growth. With this type of method, however, multiple lateral branches are allowed to grow out so that the tree is balanced all around. One central shoot is trained upwards and cut back seasonally to produce another tier of side shoots. These lateral branches are also shortened to encourage even more branching.

Dwarf pyramid trees are easy to manage and don't require the tying in that other types of trained trees do. Apples and pears are once again the fruits of choice.

If you decide to research the subject of training fruit trees, you'll discover that there are a number of variations on the basic forms into which these trees can be shaped. The Palmette Verrier, for instance, is a candelabra-shaped espalier with four or six arms; a Belgian espalier forms a diamond pattern; and an arcure consists of a series of connecting arcs. There are also single, double, and triple "U" shapes, among others.

These formal patterns are very symmetrical, requiring faithful pruning and training. Informal or free-form patterns have their following, too, as a beautiful design is created but without the strict training methods.

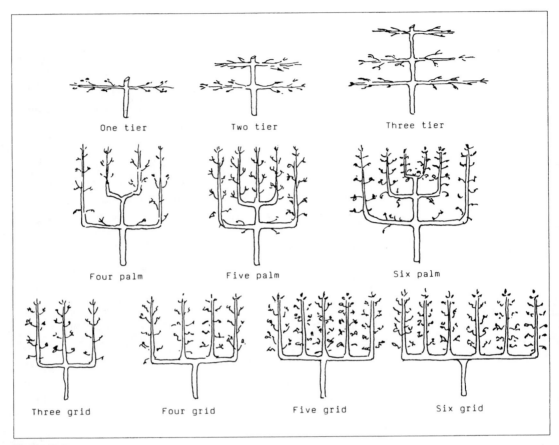

One tier   Two tier   Three tier

Four palm   Five palm   Six palm

Three grid   Four grid   Five grid   Six grid

Espalier Patterns.

Specific Training Systems

In your research you will also find references to specific ways of training trees. These systems have been developed both in this country and abroad, with objectives ranging from early production, to heavy yield, to mechanical harvesting of fruit. While those most likely to utilize and benefit from these developments are pomologists, horticulturists, and commercial fruit growers, the advantages of these systems also extend to the gardener with a physical disability. Here are a few examples.

With a standard height of 48–52", the Lincoln Canopy system is of special interest to wheelchair users. Dr. Suman Singha, Head of the Department of Plant Science of the College of Agriculture and Natural Resources at the University of

Connecticut in Storrs, tells me that the system can be "easily harvested" from a wheelchair. Originating in New Zealand, this method of training is recommended for most commonly grown varieties of apples.

Dr. Singha also notes that "a fruit hedge can be very useful for gardeners with disabilities." The hedge can be as basic as a 2– or 3–wire system, which can be worked either from a wheelchair or a standing position. The 3–Wire Trellis, for example, has a standard height of 5–6'. It is recommended for most apple varieties, and the fruit is easy to harvest. Once established, the tree then requires fairly simple maintenance.

A bit more complex is the Marchand type of fruit hedge. This system originated in France, has a standard height of 5–6', and is recommended for all major varieties of apples. Thorough knowledge of the Marchand system and disciplined care are essential for success with trees trained in this manner.

Another European method, the Bouche-Thomas system, isn't widely used, but does have potential for the gardener with a disability. In his book *Dwarfed Fruit Trees*, pomologist Harold Bradford Tukey describes the system as "a series of tiers of crossed and recrossed branches ... that has the appearance of an interwoven hedge fence." Its height can be 5, 6, or 8'. Little cutting is involved; the branches are slanted, bent, arched, and woven. Tukey suggests apricots, nectarines, and peaches in particular for the Bouche-Thomas system; apples and pears can also be used.

Grapes

Left on their own, grapes will grow and climb to enormous heights. One look at a vineyard, however, will tell you that it's entirely possible to keep the vines pruned to a manageable size. In fact, when grown on a post-and-wire system, grapes can be trained to an accessible height of about 4'. Grapes can also be planted against a wall or fence, or in an arbor if reaching isn't a difficulty.

What training system you use (Kniffen, Guyot, etc.) will depend on what sorts of grapes (American-type or European-type) you want to grow. In a manner similar to that for espaliers, fans, and pyramids, the fruiting canes are trained to horizontal wires over the space of several seasons. Since grapes fruit best on young wood, the canes are alternately tied in and pruned back, with the old wood providing a permanent framework.

Grapes can be grown indoors as well, in a greenhouse or sunroom where they can get as much sunlight as possible. The vine can be planted in a large tub; it will need pruning and training to produce fruit and keep its growth in check.

VERTICAL GROWING IN A RAISED BED, PLANTER BOX, OR CONTAINER

A New Dimension

A vertical support system of one sort or another can be a wonderful addition to a raised bed, planter box, or container: it lets you add literally a whole new dimension to your garden-

ing. The benefits of vertical growing outlined at the beginning of this section also apply to these small-space, contained gardens. Be sure, though, to position the trellis on the north side of the bed. You can, of course, judiciously use the shade from a trellis to provide some protection from the sun. Lettuce, for instance, appreciates a little shade come midsummer, while other plants require it.

Trellises for Beds and Boxes

A simple way to add a trellis to a raised bed or planter box is with three pieces of lumber. Securely fasten two vertical supports at one end of the frame with nails, bolts, screws, or pipe brackets, depending on the size of the wood. Fasten the

third piece of wood across the tops of the two uprights. Then either suspend wires or strings from the horizontal piece, or attach a section of trellis netting, lattice, chicken wire, or galvanized metal fencing to the trellis frame.

Alternately, a very sturdy support can be made using only wood. Three uprights are attached at the end of the bed's or box's frame; four crosspieces form the trellis. This vertical support system is strong enough for just about any plant, including an espaliered fruit tree.

Perhaps the simplest method of adding a trellis to a raised bed or planter box is to sink a small trellis frame into the soil next to the plant. Do this when the plant is first set in or very soon thereafter, so as not to damage the roots as they grow. Supporting stakes can be added if it seems the trellis and the plants on it need to be steadied.

The trellis itself can be either a homemade affair or a purchased one. For smaller supports, try the Mellinger's catalogue: a mini ladder trellis 42" tall and 12" wide is $8.20, and a 36" mini fan trellis is $6.30. Both are of white fiberglass.

For the best of both worlds, combine a table-top garden with a ground-level planting box to which you've affixed a trellis. This system will provide you with a lot of options for creating a unique, personal garden. For instance, with a variety of lettuces, radishes, "baby" carrots, and a few herbs growing on the table, and climbing nasturtiums and cucumbers wending their way up the trellis, you'll have all the makings for a wonderful salad right in one accessible—and pretty—garden.

Trellises for Containers

A simple clay or plastic pot with one trellised plant in it can be very attractive. Short-vined cucumbers and flowering vines are fine choices for a small trellis frame. A large plant, like a tomato grown in a half whiskey barrel, can be staked just like one growing at ground level. And, as noted above in the section on te-pees, a post-and-string tepee can be read-ily constructed using the same half-barrel container.

If you're planning to build, or have built, some basic square or rectangular wooden boxes to use as planting contain-ers, add a vertical frame to one. (Visual-ize, for example, a carpenter's tool box with an extended handle.) Try growing a cherry tomato in it, with its vines tied up to the frame, for good-looking and deli-cious results.

One handsome box-and-trellis sys-tem to buy is from Smith & Hawken's. The square planter box and larger rectan-gular one are of reclaimed redwood; the matching lattice trellis is wall-mounted ($155.00 and $195.00 a set).

A Wall-Garden

For an attractive garden that can be set up on a patio, is self-contained, and is easy to maintain, consider the wall-gar-den. A box-shaped vertical planter, wall-gardens are popular in Europe. One or two sides of the wooden planter are made of slats, which are backed either with black plastic or wire and sphagnum moss. Perforated plastic pipes for watering are fit-ted inside the box; then the planter is filled with a lightweight soil mix. Vegetable and/or flower seedlings are inserted through slits cut in the plastic.

To catch changing patterns of light and shade, the wall-garden is mounted on casters so that it can be easily moved.

Alternately, the vertical planter can be built so that it rests permanently on the ground.

If kept to a height of about 4–5', the plants will be easy to reach from a seated position. From a standing position, the top rows will be manageable, but help will probably be needed with planting the lower levels.

A more ambitious project than others described throughout this book, a wall-garden can be built at home but will require some carpentry skills. One source of diagrams and directions for constructing this vertical planter is *Gardening in Containers.*

Plant Supports While
wire plant supports are typically used with flowers in a ground-level bed, they're certainly appropriate in a raised bed, planter box, or container garden, too. The supports help keep weaker-stemmed plants from breaking, hold long-stemmed ones upright, keep large, floppy plants off the ground, and help clusters of flowers look their best.

These ingenious supports are of coated wire and come in such a variety of shapes and sizes that there's one appropriate for each annual, perennial, or bulb. There are even modular systems that link together to form almost any shape you need. Not only are the supports beneficial for the plants, but they let you get closer to the flowers for smelling and viewing, without a lot of bending or stooping.

Catalogue sources include Gardener's Supply, Walt Nicke, and Smith & Hawken; prices are reasonable. Or, make your own flower supports. For perennials that grow in a clump, try cylinders of pea fencing (look for wire that's coated in green plastic—it's less obtrusive) placed over the plant when it's very small. As it matures, the plant will grow through the mesh. For a very large plant, add a stake.

For peonies, whose large flower heads tend to droop to the ground, many gardeners use this simple trick. Place a circle of chicken wire over the tiny sprouts when they come up in the spring. As the peony grows, the wire circle will "grow" with the plant and provide support for the stems. Here, a stake is recommended.

For other flowers, any stiff wire—even a coat hanger—can be bent to form various loops and support frames.

Combination Plantings

If the pot you're using is large enough, consider adding a low-growing plant or two at the base of the climber. Not only will this be a very effective use of available space, but the plants will serve to hide the climber's base, which may be somewhat unattractive. Combining plants in this way will help heighten the visual interest of your garden, as well.

Measure Before You Plant

As a final reminder on vertical gardening in a container, planter box, or raised bed, ask yourself the questions outlined at the beginning of this chapter before you begin. Take measurements and plot out the heights of plants, trellises, and your reach. Then use this information to help determine how best to arrange and plant *your* vertical garden to make it enjoyable, productive, and accessible.

CHAPTER FOUR

Tools, and Tips for Using Them

Introduction

Have you heard it said, "A good craftsman never blames his tools"? I would suggest that the saying is only true up to a point. When you're working in the garden, having and using good tools are what will help make you a good craftsman.

For the gardener with a disability, a "good tool" is something worth searching for. These tools won't necessarily be the most expensive or fanciest ones on the market—although they might be. Sometimes the best tools will be those you've created yourself, from an old spoon, scrap lumber, or what have you. Other times they'll be a familiar old tool used in a new, creative way.

CHOOSING THE RIGHT TOOLS

Your Physical Abilities

The most important thing to consider in choosing garden tools is, as always, your physical capabilities. You know what your body can and cannot do, and you need to apply this knowledge when making your tool selections. It's for this reason that these types of tools are often called "enabling tools." They can help make it possible to overcome any physical obstacles that stand between you and an active, enjoyable pursuit of gardening.

The enabling tools I discuss in this chapter are suggestions meant to encompass a wide range of abilities and limitations. Horticultural therapists and others who have studied accessible gardening have found certain tools to be among the most useful and useable. The many gardeners who actually put these trowels, hoes, and so on to the test bear out these findings through their own experiences. While not every tool discussed here will pertain to your particular situation, I'm sure you'll find some that will be just right for your purposes.

Having and using "good tools" in the garden can make your time spent there a pleasure and not a chore. Think of your garden tools as an extension of your body and let them help it function in the smoothest, most efficient way possible. By letting the tools work with you rather than against you, you'll conserve energy and avoid unnecessary strain and fatigue. Make conservation of effort one of your gardening goals!

With that said, however, remember that your best tools are right at the ends of your arms. If possible, use your hands instead of an implement for at least part of your gardening. For some people, working with the hands rather than a tool is better exercise, and can stimulate the senses and the memory, too. Don't let a set of tools stand in the way of the connections to be made between you, your plants, and the soil.

BUYING TOOLS

What to Look For

If you're in the market to buy some new gardening tools, several criteria need to be met to help you get the easiest, safest, and most efficient use from a tool. Before you make a selection, look for these factors, then buy the best tool you can afford.

- Balance: A "good tool" shouldn't require great hand strength to hold it and to use it. Hand tools, especially, should fit your grip comfortably.

- Weight: A lightweight tool is preferred as long as it's also strong and well-balanced. Aluminum hand tools, for example, are non-corrosive, easy to clean, and wonderful to use.

- Good construction: Watch out for inexpensive, poorly made tools that will bend and break easily. They can be tiring to use and even dangerous, and will cost more in the long run. Check instead for signs of quality construction. Cheaply made tools, for instance, will often break at the spot where the handle and the metal tool join. Better tools will have solid-socket or solid-strapped construction.

• Adaptability: Wood is preferred for the shafts of tools that are used vigorously, like rakes and hoes, since they're easier to adapt: just screw a hand-grip in place. White ash is an excellent choice for handles. Also used to make baseball bats, this wood is strong, light, and durable. Before buying any wood-handled tool, check the grain. It should run straight along the handle's length, with no knots.

Any tool you use in the garden should be able to do its job with a minimum of effort required on your part. Even more useful are tools that can handle multiple tasks. Having one tool that can do the work of two or more means fewer items for you to store, transport, care for, and keep track of in the garden.

Where to Buy Tools

If you have access to a garden center, nursery, hardware store, or home center, you'd do well to check out their tools in person. Some stores may let you try out a tool, to make sure it's the right "fit" for you; it's worth asking.

Going to the store yourself isn't the only option, however. Catalogue shopping will allow you the benefits of a wider selection of tools from which to choose, plus the convenience of phone or mail ordering and home delivery. The one drawback, of course, is that you can't see and test the item before buying it. You'll have to rely on the company's reputation, accuracy of descriptions, and desire to please its customers.

Homemade Tools

Interspersed with the examples of gardening tools you can buy are some tools that you (or a handy friend) can make. Requiring just basic materials, these low-cost homemade enabling tools can help solve gardening problems for which no manufactured tool yet exists. Also, with imagination, there's no end to the adaptations that can be created for standard tools you may already own. As you'll see, Yankee ingenuity is alive and well in the garden!

STORING AND CARING FOR YOUR TOOLS

A Place for Everything

To be a good craftsman in the garden doesn't just involve having the proper tools. It also means finding a convenient place to store them, and then maintaining the tools in proper working order.

Gardening tools and supplies, first off, should be kept in an area where they're readily accessible. Whether your tools are stored in the garage, a special shed, or other location, take the time to set up a system that works for you. Hanging tools on hooks, racks, or a pegboard; winding hoses on a reel or coiling them up; locating pots and potting soil on shelves; and keeping small hand tools in plastic storage bins are just a few of the ways to organize your equipment.

Tools stored in an accessible spot are also tools stored safely. This means nothing hung so high that you lose balance or strain muscles reaching for it, or so precariously placed that a tool can come crashing down on your head. Conversely, tools should not be strewn about on the floor, waiting to trip the gardener or to be stepped on and broken.

In the same safe manner, supplies like fertilizers need to be carefully labelled if they're transferred to a lidded container or jar. Any dangerous materials such as pesticides, however, should *never* be re-packaged but rather stored in their original containers.

Tool Maintenance

Maintaining your tools involves removing the dirt after you've spent a session together in the garden, either by hosing them off or wiping them down. Plunge metal tools like shovels and spades in a bucket of sand to which a quart or so of motor oil—new or used—has been added, to keep them in good condition. Remove any rust from corrosive metals with steel wool, emery cloth, or a wire brush. This will both preserve the tool and lessen the threat of tetanus. Keep the blades of pruners, shears, and other cutting tools sharp. Not only will they be more efficient, but a sharp tool can actually be safer to use than a dull one.

Don't overlook the handles of your wooden tools. Apply oil or floor wax occasionally to prevent splintering and to keep the wood comfortable to the grip. And, to avoid finding a misplaced tool the hard way, paint brightly colored bands around the handles. This will make the tool readily visible if inadvertently left on the ground or laid in the grass.

Finally, periodically inspect your tools for loose screws or bolts. Tighten or replace any that could cause slippage and thus an unsafe condition.

A POSITION FOR GARDENING

Sitting and Kneeling

Let's start with accessing the garden itself. Whether you garden in containers, a raised bed, or a ground-level bed, many people find that some sort of a gardening bench or seat allows them to reach the plants right where they grow. If you use a wheelchair, transferring to a bench might be a feasible alternative if you find you need to get closer to the soil. Several seating options are available.

Over 20 years ago, British author Betty Massingham (*Gardening for the Handicapped*) recommended use of a kneeling bench. Such a seat can reduce fatigue by allowing you to change positions, plus it provides support for lowering or raising your body. Her advice is equally good today.

The Easy Kneeler® is one example of just this sort of bench. Standing 20" high, the tubular steel-framed seat flips over for kneeling. The legs become handles to help you lower yourself down and then push yourself back up again. It has a foam cushion for comfort and weighs under 10 lbs. (Gardener's Supply, $50.00).

A number of other companies carry versions of the Easy Kneeler®. Prices vary considerably; for example, a folding steel, 6–pound kneeling bench is $24.00 from Mellinger's, while a steel bench made in England is $75.00 at Gardeners Eden. Lightweight polyethylene models are available too (Plow & Hearth, $40.00).

If you want to avoid kneeling and bending, the four-wheeled Scoot-n-Do® could prove a real help. About 10"

The Easy Kneeler®.

The Scoot-n-Do®.

high, it has a padded seat and big plastic wheels (Gardener's Supply, $60.00). Three-wheeled garden trikes or scoots are also available (Alsto's, $80.00).

Another possibility is the Unicar Scooter from Langenbach. Made in Germany, it has a steel frame, molded seat, carry-all tray, and four wide tires. It sells for $59.00.

If you can kneel but would like some cushioning for your knees, try a foam pad that's impervious to water (A.M. Leonard, $6.00). A variety of knee protectors are available, too, from thick sponge rubber (Walt Nicke's, $10.00), to waterproof rubber with self-stick closures (Mellinger's, $24.50).

Of course you don't need to purchase a special seat for your gardening. Many a gardener has found that a child's folding chair is admirably suited to the task.

TOOLS FOR GARDENING

Hand Tools

Over the past few years it's been very encouraging to see how manufacturers are (at last!) beginning to offer ergonomically designed hand tools. For the gardener with arthritis, rheumatism, carpal tunnel syndrome, or other problems with the hands, these tools can be a godsend. There are several types of enabling hand tools that warrant consideration.

First—and most unique—are the Handform trowel and fork. These tools were created by Hubbard Yonkers, an industrial designer and gardener in New Hampshire. Tired of ending up with sore wrists after a session of digging with a conventional trowel, he undertook to redesign the tool.

Bearing little resemblance to traditional models, the trowel and fork feature curved handles that let you hold your wrist in a more relaxed and comfortable position. You get maximum leverage for your effort, but without the need for keeping a tight grip on the tool.

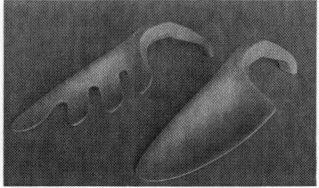

Handform tools.

Of bright yellow unbreakable plastic, the tools are lightweight and don't conduct cold from the soil, a boon for those with cold-sensitive hands (Walt Nicke's $12.00 each; Mellinger's, trowel only, $12.00).

Other ergonomically designed hand tools include the Corona Comfort line. Made of aluminum alloy, these tools feature a larger diameter, contoured handle with cushioned grips for an easier and more comfortable operation (A.M. Leonard, $7.00 each). "Super grip" or "trigger grip" hand tools are of die-cast, polished aluminum and weigh just 7 ozs. each. The trigger design on the handle makes them comfortable to hold, and gives extra leverage too. The makers suggest you try these tools if you have arthritis or another condition that makes traditionally designed tools painful to grasp and use.

Brookstone carries a set of 5 "trigger grip" tools—weeder, trowel, planter, fork, and cultivator—for $35.00. Nichols and Stokes price the individual tools at about $5.25–$5.50

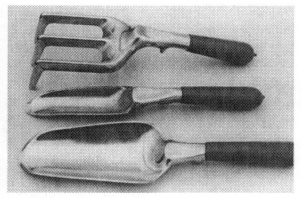

Trigger-grip tools from Johnny's.

apiece. Johnny's offers the trowel, planter, and cultivator as a set for $23.00, with the bonus of plastic coated grips on the handles. Individually, their tools are $9.00 and $10.00.

Dig This describes their plastic tools as "surprisingly sturdy" and recommends them for hands without much strength. The assorted hand tools are $2.00 each.

Cushioning Handles

Whether you decide to use ergonomically or conventionally designed hand tools, many gardeners find that adding gripping material or padding to the handle makes a tool easier to hold and use. There are many options in cushioning available, both homemade and purchased. Padded grips can, of course, be added to long-handled tools as well.

One way to cushion a handle is to wrap a piece of foam rubber around the handle and secure it with epoxy or electrical tape. Cylindrical foam padding is also available; just cut it to fit and slip it over the tool's handle. Try the adaptAbility catalogue for foam tubing in four sizes, each in a section about 1 yard long ($3.50 and $4.50).

Another way to build up a handle is with insulating pipe tape wrapped to an appropriate thickness. Other choices include self-adhesive foam, elastic bandages, rubber hand grips for crutches, moleskin, tennis racket grip tape, bicycle handle grips, or even just some soft fabric to make a tool more comfortable to the hand.

Whatever padding or gripping material you select, however, be sure it's secured firmly to the handle. A tool that slips can be a dangerous thing!

A can of air-dry plastic coating from the hardware store lets you put your own "personal grip" on a tool. Following the manufacturer's directions, cover the handle with three coats of the material. When the last coat is nearly dry, squeeze the handle, then let it dry completely. Since the coating will be molded to your own hand, the chances of the tool slipping out of your grip will be greatly reduced.

My-Grip® thermoplastic also custom molds the handle to your hand. Low heat is applied with this material, which can be easily re-molded (adaptAbility, slip-on tubing, $10.50 or spiral tubing, $15.50). A similar material is offered by Enrichments, called My-Grips™. Heat the pre-cut, slip-on soft plas-

Tools adapted with My-Grips™ from Enrichments.

tic tubing in hot water, and mold it to your grip. Three packages of two each are $9.50.

Check the Walt Nicke catalogue for Gardener's Grips. These slide onto your tool handles and are secured with the supplied glue, to provide a soft, non-slip grip ($2.50–6.00).

Cushioning Hands
Instead of—or in addition to—padding a handle, you can cushion your hands. Your local bicycle shop has fingerless, leather-palmed bike gloves, in a variety of makes and styles. Sizes range from adult down to ones small enough to fit a two-year-old. A basic glove will cost around $10.00, with prices going up to around $40.00.

Another option is to wear a pair of wheelchair cuffs. Designed to protect hands while using a wheelchair, these suede leather cuffs feature open finger and thumb areas and are easy to put on and take off (Enrichments, $25.00).

Aids for Extra Support

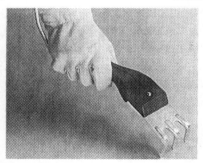

Lever Aide tools.

A new item in the 1993 Walt Nicke company catalogue is the Lever Aide, a cushioned leverage bar attached to a hand tool. This device can be a real help if you have weak wrists and hands, since the stronger arm muscles do the work. The tool's plastic handle is ergonomically designed to reduce the effort required and thus lessen fatigue. A set of three tools for weeding, cultivating, and digging is $37.00. Brookstone sells the extra leverage cultivator alone for $15.00.

An item called a Homemaking Cuff ($28.50) is available through the Enrichments catalogue. The adjustable cuff is of soft suede, with Dycem® lined straps that hold the cuff securely to any rod-shaped handle.

While its original use is with a household implement like a broom, a company representative agreed that the cuff could be used with a gardening tool, suggesting that it be a small, light one, though.

Also available in the Enrichments catalogue is a Phone Holder. This holder or cuff has a bendable, plastic-covered metal frame with a wide Velcro® wrap strap; a set of two is $14.00. Horticulture/Vocational Rehabilitation Therapist Jim

Bradford of California considers this type of cuff a "valuable tool" for gardeners who can use their arms but not their hands.

Horticultural therapist Julia Beems, author of *Adaptive Garden Equipment,* includes detailed directions in her book for making homemade devices for gardeners who need extra help holding their tools. The Tool Clip, Forearm Cuff, and the Universal Cuff feature Velcro® closures to keep the tool securely in your hand. All three use canvas webbing and other readily available, inexpensive materials. Sewing is required.

On a safety note, be sure to check for pressure or skin sores that might develop from using any adapted tools. Skin irritation from perspiration under the cuff is another possibility. Loosening the cuffs or adding padding may be all that's needed to solve the problem.

Long-Handled Hand Tools

If you garden from a wheelchair or other seated position, long-handled hand tools may be just right for you; they're especially useful for working in a raised bed. A number of fine choices are available, in a variety of lengths and prices.

Leading off is Langenbach, with three different sets of these tools available in their catalogue. First is a set made in Maine. The claw, dandelion weeder, trowel, and Cape Cod weeder have 30" handles and are crafted of steel and ash. Prices range from $14.50 to $16.75.

Next, an English-made, long-handled trowel and fork sell for $27.50 and $26.00, respectively. These 20" tools feature polished stainless steel heads, polypropylene handles, and cushioned pistol grips.

Finally, Langenbach also carries Gardena (of Germany) Combisystem hand tools. Their compact size lends them for use in small spaces, either as hand tools or, with the 30" extension handle, as long-reach tools. The handle and 4 tools are $12.00 each; the gardener's saw costs $29.00.

Check the Walt Nicke's catalogue for another set of German hand tools with extension handles. This expanded group—from Adlus—includes 7 tools ($5.95–$10.95 apiece) and 3 extension handles ($5.75–$6.75 apiece). The

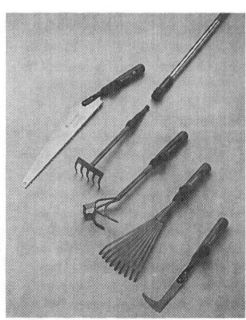

Gardena Combisystem hand tools.

lightweight handles come in 15", 30", and 38" lengths, offering the gardener a lot of options.

Walt Nicke also carries two stainless steel, heavy-duty digger trowels with longer handles. The model with the 18" handle is $10.00, and the 22" one is $12.00.

From the Kinsman Company come a lightweight 20" fork and trowel with alloy handles and stainless steel heads ($30.00 each). The angled handles let you reach and dig more easily.

Also from Kinsman are 8 different tools with 28" handles, including various weeders, trowels, and forks. These tools are made in Maine, have ash handles and steel blades, and cost $15.00 apiece. (A matching 35½" long shrubbery rake is $19.00 from Gardeners Eden.)

The British company of Spear & Jackson has been making tools for over a century, and the long-handled gardening tools they offer are fine ones indeed. The hoe, trowel, and rake have comfortable contoured hand grips, detachable wrist straps, and lightweight tubular steel handles. A set of 3 with 27" handles is $70.00 from Plow & Hearth, or $80.00 for the set with 39" handles.

With such a range of lengths from which to choose, you can probably find a long-handled hand tool to match your needs. Of course, for a really customized size and low cost, you can fit a broomstick, tennis racket handle, or piece of aluminum conduit into the socket of a trowel or fork head; conversely, a standard tool like a hoe or rake can be cut down to the length you want. For little jobs, lash an old spoon and fork onto bamboo canes, or use long-handled barbecue tools.

Children's Tools

Many fine sets of children's gardening tools are now on the market. Because of their lighter weight and smaller size, these tools are also helpful for the seated or kneeling adult gardener. Children's tools are particularly useful if you're gardening in a ground-level or raised bed, where full-size implements could be awkward and tiring to use. They can also be used when standing: just add a longer handle. Again, as with the

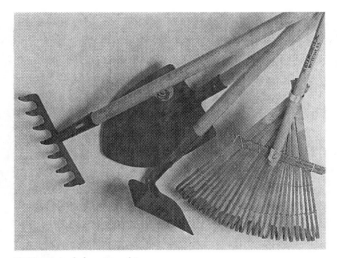

Children's tools from HearthSong.

hand tools, you might want to apply some sort of cushioning material to give you a better grip.

Various plastic tools are widely available in toy and hardware stores, but for real durability look for ones made of steel and wood. Some companies describe their children's gardening items as being smaller versions of standard adult tools, and not toys.

A shovel or spade, rake, and hoe can be had at a reasonable cost (Dig This, $8.00 each; Mellinger's, $15.00). Leaf rakes are even less expensive. A small bamboo one at the local hardware store, sized just right for my 5–year-old daughter, Rachael, was only $4.00.

In the $20.00–40.00 range are children's tools from Gardener's Supply, HearthSong, Alsto's, Walt Nicke's, and Langenbach. The tools average in length from 28–32"—a few run as long as 40"—and are often sold in sets. Particularly handsome are the English-made Sheffield Pride children's tools, described as worthy of being passed from generation to generation (Walt Nicke's).

By the way, if you're actually buying these tools for a child, don't forget a pair of work gloves. Of cotton duck with leather palms, they come in sizes for ages 3–13 years (HearthSong, $6.00). Adult work gloves can be found just about anywhere.

Adapting Tools

If you'd like to turn a standard-issue tool like a fork or spade into an enabling tool, here are two good ways to go about it. For the first method, fit a D- (or T-) shaped handle halfway along the shaft

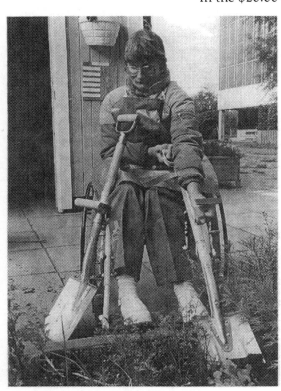

Using a spade with a T-shaped handle.

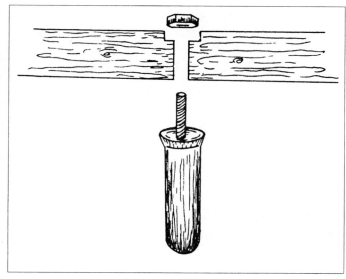

Attaching a support handle.

and you'll eliminate some bending as you work. Instead of leaning over to reach farther down the shaft, you'll be pulling on the D-shaped handle instead and getting better leverage for your effort. Try a hardware store for this handle, or send for a "Helping Handle" (Walt Nicke's, $9.00)

For the second, adding a support handle to a long-handled spade or fork lets you lean on it and avoid stooping. Pick up a 4–5" support handle and a corresponding ¼" bolt and washer at the hardware store. About 30" from the top of the blade, drill a hole through the handle. Then countersink to about ⅜" the side opposite the handle. Insert the support handle and its bolt through the hole, fastening it firmly with the nut. This tip comes from the therapists of the Chicago Horticultural Society.

If you find these adaptations helpful, you may even want to add both a D-shaped *and* a support handle to the spade or fork. Experiment first to find just the right leverage points for you before attaching the handles.

PREPARING FOR PLANTING

Digging and Cultivating with a Spade

Digging in the garden can present problems in terms of the difficulty of the work, and stress and strain on the muscles. A spade, with its smaller blade, will probably be easier to manage than the standard round point shovel. A child-sized shovel, though, may be just right.

When shopping for a spade, look for a combination of light weight plus sturdy construction. Weighing just 4 ½ lbs., the Leonard Iowa Pattern spade has a "D" handle grip, and the shorter, 27" handle of a traditional spade. The Nursery/Garden spade is also 4 ½ lbs. with a "D" grip, but has a longer, 47" handle (A.M. Leonard, $46.25 and $30.75, respectively).

More expensive are three spades that are available in 54", long-handled models, as well as the standard short lengths. The spades are of tubular all-steel make, are zinc plated, have "D" handle grips, and weigh around 6 lbs. Prices for A.M. Leonard's long-handled Standard, Extended Blade, and Diamond Point models range from $79.00 to $83.50.

Spear & Jackson makes a beautiful, high-quality spade of solid forged steel, with a hardwood shaft impregnated with a strong weatherproofer. This long-handled spade measures 59" and weighs about 4 lbs. (Langenbach, $42.00).

Another British-made, long-handled spade is available from Kinsman. Manufactured by Sheffield Pride, this tool is 59" long, weighs about 6 lbs., and has a forged carbon steel head. Its price is $44.00.

Digging and Cultivating with a Fork

Many gardeners consider a good fork to be as indispensable a tool as a spade or shovel for working the soil. Again, a strong but light tool is best.

Spear & Jackson makes a long-handled fork to match the spade described above. It too weighs 4 lbs. and is 59" long. Buy the fork from Langenbach for $44.00, or get both the spade and fork for $79.00.

Kinsman has the Sheffield Pride long-handled fork to match the spade, with the same length, weight, and price of $44.00.

Other Tools for Digging and Cultivating

The Soil Digger is a tool that can keep you upright while you cultivate and aerate the soil. Shaped like an over-sized garden fork with 2 handles and a cross-bar, it weighs 15 lbs. and is recommended especially for raised beds. You step firmly on the cross-bar and then rock back, thus lifting and loosening the soil (Gardener's Supply, $70.00).

Langenbach's Soil Tilling Fork does a similar job. To prepare beds for planting, push the fork into the ground with your foot, then pull the handle down. You'll need to bend over, but without the back strain usually associated with bed preparation. This fork costs $74.00.

The Soil Tilling Fork from Langenbach's.

From Solutions comes the Garden Claw, at $34.50. Push the 3', steel device into the soil, and use the handle to turn the claws, or tines, to break up the dirt. Pull the Garden Claw up, and the soil easily falls away. This tool will also uproot weeds.

A soil miller, or rotary tiller, is useful for cultivating fairly light soil as the star-shaped metal blades break up and loosen the ground. A Swiss-made tool comes with both a 60" and a short handle (Langenbach, $30.00). Dig This offers also offers a soil miller, for $20.00.

If you read any gardening books from Great Britain, you may find reference to a tool called the Wolf Terrex spade. British gardening writers often recommend the spade as particularly helpful to the gardener who must avoid bending or stooping. This tool boasts a unique lever action with a foot pedal that acts as a fulcrum to throw the soil forward.

Tracking down the Terrex spade required a bit of international detective work. Wolf Tools, I found, are manufactured in Germany and distributed in the U.S. by the Scotts Company. Unfortunately, however, the trail ends here as the Terrex spade is not sold in this country. Should you ever find yourself in Betzdorf, Germany, perhaps you could buy one at the source.

The Garden Claw from Solutions.

A soil miller from Langenbach.

Home Garden Tillers

Preparing a ground-level garden for planting doesn't have to be done by hand, of course; you can rent or buy a tiller, or hire someone to do the tilling for you. Check your local paper or shopper's guide for ads that offer this service—it needn't be expensive.

Remember that the best tillers will have rear-mounted tines; that is, the tines are mounted behind the wheels. That way the newly tilled soil won't be packed down again by the

machine's weight as it rolls over the ground. If you have a
friend or neighbor with a garden tiller, you can also consider
trading services for their equipment and/or help.

For small-size, home garden tillers, two of the most popular names on the market are Troy-Bilt and Mantis. The Troy-
Bilt Mini Tiller, which is manufactured by Garden Way Inc.,
weighs 23 lbs. and lists for $329.00. I asked Garden Way if
they knew of any gardeners with disabilities who are using a
Troy-Bilt tiller. They told me that they "cannot encourage"
anyone with a disability to use their power equipment; on the
other hand, the company noted that "some people with minor
disabilities may own our products."

The Mantis Manufacturing Co. offers a 20–lb., 9–hp gas
tiller for $359.00 and an electric model, at 27 lbs. and ½ hp,
for the same price. When I asked Mantis about any gardeners
with disabilities who have one of their tillers, I was sent a copy
of their *Savvy Gardener* magazine.

In the Winter 1992 issue was an article describing use of a
Mantis tiller by residents and staff of Echoing Hills Village in
Warsaw, Ohio. According to John Swanson, assistant executive director of this residential home for people with developmental disabilities, they found the tiller "'easy to use and very
helpful.'" Apparently they've even used the tiller—which was
donated by Mantis—in raised planter boxes.

Gardener's Supply Company out of Burlington, Vermont
has also entered the small tiller market. Their model has 1.6
hp, weighs 25 lbs., and sells for $260.00. A company repre-
sentative described the tiller as being "designed for a certain
flexibility" in meeting the needs of a diverse population. Many
gardeners with a physical disability, she felt, could find their
tiller easy to use.

Yet another small tiller/cultivator is offered in the Stokes
gardening catalogue. The Garden Way Speedy Hoe weighs 23
lbs. and has 1.6 hp; it goes for $340.00.

A variety of attachments are available at extra cost for
these four tillers, and you may be able to find a sale price or
special offer on the tiller itself. But before investing, I would
strongly urge you to proceed with caution: even a small, lightweight machine may be too much to handle.

If you have any doubts about your physical capabilities in
operating a tiller, see if you can—carefully—try a friend's out

first. Otherwise, either work the garden by hand or get some-one else to help. When health and safety are involved, some things just aren't worth the risk!

PREPARING THE SEED BEDS

Rakes

An iron-pronged garden rake is essential to smoothing out the soil once you've dug it up, whether with hand tools or by machine. A sturdy rake can also break up dirt clods, culti-vate, and do light weeding. (Plastic- and rubber-pronged rakes are best for yard work.) Here are three suggested models.

Weighing in at only 2 lbs. is a good-looking metal rake from England. The head is stainless steel, with a 54" alumi-num alloy tubular shaft and a cushioned grip (Langenbach, $39.00).

The swan neck design and 60" handle of this 4–lb. rake will help you keep your back straight while you're working. It has curved, pointed tines and is made in Holland (Gardener's Supply, $35.00).

Also at 60" is a rake with 14 bolstered teeth, which look like big nails (Kinsman, $31.00).

Hoes for Furrows

After the soil is smoothed you'll be ready to make plant-ing furrows. While some gardeners use the back of a small rake, furrows are probably most often made with a hoe. Alter-nately, you could pull a dibble through the soil to make a fur-row (see below).

While any hoe you can easily draw through the dirt can make you a furrow, some designs are better suited for this pur-pose than others. Try, for instance, a warren hoe with its trian-gular-shaped head. A.M. Leonard's model has a 45" handle, weighs just over 2 lbs., and is $21.00. For a warren hoe with a longer, 60" handle, see the Smith & Hawken catalogue, where a model made in England by Bulldog costs $34.00.

Other hoes with triangular heads include a 42" model from Gurney's at $12.75 and a 56" Farmer's Hoe from Langen-bach at $19.00.

A triangular warren hoe from Smith & Hawken.

Also from A.M. Leonard is a cultivation hoe with a tapered blade that is "perfect" for digging furrows. It has a 48" handle, weighs 2 lbs., and costs $17.00.

A Swiss-made goose foot hoe with a 60" handle can be used to make furrows, too, thanks to its pointed tip (Langenbach, $30.00). A hoe with a diamond-shaped head that's sharpened on all 4 sides is suitable for this use as well (Langenbach, $29.00).

By the way, I've noticed that the names for various types of hoes aren't entirely consistent, so don't buy a hoe by name alone—you may not get the one you had in mind!

Other Furrow-Making Tools

Master gardener Jim Crockett of "Victory Garden" fame uses a homemade 4' long, 4" wide planting board to measure out planting spaces and to make a furrow. Small and large notches are cut at 6" and 1' intervals to mark positions for planting. A 45–degree bevel is also cut on one of the board's long sides, and the resulting point used for furrow-making. Adaptations such as a longer or shorter length, or adding a handle, may be necessary for the gardener with a disability to comfortably use this tool. For deeper furrows you can make a seed-trencher, as described by Michael Wright in *The Complete Book of Garden-*

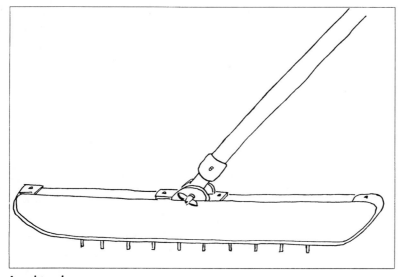

A seed-trencher.

ing. Start with a piece of wood about 3' long, 4" wide, and ¾" thick, and cut it to look like the rocker on a rocking chair. Attach a thin metal strip to the curved edge and hammer in 8 nails, leaving about ½" showing; cut the nail heads off. Firmly mount a 4' pivoted handle to the other side.

To use the seed-trencher, push it back and forth in well-tilled ground. This tool makes a narrow trench or furrow 3" deep.

MAKING HOLES FOR PLANTING

Dibbles

Do you know what a *dibble* (or dibber) is? The dictionary tells us that the word comes from the old English "debylle," a small hand tool used for making planting holes for seeds, plants, and bulbs. In *Crockett's Victory Garden,* Jim Crockett describes a dibble simply as a "hole-poker," and that's exactly what it is.

Look for a dibble in your garden or hardware store, or pick one up by mail. Kinsman, for instance, has an English-made dibble with a wooden T-handle and metal tip for $6.00. If you garden while standing, there's even a long-handled dibble available (Langenbach, $18.75).

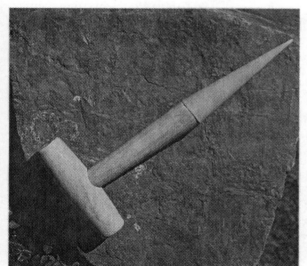

A dibble from Kinsman.

Scout around the house and you may find your own version of this tool. How about a turkey baster from the kitchen, or a pencil, or a piece of dowel rod? Or try a sharpened broomstick, inserted into a square or rectangular piece of wood, if the broomstick alone is hard to hold. If you walk with a cane or have an old one in the closet, use it to make planting holes, and then to cover up the seeds. Remember that an enabling tool can be a conventional item used in an unconventional way—that's the challenge and even the fun!

Multi-Dibbles

For making more than one hole at a time there are different versions of multi-dibbles. One type is a 15" long, handheld device with 4 adjustable probes. Push the tool down into the soil and you've made 4 holes, 4" apart. The probes can be repositioned for other spacings, too (Kinsman, $13.00).

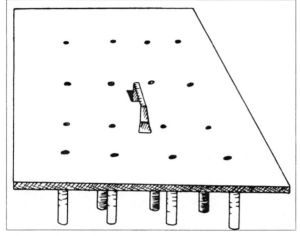

A homemade multi-dibble.

In the Victory Garden, 2 multi-dibbles are used to make from 8 to 16 holes at once. Short pieces of dowel are fitted into a board at regular spaces, depending on how far apart the planting holes are to be. A smaller one for smaller hands might have only four dowels mounted in a short piece of board.

Here are more specific directions for making a multi-dibble, from *Raised Bed Gardening*. Mark a 12" x 12" piece of plywood off in square inches; then, every 2", rout out a ⅜" hole. Also drill holes for a 4¼" handle in the middle of the board. Next, cut a 5' length of ⅜" dowel rod into 36 pieces, each ¾" long. Use wood glue to fasten the dowel rod pieces in the holes and let the board dry overnight. Finally, fasten the handle in place.

To use this multi-dibble, press it into the dirt and drop your seeds into the resulting holes. You can vary the depth of the holes to suit different seeds' requirements, by how hard you press the board into the ground. If you want a different spacing or pattern for planting your seeds, either make more than one multi-dibble, or just fill in the unwanted holes with soil.

Using a multi-dibble.

One more idea comes from a woman who uses her garden fork to plant peas; I suppose you could call it another type of multi-dibble. This gardener painted a bright red line on each tine, at the proper planting depth. Then all she has to do is insert the fork into the ground, up to the red lines, and she's made four holes for seeds.

Digging Holes

Digging holes for transplants can be accomplished with any of the short- or long-handled trowels, children's shovels, or spades described above. Another small-bladed spade called a rabbiting tool (as in digging out rabbit warrens) could be useful for digging holes. Made by Sheffield Pride, the spade is 36" long overall, so it's probably best for the seated gardener (Kinsman, $43.00).

A cross between a scoop and a spoon, a scoon looks like a small bowl with a rounded handle or lip curved about one side. Useful for transplanting and other jobs, this design might be helpful if your hands are stiff. Smith & Hawken offers the stainless steel scoon for $10.00.

Two common kitchen items can also be pressed into service for digging holes. A big spoon can be used as is, or attached firmly to a sturdy pole or stick. A large-handled plastic mug can be a scoop. By slipping your hand through the handle, you can cradle the mug without having to actually grip it, which is helpful for weak hands. Besides scooping dirt, a mug can be used for transferring fertilizer or water, too.

PLANTING

Hand Seed Dispensers

Now that you've prepared your garden bed, it's time to look at tools that will help you plant your vegetable and flower seeds. Several ingenious devices are available, beginning with the modestly priced hand-held seed dispensers. If you need help getting seeds—particularly tiny ones—out of the packet and into the ground where they belong, try one of these easy-to-use tools. One of the smallest seed dispensers is also simple in design: a little round plastic box with a cover and spout (Walt Nicke's, $2.50, and Kinsman, $3.00). The Tiny Tim sower resembles a hypodermic needle and puts mini seeds such as carrot seeds right where you want them (Gurney's, $5.30).

Several companies offer the Seedmaster® dispenser, which is shaped like a trowel. When the ratchet wheel on the handle is turned with your thumb, the resulting vibrations jiggle the seeds out. It has four baffles to handle various seed sizes (Mellinger's, $6.00; also Park, Walt Nicke's, and Gurney's, with comparable prices).

Seedmaster® seed dispenser.

Long-Reach Seed Sowers

A rolling seed sower has a hopper to fill with seed, and four changeable plates to adjust for different seed sizes. Push it along on its 46" handle and the seeds will be set out at the correct intervals (Park, $20.00). The beauty of this tool is that there's no bending or kneeling required on your part.

For "fast and easy" planting of larger seeds like corn and squash there's the "Easy-Plant" jab-type planter. To use it, insert the planter into the soil, then drop your seeds down the metal barrel. Lean the device forward so the spring-operated lever releases the seed, step forward, and repeat. The planter is 34" high overall and weighs 3¾ lbs. (Johnny's, $60.00).

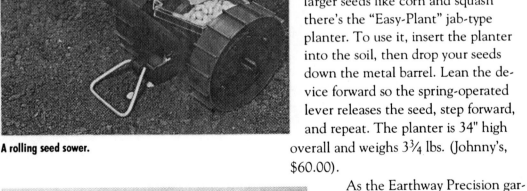

A rolling seed sower.

As the Earthway Precision garden seeder rolls along it will furrow the soil, space, plant, cover your seeds, and mark the next row, all in one pass. It comes with six seed plates, with five other plates and a fertilizer applicator available as well.

The Easy-Plant jab planter.

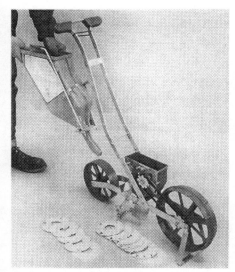

The Earthway Precision garden seeder.

If you have a big garden, it could be worth the investment (Johnny's, $70.00).

A Homemade Seeding

Helper
Getting seeds into the dirt in a ground-level garden can pose a problem if you're gardening from a wheelchair or erect position: how do you make contact with the soil if you can't reach it? The solution lies with a length of either hollow metal tubing, 1" PVC pipe, or bamboo. Just aim the bottom end of the tubing in the furrow or planting hole, then let a seed slide down the tube to the ground. Simple and effective!

Some gardeners have further refined this tool by adding a funnel to the top of the tube, taping it securely in place. The funnel makes it even easier to drop seeds down the tubing, especially if you have trouble with fine motor control.

Yet another practical modification is to tape a pointed stick (like a pencil, sharpened dowel, or skewer) to the tube so that it extends 3" or so beyond the bottom edge of the tube. Use the stick as a dibble to make the planting hole, then slide the seed down.

Finally, if you use a cane or broomstick as a dibble, consider creating a combination tool by taping it and the seeder tube together. Again, let the dibble extend some 3" beyond the tubing.

Planting Boards
When you can connect directly with the soil, a planting board can help you properly space the seeds to be sown. This device is especially useful if your vision is poor, or your hands stiff or shaky.

In a piece of masonite (about 12" square is a good size), drill a number of ⅛" or ¼" holes. Although it's not essential, at-

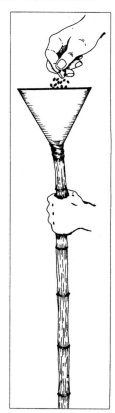

A homemade seeding helper.

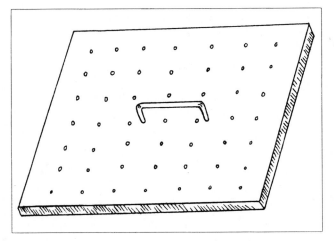

taching some sort of handle in the middle of the masonite will help in lifting and placing the board. Painting your planting board a light color will enable you to see the holes more easily.

A section of pegboard can be used instead of the masonite, with the advantage, of course, that the holes already exist. To get the right spacing for your seeds, stick strips of masking tape across some of the holes. Then, with either type of planting board, simply lay it on top of your prepared soil, drop the seeds in the holes, and lift the board up.

Another easy way to be sure your seeds are properly spaced is with a piece of one-inch chicken wire. Either flatten it inside a wooden frame, or else lay it down on the soil as is. Dropping a seed through each hole will put them one inch apart. For a 2" or 3" spacing, just skip a few holes in the wire before sowing the seed. Remove the wire, then sprinkle soil to cover the seeds.

Therapist Jim Bradford suggests trying plug trays, which are a type of multi-sectioned plastic tray used by commercial growers (check a gardening supply store). These clearly show both where the seed is to be placed, and then, where it has been placed. After planting, lightly coating the seeds with a layer of fine sand helps ensure quick growth.

Other Ways to Seed

Tiny seeds can also be mixed with sand, fine dirt, or used coffee grounds, and then carefully broadcast either in a salt shaker, a canister with holes punched in its lid, or by hand in the seed bed or row. If your vision is limited, a magnifying glass—either a hand-held one or the type that hangs around the neck by a cord—can be useful.

A few companies carry pelleted seed, where each seed is enclosed in a little clay ball; this can be especially helpful if you have problems with your hands. More varieties of flowers and vegetables are available as seed tapes. Here the seeds are sandwiched between two layers of biodegradable paper, at just

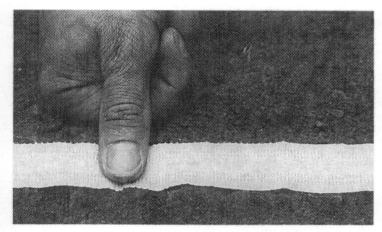

the right spacing. For many gardeners, seed tapes may be ideal. For more information on sources for tapes and pelleted seed see Chapter Five.

If you want to make your own seed tapes, here's a method one gardener devised. She cuts newspaper strips about one inch wide and whatever length she wants for her garden plot or bed. Next she makes a flour-and-water paste and puts a dab of it on the paper strip, spacing the dots at the proper planting intervals for that particular variety. Finally, she puts one seed on each dab of paste. (Tweezers could be helpful here.)

During the winter this gardener is busy preparing her seed tapes. Then, when spring comes, she's ready to lay the tapes

in a furrow, cover them up with soil, water them, and wait for germination. It's a method, she says, that "really works."

A final seeding tip, from Jim Bradford, is for those who are unable to use hands or arms. He recommends a bird-beak type mouthstick for planting seeds, noting that he's had "a lot of success" with this tool, purchased through the Enrichments catalogue.

Covering the Seeds

If you can manage it, the only "tools" you need to cover up the seeds and gently tamp the soil over them are your hands and/or feet. Otherwise, you can use a small rake to draw dirt over the seeds, then flip it over to firm the soil. A small hoe will also do the trick.

Now, before you forget what's planted where, label the rows. Any sort of system is fine, from popsicle sticks and indelible ink, to laminated seed packets taped to a stake. Just be sure to include the crop (green beans), the variety (DERBY), and the date you planted the seeds (if for some reason your seeds don't germinate in a timely manner, you'll need to re-plant).

Thinning

Does any gardener really like to thin out flower and vegetable seedlings? Somehow it goes against our nature to pull out any of those beautiful little plants we've started from seed and then nurtured along. And yet if we don't, we'll wind up with overcrowded plants that will be prone to disease, will have reduced blooms and crops, and in general won't thrive the way they should.

Pulling out the extra seedlings by hand is one way to manage thinning. From a sitting or standing position, thinning can also be accomplished with a small hoe with a sharpened, diamond-pointed head. Try the warren hoe you used for furrow-making, or a 55" gooseneck hoe with three very sharp working edges (Walt Nicke's, $15.00).

A metal garden rake can be used for thinning, too. When the seedlings are under one inch tall, carefully pull the rake across the seed bed to remove the extra plants.

However you do your thinning, you'll find it's easier if the soil is moist rather than dry. That way, there's less chance of damage to the seedlings you want to stay in the garden. You might be able to transplant some of the thinnings; otherwise, throw them on the compost pile. Be sure, though, to add those lettuce and spinach thinnings to the salad bowl!

When the seedlings you've started in a cell-pack or other container are ready to set out in the garden, don't try to separate any that you planted in pairs. Since the seedling roots have probably grown together, you risk hurting your potential transplant if you try to thin by pulling the extra plant out. Instead, decide which seedling looks the strongest, then simply snip off the other one at the soil line.

If every seed you planted were to germinate, thinning wouldn't be necessary. All you'd have to do was plant each seed at the right spacing, then step back and watch them grow. Since 100 percent germination can't be guaranteed even for good, fresh seed, however, sow the seeds as carefully as you can. Taking the time initially to space the seeds properly will save you most or even all of the need for thinning later on.

Setting out Plants

Whether you've been growing your own seedlings indoors into husky little plants, or have bought them at the local garden center, setting transplants out into the garden really brings the growing season into focus. Unlike the patient wait required for seeds to sprout, transplants quickly make a garden *look* like a garden, with promises of crops and harvests to come.

Use your hands if you can to tuck the plants into the ground; a trowel can assist. If the ground is out of reach, use a long-handled trowel, a child-sized shovel, or a spade to lower the plant into its hole, and then fill in and firm the dirt around it.

If the rootball is firm and the transplant sturdy enough, a

plant can be set in with the aid of a long-reach grabber. The Baronet weed puller described below can also be used as a planting aid.

An ingenious New Jersey gardener has devised another method to set out transplants. Working from his three-wheeled electric scooter, he first uses a small hoe to dig planting holes. Then he maneuvers a 5' length of drainpipe into position and slides a plant down to the hole, where the transplant is tamped into place.

Planting Bulbs, and More

You may be already familiar with the small bulb planters you push into the ground, then pull out again to remove the soil for planting. Long-handled models are available, too, although not so inexpensively. If you have a lot of bulbs to put out, however, and must avoid bending and stooping, a long-handled, step-on planter could be well worth the cost. The planter can also make holes suitable for setting out small plants and seedlings, and can even be used for weed removal, too.

One model is 34" long with a T-shaped handle, and will cut a hole 8" deep and 3" in diameter (Alsto's, $45.00). Jackson & Perkins has a 36" steel planter with a rubber-coated handle for $20.00. Another bulb planter is a little longer at 39". From Bulldog Tools, it weighs 4 lbs. (Smith & Hawken, $55.00).

Other long-handled bulb planters include 2 from Langenbach, with 2½" and 3" diameter cutting cups ($39.00 and $44.00, respectively). Similarly designed, with a long, cushioned "T" handle, is a planter from Kinsman for $41.00, one from Walt Nicke's for $45.00, and one from A.M. Leonard for $29.00. All 5 bulb planters are 35–36" in overall length.

An alternative to this type of bulb planter is an auger that's used with your electric drill. These tools let you create planting holes quickly and efficiently, and with less strain on your hands and wrists than the same job would cause with a trowel.

A soil auger from Solutions.

There are several different sizes of augers for making various-sized holes—just be sure the auger will fit your drill. These augers can also be used for taking soil samples, deeproot fertilizing, planting seedlings, etc. Check with the company before you buy if you plan to use an auger in heavy clay or very rocky soil, to be sure it can hold up to these conditions.

Solutions offers a planting auger in 2 sizes, 7" ($19.50) and 12" ($24.00), to drill holes 3" in diameter. Made of heavy-duty steel, this auger is said to work "in any soil."

Augers can also be found in the Brookstone, Mellinger's, Jung, and Alsto's catalogues, among others. These four companies also offer longer, 24" augers.

CULTIVATING AND WEEDING

Two Important Jobs

Besides helping air and water to reach your garden plants' roots, cultivating the ground will also uproot any weeds that may have sprouted. And, whether you're a novice or an old hand in the garden, you know it's important to keep weeds under control. Left to grow unchecked, weeds will rob your vegetables and flowers of nutrients, water, and sun and air space. And if you let those weeds go to seed, you'll be asking for trouble. "One year's seeding, seven years' weeding," goes an old saying—heed it!

On the other hand, don't let a constant concern over weed control ruin your enjoyment of your garden. Except to the most aesthetically fussy, a few weeds here and there aren't worth worrying about. Also, if you weed fairly diligently in the spring, you'll find there are fewer weeds to contend with later on, when your garden plants are bigger and better able to fend for themselves.

Depending on the size of your garden and your physical capabilities, weeding by hand may not be either practical or feasible. Consider, then, the following tools to help you in this task.

Hoes for Cultivating and Weeding

The hoe is the first tool people think of when they set out to do some weeding. Unfortunately, hoeing has the reputation for being a tedious and muscle-straining—if necessary—chore. Using a hoe doesn't have to be difficult, however. Choosing the right *type* of hoe can make all the difference.

The standard draw hoe is the model most associated with backaches, since the gardener is continually employing a lifting and chopping motion. If you're using a push-pull movement, however, you can accomplish as much, or even more, with less effort. The hoe that lets you do this is known as an oscillating hoe.

An oscillating hoe.

The oscillating hoe has a metal stirrup-shaped head that's sharpened on both sides, which means you'll be slicing weeds off just below the surface on both the push and the pull motion. And, for the standing gardener, a 66" length means less strain and fatigue on the back (Johnny's, $26.00). Natural Gardening's Swiss-made oscillating hoe has a 60" handle, a smaller blade, and costs $25.50.

Another type of hoe to look for is the collinear hoe. This design features a blade parallel to the ground, to skim weeds off right below the soil surface while you stand upright. Try Smith & Hawken's 58" hoe for $21.00, their 64" one for

$22.00, or Natural Gardening's collinear hoe from Switzerland with a 60" handle for $21.00.

Brookstone's Glide and Groom hoe also works just below the surface, with an easy push-pull motion. Shaped something like an elongated triangle, the blade is sharpened on both sides, has a 56" handle, and costs $22.50.

Helpful too for less-stressful weeding is the swan neck hoe, where the curved neck on a 60" handle lets you draw the blade through the soil with little effort (Gardener's Supply, $27.00). Of course, the hoe you used for making furrows may be just right for weeding jobs as well.

Other Tools for Cultivating and Weeding

Also useful for weeding and cultivating are the soil miller and small electric or gas garden tiller mentioned previously, and a three-pronged cultivator. This latter tool has been around a long time, because it's good at what it does. Three-pronged cultivators are widely available at garden centers and hardware stores. The cultivator can also be found in catalogues, including one in a 48" length (A.M. Leonard, $26.00), a 54" (Walt Nicke's, $33.00), and a 60" (Natural Gardening, $22.50).

Of course, for raised beds you'll want to use your long-handled hand tools: the fork, cultivator, and the various weeders. Remember, too, the child-size hoe for your weeding chores.

For really tough weeds, like woody-stemmed seedlings, try yanking them out with a pair of pliers—they'll give you extra leverage.

Long-Reach Weeders

Cultivating as frequently as once a week will go a long way to keeping weed growth down and thus manageable. For those big weeds that sprang up while you were on vacation, however, some extra help may be in order.

A 35" long-reach weeder lets you extract weeds and their roots without the need to bend or kneel. The one-handed, upright operation involves

Long-reach weeder from Brookstone.

placing the jaws over the weed, stepping on the plate, releasing the trigger, and pulling out the weed. Of enameled steel, this tool is available through the Brookstone catalogue for $29.00.

Expensive but beautifully made is the Baronet of Sheffield firm grip weed puller. This English tool is lightweight, 34" long, and can be operated with just one hand. Excellent for use from a wheelchair, or in a standing position with no bending required, it can also be used to set out plants (Walt Nicke, $60.00).

MULCHES

A Helpful Barrier

Perhaps you're wondering at this point whether there's an easier way to keep down weed growth in your garden. There is: it's called mulching.

A mulch is defined as a "protective covering" in the garden. It can either be homemade and replaced yearly, or purchased as reusable plastic or paper barriers. Mulch has a great many benefits in the garden, including:

- Inhibiting weed growth
- Keeping moisture in
- Preventing erosion
- Keeping crops from rotting from soil contact
- Encouraging soil fertility
- Reducing soil compaction
- Keeping crops cleaner from rain-splashed dirt
- Encouraging earthworms
- Helping to maintain an even soil temperature

While not a panacea (slugs, for instance, are a problem with mulching in some areas), mulches can go a long way towards keeping your garden healthy and productive, and with less overall effort for upkeep required on your part.

Organic Mulches

Some of the most popular and readily available materials for mulching the garden are hay and straw, leaves (shredded first with the lawn mower), dried grass clippings, wood chips and sawdust, shredded bark, and newspaper (black and white only as the colored ink dyes are poisonous). Depending on where you live, more exotic mulching materials could include peanut shells, cocoa bean hulls, seaweed, Spanish moss, and so on—just think about what you might find locally.

Before spreading your mulch, be sure the soil is damp so that moisture will be kept in the ground, not out of it. A general rule is that the lighter the mulch, the more of it will be needed to create a truly useful covering. For instance, a hay mulch should be from 6–8" thick, whereas only about 2–3" of wood chips would be required. Rocks or dirt may be necessary to prevent the wind from carrying away some mulches, like one of newspapers.

Commercial Mulches

Plastic and paper mulches have the advantage of durability; that is, they won't need to be replaced or added to during the growing season as some organic mulches might be. And, depending on your abilities, these mulches in the forms of mats, fabrics, and rolls *may* be easier to handle. (However, unlike the organic mulches, the plastics won't be adding any nutrients to the soil.) The commercial mulches can also be used in conjunction with organic ones, as around shrubs and under trees.

Miracle Mulch™ is one popular brand of commercial mulch. The sturdy plastic is covered with microscopic holes to let in water and air. Heat and moisture are retained while any weeds are smothered (Gardener's Supply, $9.00 for a 3' x 50' roll).

Weed-X is a multi-ply mulch of plastic and fabric that comes with a 5–year guarantee against weeds. It's designed to let water in and hold enough of it there to make your plants grow well. You cut the mat with scissors to install it, then add mulch on top to anchor it (Park, $15.00 for a 3' x 50' roll).

As described in the Gardens Alive! catalogue, the Weed Barrier Mat is a non-woven geotextile fabric that allows for passage of water and air to the soil. It helps keep plants and crops clean, comes in four sizes, and can even be walked on. The Mat is available in a medium weight, which is guaranteed for three years, and a heavy weight, with a five–year guarantee. Prices start at $13.00 and $18.00, respectively.

A biodegradable mulch called Horto Paper is made from a mix of peat moss and recycled cardboard. It keeps moisture and warmth at an even level in the soil (Gurney's, $7.65 for 25').

Plain black plastic mulches are widely available, too, and can do a good job at keeping down the weeds. They come in various thicknesses; the thinner plastics may be more difficult to preserve for subsequent growing seasons.

WATERING

How Much Moisture?

Your garden will need one inch of water a week. To measure how much rain you've actually been getting, either buy an inexpensive rain gauge, or mark off inches on a coffee can and leave it in an open, level spot in the garden. A jumbo rain gauge with large markings and a red float that can be seen from yards away may be a handy item to have (Alsto's, $9.50).

If it doesn't rain often enough to supply that one inch, you'll need to provide the moisture. Schlepping heavy buckets of water, or struggling with unwieldy hoses, is a scenario any gardener—especially one with a physical disability—will want to avoid. Fortunately, there are alternatives, as described below.

Remember that if you've been mulching your garden, you've already cut down or maybe even eliminated your watering chores. Plants grown in containers also benefit from a good mulch. Since they dry out so quickly, anything you can do to help them hang on to the moisture in the soil means you've saved yourself both time and effort.

When you do need to water, don't waste time and precious moisture by letting water escape from your plants. Mound up a 3" earthen dam or ring around each plant, then water at the base of it. The dam will hold the water so that it soaks down to the roots rather than running off. Mulch can still be applied around the plant—just leave the ring open so that the base of the plant is exposed to receive the water.

Soil Additives

Adding special materials to your soil is another way to cut down on the need for frequent waterings. And because the plants will be less subject to water stress from alternating wet and dry periods, they'll grow healthy and strong.

HydroSource crystals absorb up to 400 times their weight in water, releasing the moisture as your plants need it. The non-toxic polymer crystals last up to 10 years and can be used on houseplants, in containers, or in an outdoor garden. Gardener's Supply sells a pound bag for $10.00.

Jackson & Perkins sells "moisture crystals" too, under the name Solid H_2O. **This brand absorbs up to 500 times its weight and is effective for at least 5 years. At a cost of $15.00, 1 jar will treat 150 gallons of soil, 60 square feet, or 60, 12–inch pots.**

A new additive called Dialoam, made from diatomaceous earth, is also sold by Gardener's Supply. This material is highly porous and holds moisture so well that the need to water is reduced (10 lbs. of Dialoam cost $13.00).

Garden Hoses

Making your garden hose easier to use begins with locating it in an accessible spot, where the spigot can be placed 2–3' above the ground. The area should have some sort of ground cover, paving, or carpeting so there's no possibility of slipping in mud. Snap connectors are less awkward to use, as are hand levers for turning the water on and off, which are preferred over the standard round handles.

As to the garden hose itself, be sure it's a good sturdy one that will stand up to a bit of abuse. Consider a hose cart to keep it neatly wound and so avoid the chance of tripping and falling over the hose. And if you need to drag a heavy hose through the garden, try pulling it through the D-shaped handle of a spade or fork.

Soaker Hoses

For ground-level gardening, consider installing a drip irrigation system of soaker hoses. The hoses, which are often made from recycled tire rubber, are perforated with tiny holes to let the water seep out. Depending on the brand of soaker hose, you place the hoses either above or below ground, next to your plants.

Since the plants won't suffer stress from fluctuating supplies of water, they'll grow bigger and healthier, and produce greater yields. And, because the plants will get water where and when they need it, you'll end up using *less* water in the garden.

Brands of soaker hoses include Hydro-Grow, Earthquencher, Moisture Master, Kourik, Aquapore, and Irrigro. Prices for 25' of hose typically run under $15.00; 50', 100', and 250' lengths are also available, as are various kits and accessories. Check these catalogues for more information: Gardener's Supply, Plow & Hearth, Smith & Hawken, Mellinger's, Solutions, Natural Gardening, and Jung.

Of special interest is the Kourik Drip Irrigation System, designed by Robert Kourik, a national expert on drip irrigation. Described in detail in the Natural Gardening catalogue, this system can be purchased as a kit (starting at 100' for $109.00) or as separate components for custom design or kit modification. Natural Gardening also carries Kourik's book *Drip Irrigation: For Every Landscape and All Climates.*

Yet another solution to watering is an accessory to add to the raised bed kit from Gardener's Supply, as discussed on page 17. New for 1993 is their root zone irrigation kit, which uses a pressure-compensating dripper line. A kit for a 4' x 4' raised bed costs $15.00, or $19.00 for a 4' x 8' bed.

A Homemade Drip Irrigation System

A simple but tried-and-true way to water your plants with a drip or trickle system involves these two household items: coffee cans and plastic milk jugs. For the coffee cans, punch very small holes in the sides, sink them most of the way into the ground next to your plants, and fill them up with water. For the jugs, poke a tiny hole in the bottom, then set them into the ground and fill.

The water will slowly drain from the can or jug, providing the roots with a steady supply of moisture. And, since you're only filling the container—not watering the entire area surrounding the plants—you'll save both time and effort, and water.

Spray Wands

Spray wands attach to your hose nozzle and let you extend your reach up to 36". The wands are particularly handy for watering hanging baskets and container gardens, and for use from a wheelchair. Models with a shut-off valve keep you from wasting water as you move from plant to plant.

The Gardena Soft Spray Wand.

Gardena of Germany makes a variety of tools and accessories for watering, including a Soft Spray Wand. This wand comes in lengths from 31" to 36" and features a trigger lock and control and adjustable sprayhead (Shepherd's and Gardener's Supply, $20.00 and Langenbach, $24.00).

A little shorter but still very handy for watering container plants is the Pot Waterer from Natural Gardening. It has a thumb-operated shut-off valve and is available in two lengths. The 14" waterer is $16.00, and the 24" one is $19.50.

In the under-$20.00 category, other spray wands can be found in the Smith & Hawken, Nichols, Johnny's, Jung, and Walt Nicke's catalogues. Check Plow & Hearth, Natural Gardening, Walt Nicke's, Brookstone, and Smith & Hawken for spray wands ranging from $22.00 to $56.00.

Plant Pulleys

There's a handy gadget called a plant pulley that will also help you water hanging baskets. Like the spray wand, it's particularly useful for someone gardening from a wheelchair.

The Hi-Lo pulley has a ratchet device to let you lower a hanging basket down 3', or it will stop at any point in between. An automatic locking cam holds the basket where you want it. Then, when you're done watering or grooming the plant, release the catch and the basket will return to its raised position. The pulley holds up to 25 lbs. and is quite weatherproof (Alsto's, $10.50).

Watering Cans

Although catalogues offer a wide range of watering cans, this is one item in particular that should be given a test run before purchasing. A watering can that is comfortable for the standing gardener to use may be awkward for someone working from a wheelchair. Likewise, the gardener with hand and arm weaknesses may require a small, light watering can while someone with more upper body strength could manage a larger one.

Check to see that the can is well balanced, with a spout that's long enough for your watering needs. Attractive and functional watering cans are made in both metal and plastic, so you can select the weight that's easiest for you to manage. Remember when you're filling the can that 1 gallon of water weighs 8 pounds.

Other Ways to Water

Some gardeners find that a partly filled plastic gallon milk jug makes a good watering can, with its built-in handle and screw- or snap-on top. For watering seeds and seedlings, a rubber squeeze bulb provides a gentle spray (Park, $7.00). And if even a small watering can is too difficult to handle, a sponge soaked in tepid water can be squeezed over a plant.

Finally, there are the self-watering containers described on page 46.

CUTTING AND PRUNING

Scissors

A good pair of garden scissors is useful for any number of jobs. The soft vinyl handles of Never-Dull scissors are said to be comfortable for someone with arthritis and can be used with either the left or right hand. As the name implies, these scissors won't need re-sharpening over a lifetime of use (Gardener's Supply, standard $15.00, extra-long $16.00). Another style of scissors is sharp, light, and 7½" long (Johnny's, $11.00).

Florist's pruners are also an option, and come in small and large sizes. They have the advantage of open handles, which can be a boon if you find it uncomfortable or painful to fit your fingers into a handle.

Flower Gatherers

These clever tools let you pick flowers with just one hand. The scissors-like Gardena flower gatherer will hold the flower stem, cut it, strip off thorns, and crush the stalk ends if desired (Stokes, $9.00).

The Victorinox flower gatherer (from the makers of the Swiss Army Knife) has two spring steel bands to hold the stem as it's cut. A model by Johnny's has open, wooden handles ($12.00).

Long-reach flower gatherers are available too and are especially suited for use from a wheelchair or other seat, or from a non-bending standing position. Handy for reaching in among thorny bushes and across flower beds, the gatherers can also be used with hanging baskets and in the greenhouse. One version features a spring-loaded action to cut and hold flower stems, with serrated jaws to prune branches as well (Smith & Hawken, 2' length for $46.00, 5' for $56.00).

Probably top of the line is the Baronet of Sheffield flower gatherer (the British call it a *secateur*). Made in England, it's 31" long and weighs 14 ounces. The stainless steel blades cut and hold the flowers until they're brought within the gardener's reach. Besides cutting flowers and dead-heading, this tool is also useful for light pruning, and can be operated with one hand (Walt Nicke's, $60.00).

Pruners and Shears

For general pruning jobs around the yard and garden, ratchet pruners and shears are wonderful if you have limited arm and hand strength. These tools offer a lot of cutting power with little effort required on your part.

Give the handles a brief squeeze, and the ratchet mechanism will hold the branch in the pruner's blades. Release your grip and the ratchet will move to the next notch, increasing your leverage. Repeat until the branch is quickly and easily cut through. This 7" long ratchet anvil pruner has fiberglass handles and a steel blade (Gardener's Supply, $15.00).

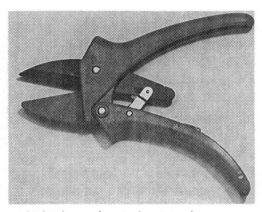

Ratchet hand pruner from Gardener's Supply.

Also easy on the hands is the Sheffield shear, originally designed over 250 years ago for shearing sheep. Available in two sizes, the smaller shear is particularly suited for easy, one-handed use. This quality tool is of fine Sheffield steel, and its lightweight, open-handled design makes it comfortable to use for many trimming and cutting jobs. Moreover, the shear makes a pleasant "singing" sound as it's being used. The large shear is $24.00 (Smith & Hawken), the smaller one, $29.50 (Langenbach).

The ratchet-cut design is used too for longer-handled shears and loppers. These both have a hook nose feature that helps keep the branch from slipping away. The regular lopper is 19" long and will cut branches up to ¼" in diameter; the maxi is 27" and cuts up to 2" (Alsto's, $55.00 and $140.00).

A lightweight, aluminum long-reach pruner with a trigger-type handle comes in 6' and 10' lengths. The steel blades come in two types: the standard bypass pruner, and the "snip and grip" that will hold the cut material (Natural Gardening, from $75.00 to $140.00).

Other cutting tools include long-handled grass or edging shears. Since they can be used while standing, these shears would be a help if bending is difficult. Handy for all sorts of trimming, this grass shear is 43" long overall. It has light tubular steel handles and horizontally mounted carbon steel blades (Gardener's Supply, $25.00).

Cleaning Up

Now that you've dead-headed your flowers and pruned back your shrubs, what can you do with that pile of clippings around your feet? A device called a long-handled pick-up grab may be just the tool you're looking for. I've only come across references to a grab in British gardening books, but apparently it's been around for a long time. Michael Wright in *The Complete Book of Gardening* calls the grab a "time-honoured design [that has been] used for generations."

A grab consists of two rectangular pieces of wood or metal to which 3–foot scissor-action handles are attached. Think of picking up a pile of leaves with a giant pair of tongs with snow shovel-like blades, and you'll have some idea of how this tool works. The grab can be used from either a seated or a non-bending standing position.

Curiously enough, I had already written this section when I received Walt Nicke's latest catalogue. In it I found a new item for 1993 called an Easy Gripper, which, sure enough, turned out to be a long-handled pick-up grab. Their version has galvanized tubular steel handles, galvanized sheet met-

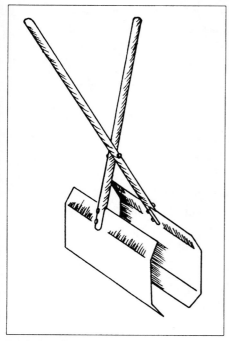

A pick-up grab.

al blades, and vinyl grips ($25.00). It seems this "time-honoured design" is making its appearance in American markets!

Here's a way to make your own pick-up grab. Start with two sheets of 7" x 12", 16–gauge aluminum. Sandwich one piece between two boards, leaving a 2" wide strip protruding, and secure in a vice. Hammer the 2" strip to a 30–degree angle, then repeat on the other edge so that both strips are angled in the same direction. Do the same to the other sheet of aluminum.

Now take a broomstick handle and slot and screw it to the middle of one blade, at a 60–degree angle to the top; repeat with another handle and blade. Join the handles with a ¼" bolt, nut, and two washers so that they pivot. Gripping material can be added to the handles if desired.

TRANSPORTING

Wheelbarrows and Garden Carts

A wheelbarrow is probably the first item that comes to mind for moving things to and from the garden or yard. It's doubtful, however, that the conventionally designed wheelbarrow, with its two handles and single wheel, will be at all useful to the gardener with a disability. This wheelbarrow requires a certain upper-body strength, offers no support while walking, can tip easily, and can't be pulled behind a wheelchair. Look instead to other options.

Several good styles of garden carts are now on the market, with most featuring two large wheels and a lawnmower-style handle. This sturdy design is easier to push and can even be used as a walking aid. As described below, several catalogues offer a range of models and prices of these carts. (Do note that assembly may be required.) As another option, national retail outlets like K-Mart and Frank's have begun carrying this type of garden cart, as well.

Carts from Catalogues

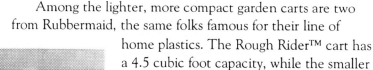

Among the lighter, more compact garden carts are two from Rubbermaid, the same folks famous for their line of home plastics. The Rough Rider™ cart has a 4.5 cubic foot capacity, while the smaller Easy Rider™ cart handles 3 cubic feet; both can carry 200 lbs. The two carts are of gray plastic, have wide wheels, a comfortable handle, and a built-in tray and slots for holding garden tools.

The larger model retails for $65.00, and the smaller one for $55.00. Look for them in most major retail chains and in some nurseries, or call (316) 221–2230, ext. 219 for an outlet in your area.

New for 1993 is a lightweight (25 lbs.) garden cart with a polyethylene body and big semi-pneumatic tires. Its capacity is 5½ cubic feet, holding up to 250 lbs. (Gardener's Supply, $60.00).

Moving up in size (and cost) are two sturdy carts with tough polyethylene tubs and large tires (Gardeners Eden, $189.00 and Johnny's, $170.00). Similar designs in larger carts can be found in the Walt Nicke's, Langenbach, and Stokes catalogues, with prices ranging from $229.00 to $259.00.

Rectangular bed carts with plywood sides and spoked wheels are available from Alsto's, Plow & Hearth, A.M. Leonard, Gardener's Supply, and Smith & Hawken. Most models feature a removable front panel; handle placement varies. Prices range from $125.00 for a smaller cart to up to $200.00 for one that can carry 400 lbs.

Still with the lawnmower-style handle is a collapsible garden cart. Made of strong but light aluminum, the cart has 20" pneumatic tires and a removable tailboard, and can carry up to 330 lbs. Pressing the handles together folds it flat for storage. Plow & Hearth, Brookstone, and Natural Gardening all sell this model for around $200.00.

A few of the many garden carts available from catalogues. top: Rubbermaid, middle: Gardener's Supply, bottom: Solutions.

Described as a "reassuring walking aid in the garden," a smaller-sized cart or barrow has a golf cart-style handle, with rubber tires and a steel body (Dig This, $70.00). It's possible it could be pulled along behind a wheelchair, although more of a hook to the handle might be needed.

Also with this golf cart-style handle is a folding cart that can be used either with the basket opened up or as a platform cart. The Pop Kart has solid rubber tires, a polypropylene basket, and can hold up to 100 lbs. (Solutions, $49.00).

More than one gardener has found a child's wagon to be a help in moving things around the garden. But did you know that the classic Radio Flyer also refers to a child's wheelbarrow? It has one rubber tire, a steel body, and hardwood handles (Mellinger's, $21.50). The color? Bright red, of course!

Wheelchair Transporting

If you're gardening from a wheelchair, some sort of lap board or tray can be handy for collecting and transporting supplies. To keep it from slipping, glue on rubber jar openers or bathtub appliques. Even something as simple as a cut-down cardboard box makes a useful, lightweight container.

Likewise, a basket can be carried on your lap; choose from among a great variety of sizes and shapes. For instance, a tough woven willow basket with 4 compartments could also make a handy lap carrier (Gardeners Eden, $13.50).

A bag, bicycle basket, pocket, or box hung from the back of the wheelchair or from the armrest can be used as well for carrying tools, seed packets, etc. To hold a watering hose, attach two hooks on the armrest so that only one hand is needed to use the hose.

Ambulatory Transporting

If you're ambulatory but need your hands for holding crutches or other aids as you walk, here are two ideas from fellow gardeners. One woman cut down a one-gallon plastic milk jug—leaving the handle on—and covered the cut edge with duct tape to prevent scratches. She then belted the container around her waist and was ready to carry her tools to the garden.

Another woman took a carpenter's canvas apron and turned it into a gardening apron by adding a variety of large and small pockets with Velcro® closures. The largest pocket was lined with a plastic bag, and in it she put her clippings, trimmings, and other debris from the garden.

A ready-made apron is available from Dig This for $24.00. It has extra-long ties for tying in front, large pockets, and is machine washable. One of the pockets is made just for carrying string or twine: it has an eyelet out of which the string can be run.

If you use a walker, a bicycle basket or other type of container can be easily attached to its frame.

Transport Plus Storage

Instead of constantly carrying small items back and forth, try setting up a mailbox in the garden for easy storage of your supplies. Mount it on a post at an accessible height, and you'll save yourself some trips back to the house.

If you're gardening on a patio area, or have paved walkways around the garden, a small wheeled cart or table can be very helpful. Stocked with hand tools, compost, pots, and so on, the cart can be pushed along with you as you work.

Tarps and Bags

Grass clippings and other items destined for the composter can be hauled off with a tarp, instead of in a wheelbarrow or cart—just be sure to keep the loads small enough to manage. A 6' x 6' polytarp has handles at each corner (Dig This, $17.00); a similar 7' x 7' BosSheet is $15.00 from Kinsman.

A large, lightweight, collapsible polypropylene bag could be handy as well for those clean-up chores (Dig This, $10.00). BosBags are also sturdy and light, folding flat for storage. Since they'll stand up on their own, your hands are free to toss in raked-up leaves, trimmings, or clippings. A bag 19" x 19" x 17" high is $13.00 from Kinsman, Natural Gardening, and Walt Nicke's.

An old sheet, bedspread, tablecloth, or shower curtain
can be used as a tarp, too.

HARVESTING

Gathering the Crops

Since you've carefully planned your garden for accessibility—whether it's ground level, raised beds, or containers—you've already taken into account just how to get your hands on the fruits of your labors. If something has grown out of reach, however, it should be easy finding a helper who would be willing to exchange a little labor for a share of the goods. Just remember to keep any miscalculations in mind when planning *next* year's garden.

To collect your fresh produce, the same baskets and bags that you used to carry supplies will serve equally well to hold your fruits and vegetables. A long-reach grabber can be pressed into service as a harvesting aid; a cut-and-hold flower gatherer can harvest herbs.

To free your hands for picking small items like cherry tomatoes or berries, a tin can or a cut-down milk carton or jug can be suspended by a string around your neck. Add a piece of foam rubber if the cord becomes uncomfortable against the back of your neck or shoulders.

The gardeners in Sweden who constructed this tomato trellis left enough space between the crossties to hang a harvesting basket. A vinyl-coated wire bicycle basket like the one in the photo would be a handy aid for the gardener at picking time.

Fruits and Nuts

For harvesting fruit from a tree, wire fruit picking baskets are widely available. Or, check the Stark catalogue for a vinyl-coated one with hooked "fingers" to gently separate the fruit from the tree. The basket bottom has a foam pad; you supply the pole or broomstick ($13.00).

If you need an extra-long reach, Alsto's fruit picking basket has a wooden handle that comes in 2, 4' sections. This total length of over 8' could allow you to reach 14' for harvesting your fruit ($19.50).

Picking up nuts from the ground can be tough on the knees and back, so you might want to have a nut picker-upper from Gurney's. The looped wire holder (which looks a lot like a child's Slinky® toy) is said to pick up all types and sizes of nuts while you stand upright ($9.00).

Whole-Plant Harvesting

Here's an idea that may appear wasteful at first, but makes good sense if you find it's too tiresome or difficult to harvest certain crops in the usual way. For instance, yellow and green beans are typically picked over a period of a week or two, yet the bulk of the crop often comes on at one time. Instead of straining to reach those few extra later beans, simply pull up the plants and harvest the main crop. Then add the bean plants to your composter.

In the same way, if cutting off single leaves of lettuce is too hard, just take the whole plant instead. Since most gardeners make successive plantings of beans and lettuce anyway, this method of harvesting may be an entirely acceptable trade-off for you.

MISCELLANEOUS TOOLS

Long-Reach Grabbers

Do you use a long-reach grabber, or reacher, around the house? If so, think about how you could use it in the garden, too. Try pulling a weed, or setting out a plant, picking up a

dropped tool, or planting a large seed, for starters. Grabbers are as handy for children as they are for adults—Rachael learned how to handle hers when she was just two.

Some catalogue sources for long-reach grabbers include A.M. Leonard, adaptAbility, and Enrich-

ments, for models under $20.00. Look for grabbers over
$20.00 in the Brookstone, adaptAbility, Alsto's, Dig This, and
Enrichments catalogues.

There are a variety of styles, lengths, and options: some
grabbers have magnetized ends; some fold; one model has an
optional wrist support (Enrichments); and a child's grabber is
available, too (adaptAbility).

THE ART AND SCIENCE
OF COMPOSTING

Bringing Your Garden Full Circle

Jim Crockett called compost "brown gold" and "the gardener's best friend": high praise indeed for what is essentially
decayed organic refuse! He was, of course, more than accurate in his descriptions, considering all that compost does for
the garden.

• Compost enriches the soil by adding not only the major
elements but also the minor trace elements, both critical
to healthy plant growth.

• Compost lightens the soil, which is especially important
if you're trying to garden in heavy clay.

• Compost increases the soil's capacity to retain moisture,
again especially important if you're gardening in a very
sandy area.

Creating and maintaining a compost pile has its own set
of benefits, too.

• Composting keeps organic "garbage" out of our ever-
dwindling landfill space.

• Composting saves money: it's cheaper than buying commercial fertilizers.

• Composting is a relatively guilt-free way to use up food
scraps.

• Composting even provides some exercise.

Making compost is neither hard nor complicated. Leaves,
grass clippings, kitchen scraps, weeds, plant refuse, and other
organic materials are layered, kept damp, and turned to allow

air circulation. When the decaying process is completed—in a matter of weeks during the summer—the results will be brown, crumbly compost that's ready for the garden.

Just about any of the excellent general gardening books or magazines on the market will tell you in detail how to make compost. Look too for specialized books devoted just to this subject.

Composters

There are many fine composters available for a gardener to purchase, either at a local garden center or through a catalogue. You can also find plans for making your own composter, like Jim Crockett's three-bin arrangement in *Crockett's Victory Garden,* for instance.

Now, unfortunately, after all these positives come the negatives. Most composters are not suitably accessible for use by the gardener with a physical disability. Typically, composters are designed as some sort of a bin or cylinder that requires reaching down and in to build and maintain the compost pile, and then removing the finished compost from under the container at ground level.

If, after seeing a few models of composters, you decide that they would be difficult or perhaps impossible to handle, here are a few suggestions that might prove easier for you to use.

The Tumbler

The Green Magic Tumbler is made in England of recycled plastic and is mounted on a steel and aluminum frame. It features vent holes for aeration, a wide opening for loading

and emptying, and a screw-on lid. This tumbler holds 5 bushels and is 27" wide x 34" deep x 48½" high, making it smaller than others on the market (Gardener's Supply, $120.00).

To use the tumbler, you load in your organic material and water it well. Then you turn the tumbler once or twice every 3 to 4 days, and in as little as a few weeks, you'll have compost. The staff at Gardener's Supply say that making compost is "quicker and easier" with this device "than any other method [they've] tried."

Given its compact dimensions, the Green Magic Tumbler should be fairly easy to turn, even from a seated position. And, since it's held off the ground, you don't need to try to work at that level to remove the finished compost. The contents can be emptied out—completely or some at a time—into a container and then transported to your gardening area.

Worm Composting

Another possibility for an easier-to-manage composting system is a worm composting kit. Children in particular will be fascinated to see how worms transform kitchen scraps into compost.

For this project you'll need to buy red wiggler worms—the common nightcrawlers from the garden won't do. Either assemble the components yourself, or purchase a ready-made kit like the one described here from Gardener's Supply.

A green plastic bin (24" long x 19¼" wide x 13½" high) is fitted with a lid, aeration grid, foam filter, and drip tray. A special potting mix is used for bedding, then worms are added along with scraps from the kitchen. The resulting compost is typically ready to use in a few weeks. Keep feeding the worms, and they'll continue making you compost.

The bin can be kept wherever the temperature range is 40–80° F., say in your garage or basement. The bin plus worms sells for $70.00; the bin, worms, potting mix, and a book on worm composting are also sold separately.

An older California gardener who is hooked on worm composting notes that a pound of worms can consume a pound of organic refuse each day. And, as she points out, worms make *very* quiet pets!

Small-Scale Composting

If these two methods of composting still sound challenging, here's a compact, easy-to-handle way to make your own compost. Put 3" of potting soil in the bottom of a large clay pot, then put the pot in a sunny, convenient spot outdoors. Now begin collecting kitchen scraps—no meat or dairy products, though. A lidded plastic container is fine to round up those parings and peels. (Chop large or tough scraps into smaller pieces, first.)

When you've accumulated enough organic matter to make a 3"–layer in the clay pot, dump it in. Keep alternating layers of soil and refuse, turning over the contents every few days with a trowel or fork. Cover the pot with a sheet of cardboard or plastic and add a little water as needed to keep the mixture moist.

Six weeks later, when the compost is ready to use, you can start the process all over again. Or, to keep the supply going, have several pots in operation at once, staggering the times when you begin layering the "ingredients."

CHAPTER FIVE

Choosing Your Plants: Vegetables, Herbs, Flowers, Ornamental Shrubs and Trees, and Fruit Bushes, Vines, and Trees

Introduction

The plants discussed in this chapter represent both older, familiar varieties, and the newer breakthroughs in plant breeding. The vegetables, herbs, flowers, trees, and fruits described below were selected because of the special characteristics they offer the gardener with a physical disability. Many are smaller, more compact varieties suitable for container growing; others are shorter and thus easier to reach from a wheelchair. Conversely, some plants are taller and so good choices for growing on stakes, poles, or trellises.

Naturally, the plants suggested here don't include all your choices; what follows, however, will give you enough information to get your garden up and running. And even if you've been gardening for years, there may be a few surprises that will give you some fresh ideas for your garden. Experimenting with new varieties can be one of the best parts of gardening!

You'll note that a number of the vegetables, herbs, and flowers discussed are described as being AAS Winners. An All-America Selection designation means that this particular plant has been selected by plant breeders around the country and judged by professionals to be superior to other current varieties. Any of the AAS Winners will, of course, make an excellent addition to your garden.

SEEDS, PLANTS, AND SOURCES

The Seed Catalogues

The dozen or so seed catalogues I studied represent some of the most famous names in the business, plus some personal favorites. Other good companies are listed in the Appendix, so you can request your own copies of their catalogues to look over. As you start collecting and reading the various catalogues, remember that the seed companies are in the business of selling seeds. In other words, don't get *too* carried away by the flowing prose and enticing pictures. Since every garden represents its own unique microclimate, what is produced in your garden may or may not duplicate the seed companies' own efforts. Consider my suggestions, read the catalogues on your own, and then make your best choices.

I haven't included prices for the herbs, flowers, and vegetables as most catalogue seed packets cost between $1.00 and $2.00. You can, of course, find cheaper seeds in your local stores—I've seen them for as little as 10 cents a packet. Whatever the price, though, experienced gardeners agree that to get the best results, start with quality seeds.

Considering how many seeds are included in one packet, they really are the least expensive part of gardening. Most seeds, moreover, can be saved for a year or two if you don't use the entire packet the first season. Just keep them in their original packet in an airtight jar stored in the refrigerator or other cool place.

Starting with Seeds

To help you start your seeds indoors, refer back to Chapter Four for helpful tools and techniques for handling the seeds. Many seeds germinate easily and transplant well. However, unless your growing season is very short, some seeds are just as easy to start outdoors, right in the garden. Other seeds, though, simply don't transplant well. Instead, sow them in the spot where they are to grow. The seed packet or the seed catalogue will tell you how best to plant that particular type.

An easy alternative to assembling the supplies you'll need is to purchase seed-starting kits. Burpee's Seed 'n Start® kits, for instance, come with everything you need to grow a guaranteed ten seedlings. Each kit includes a 10–cell plastic pack with a transparent top and a bottom-watering tray, seed-starting formula, and seeds. With some 85 choices in vegetables, herbs, annuals, and perennials, you and your garden can be off to a good start. Most of the kits—which are also available without the seeds—are $3.00.

Be sure to check out the Gardener's Supply catalogue, too. They carry many seed-starting materials, from a variety of kits, to special fertilizers and soil mixes, to mini-greenhouses, and more. Gardener's Supply's showpiece is the Accelerated Propagation System for starting seeds, which they describe as "easy and virtually foolproof." You provide the seeds, which allows the greatest freedom of choice. Prices start at $10.00 for a kit to grow anywhere from 6 to 40 seedlings.

If you can't or don't want to start the seeds yourself, maybe a friend with a sunny windowsill, grow lights, or a greenhouse could help you out. It might even be worth contacting a local nursery to see if they would be willing to start a few seeds for you.

Starting with Plants

Purchasing plants ready to set into your garden is an even quicker and easier way to get started. While they cost more than seeds, putting in transplants gives you a real head start on the growing season.

The seedlings at the garden center or nursery will be varieties that are suited to your area. Just make sure the plants you pick are sturdy, well-shaped, and healthy. The disadvantage, of course, is that unlike with seeds, your choices will be limited. A good compromise might be to start some seeds yourself indoors, direct-sow other seeds into the garden, and then fill in with purchased plants.

VEGETABLES (AND A FEW FRUITS)

Tomatoes

Tomatoes have come a long way since the days when they were considered poisonous to eat. Now we can hardly imagine a garden without them; in fact, tomatoes are the favorite garden plant in the United States. While technically a fruit, the tomato is commonly regarded as a vegetable, one basic to so much good cooking.

Breeders lavish a lot of attention on tomatoes, and so we can now choose from a great variety of sizes, colors, and tastes. Other breeders have worked to preserve many of the older, heirloom tomatoes so that today's gardeners can enjoy them as well, along with the newest types.

To give you an idea of how many choices are available, Vermont Bean Seed Company has put together a catalogue called "Totally Tomatoes." It lists 250 varieties of tomatoes, from heirlooms to 1993 hybrids—with 50 types of peppers thrown in for good measure!

Tomatoes are classified as either determinate or indeterminate plants. Determinate tomato plants are bushy and usually don't need staking, with growth slowing down after the fruits have formed. These plants bear a more concentrated crop of tomatoes, over a 3–4–week period.

Indeterminate plants are larger and keep on growing after the fruits have set, and so should be pruned and staked. The indeterminates bear their crop over a longer period of time, up until frost. Which you choose will depend on your physical abilities and willingness to care for each type, and how and when you want your crop to ripen. Or, select plants of both types.

Tomatoes for Containers

The seed companies are turning more and more attention to plants suitable for container growing, and tomatoes are no exception. Shepherd's offers "SUPERB" SUPER BUSH tomatoes that grow 2½' to 3' tall and are described as "perfect" for pots and patio containers.

Other patio-type tomatoes come from Stokes: STAKELESS, pink DWARF CHAMPION, and LUNCH BOX VF, with the last two Stokes exclusives. These plants range from about 1½' to 2' tall.

More tomatoes for containers and small gardens are found in the Park catalogue. RED EXPRESS 238 VFN and PATIO PRIZE VFN have large and medium fruits, respectively, on 2' plants.

Seeds for STAKELESS are sold by Gurney's, too, which also offers several varieties for sale as plants. For an extra-early tomato suitable for containers, try GEM STATE from Johnny's.

"Dwarf Indeterminate" Tomatoes

Park offers an especially interesting type of tomato they call the BETTER BUSH™ VFN Hybrid, a "breakthrough in tomato breeding." It's described as a sturdy, compact bush 3–3 ½' tall, bearing large tomatoes right until frost—a combination of qualities from the big, vining plants and the smaller, patio-type ones. With the support of a single stake, this Park exclusive is good for both small-space gardens and for containers.

Stokes, Mellinger's, Jung, and Park have seed for the HUSKY HYBRID tomato, a similar plant to the BETTER BUSH™. It comes in GOLD (an AAS gold medal winner), RED, CHERRY RED, and PINK colors. Vermont Bean Seed has the HUSKY tomato, too, calling it a "dwarf indeterminate."

Like the BETTER BUSH™ tomato, the HUSKY series features continuously bearing plants that are compact in growth and need no pruning. The attractive plants need a short stake or cage, grow to 4 ½', and produce standard-size fruit. Try them in containers, raised beds, or planter boxes, or in the ground-level garden.

Cherry Tomatoes

A good selection of small-fruited, cherry tomatoes is available through the seed catalogues. The color range includes red, orange, pink, and yellow, in round, oval, plum, and pear shapes. Some, like SWEET 100 HYBRID (Vermont Bean Seed, Cook's Garden), need to be staked. Others, like WHIPPERSNAPPER (Johnny's) and the new TUMBLER HYBRID (Burpee), are good in hanging baskets.

The Stokes catalogue has 12 cherry tomatoes, both bush and staking, for containers, baskets, and ground-level planting. A deep orange cherry from Johnny's called SUN GOLD is said to be exceptionally delicious, with a "tropical" or "winy" taste.

Cherry tomatoes have even been developed to grow in pots just like a windowsill plant. These tomatoes grow only about 6" high, making them a wonderful choice for containers, baskets, and window boxes.

The pot hybrids RED ROBIN and YELLOW CANARY are both offered by Park and Stokes; the latter also has TINY TIM and CHERRY GOLD varieties. Or try MICROTOM from Gurney's, which grows 5–8" tall and produces lots of little red tomatoes.

Early Sunglow corn from Burpee.

Sweet Corn

Your own sun-warmed, fresh-picked tomatoes have no equal in the supermarket; neither does your home-grown corn. Recent advances in breeding have produced corn that retains its remarkable sweetness even after harvest. (The terms "sugary enhanced" and "super sweet" identify these types.) Nonetheless, there's just no substitute for sweet corn that goes right from your garden to the table.

The problem is that if you're gardening from a wheelchair or have trouble reaching, most sweet corn grows too high. The classic SILVER QUEEN, for instance, can grow 9' tall! This presents an obvious difficulty should you need to protect the individual ears against earworms, and at harvesting time.

Fortunately, however, there are some types of sweet corn that come in at a more accessible height. Try GOLDEN MIDGET, which produces very small, very sweet ears on a stalk only 3' tall, or GOLDEN CROSS BANTAM, with larger ears on a 5–6' stalk. Seed for these two traditional varieties is available from Vermont Bean Seed.

A sugary enhanced yellow corn called SUGAR BUNS is tender, early, and grows 5–6' tall. NORTHERN XTRA-SWEET is a yellow, super sweet type of corn with a 5' stalk. Both are carried by Johnny's.

Three other shorter sweet corn varieties are from Burpee. ILLINI GOLD has large ears and grows to 5'; the new SENECA GOLD 'N PEARL is an early bicolor that grows 5–5½' tall. EARLY SUNGLOW is a delicious early corn that is just 4–4½' high.

Park (and Shepherd's) carries EARLY SUNGLOW as well. Also from Park are MERIT, a yellow, 5'–tall, regular hybrid corn and STARDUST, a sugary enhanced hybrid white corn growing 5–5½' high.

Four varieties of short sweet corn can be found in the Jung seed catalogue: yellow SENECA HORIZON and SENECA WHITE KNIGHT HYBRID, both at 5–5 ½'; EXTRA EARLY GOLDEN BANTAM at about 5'; and yellow and white XTRA SWEET 4427 BICOLOR HYBRID at 4–5' tall. Two final choices come from Gurney's. EARLY GIANT GOLDEN BANTAM is very hardy and grows about 5', while HYBRID QUICKIE is an early, sugary enhanced corn at the same height.

I'll admit to being pleasantly surprised at the number of choices available in shorter-sized sweet corn—and this isn't even an inclusive list! Since Burpee introduced GOLDEN BANTAM back in 1902, we can thank plant breeders for continuing to develop new options in "accessible corn."

Lettuce

Lettuce is both quick and easy to grow in the open garden, in containers, and in window boxes. By matching the variety to the growing season and making successive plantings, you'll be sure to have a steady supply of greens for the table. Even fall and winter lettuces are available—check the Cook's Garden catalogue for information.

While lettuce is a rather small-growing crop to begin with, some varieties are especially suited to compact container growth. Look for RED SALAD BOWL, WINTER DENSITY, ANUENUE, and BUTTERCRUNCH from Johnny's; TOM THUMB from Vermont Bean Seed and Gurney's; and DIAMOND GEM from Cook's Garden.

Also try MIXED RED AND GREEN FRENCH lettuces for containers from Shepherd's; LITTLE GEM from Park and Thompson & Morgan; and WARPATH from Burpee. All these suggestions include a mix of beautiful shades of light and dark green, and red.

Of special interest are two ways of making tiny lettuce seeds easier to handle and to space, which will practically eliminate the need for thinning. Pelleted lettuce seeds in six varieties are available from Johnny's Selected Seeds. A clay coating surrounds the little seeds to make them larger and thus easier to manipulate.

Seed tapes, though, might be an even better choice if your hands are stiff. Available through the Burpee catalogue, the 15' paper tapes will dissolve in the soil, leaving the seeds at just the right spacing. Ten varieties of lettuce are offered, including the container-sized WARPATH.

Remember, too, the information in the previous chapter, with directions on making your own seed tapes and sources for hand seeders for lettuce, carrot, and other tiny seeds.

More Greens

If you're an aficionado of Chinese cooking, consider planting some pac choi (also spelled variously as bok choy or pak choi). The new hybrid MEI QUING CHOI is a true "baby" pac choi. Since it matures very early and grows to a compact 6" size, this delicious pac choi lends itself to succession plantings. Seeds can be found in the Park, Johnny's, Stokes, Cook's Garden, Vermont Bean Seed, Thompson & Morgan, and Shepherd's catalogues.

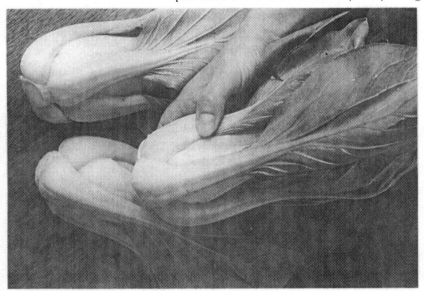

Mei Quing Choi pac choi.

Chard, or Swiss chard, is adaptable to a wide variety of soil and weather conditions. Shepherd's describes it as an "excellent choice for containers" and offers a mixed packet of seed for growing green ARGENTATA and RUBY RED chard. Park's SILVERADO is an upright, dwarf chard with slender white stalks and dark green leaves.

A vegetable especially high in vitamins, kale's flavor is actually enhanced by frost. For short varieties try DWARF BLUE CURLED VATES (Burpee), DWARF GREEN CURLED (Thompson & Morgan), or DWARF BLUE CURLED SCOTCH VATES (Park).

CHIDORI ORNAMENTAL KALE is a fancy new Japanese hybrid from Shepherd's that looks like big, beautiful flowers, and is very attractive in containers. It tastes like kale but with more of a mustard flavor.

Other greens include GREEN CURLED ENDIVE from Burpee, a pretty addition to a window box and a slightly pungent one to a salad.

For baby mache there's ELAN, a small plant with an upright habit. Shepherd's carries this green, along with a seed collection of "windowsill greens" for window boxes or containers. This company also offers arugula (rocket), a piquant green suitable for containers or window boxes. Arugula is an especially easy crop to grow.

CURLY CRESS (PEPPERGRASS) can be grown indoors on a windowsill, in pots or flats. UPLAND CRESS is fine for containers and much easier to grow than watercress. Both are sold by Johnny's.

Cress EXTRA CURLED is available from Thompson & Morgan, or try Shepherd's French variety, CRESSON. These two can be grown outdoors in the summer and indoors on a windowsill in winter.

VI-VEGETA is a new and different green in the brassica family. Its brightly colored, deep green leaves grow in an upright bunch, and are full of flavor. It can be ordered from Johnny's.

For a gourmet crop of greens you can choose Shepherd's Mesclun salad mixes. Referring to a variety of mixed greens and lettuces that are picked while young and tender, mesclun can be grown in containers for a wonderfully different salad.

Finally, parsley—available everywhere as seeds or plants—can be grown all year round in any sort of container, indoors or out.

Carrots

THUMBELINA, a 1992 AAS Winner, is probably the best-known of the round carrots that have become popular for container growing. Many seed companies carry it, includ-

The Thumbelina carrot.

ing Burpee, Johnny's, Cook's Garden, Jung, Gurney's, Stokes, and Park, among others.

Two other small, round carrots are PLANET, a French variety from Shepherd's, and ORBIT from Vermont Bean Seed. These ball-shaped carrots don't need deeply prepared soil and so are good choices for containers and even window boxes.

"Baby" or "mini" carrots grow 3–4" long, making them candidates as well for growing in pots or boxes. Try Park's BABY SPIKE, Shepherd's CARAMBA, Gurney's LITTLE FINGER, Thompson & Morgan's KUNDULUS and SUKO, Cook's Garden's MINICOR, and Johnny's KINKO. Four varieties of "baby" carrots are offered by Stokes.

Like lettuce, carrot seeds are tiny and somewhat hard to plant. Pelleted carrot seed is available from Johnny's, but only for three, 7–8" long varieties.

Burpee, though, offers six carrots in seed-tape form, including THUMBELINA and the small-size LITTLE FINGER and SHORT 'N SWEET.

Although slow to germinate, sweet and crunchy home-grown carrots are worth the wait!

Peas

Because peas begin to lose their sweetness as soon as they're picked, buying them at a farmer's market or roadside stand still won't get you the quality of peas harvested fresh from your garden.

While most Northern gardeners plant peas early in the spring, don't forget about a fall crop, too—it can be even better than the spring one since the peas will mature in the cooler weather. Just count backward from your first expected frost date to figure out the right sowing time for the variety you're planting.

The main concern for the gardener with a physical disability will be reaching the pea pods at harvest time. For this reason consider some of the dwarf varieties for growing in raised beds and planter boxes. Or, if it's easier for you to reach plants trained on trellises or poles, choose some of the taller, vining types of peas.

The shortest peas will grow about 1½' high. Look for LIT-TLE MARVEL (Burpee), IMPROVED LAXTON'S PRO-GRESS (Stokes), LAXTONIAN (Gurney's), PROGRESS NO. 9, and EXTRA EARLY LITTLE MARVEL (Jung), or KELVEDON WONDER, DAYBREAK, and FELTHAM FIRST (Thompson & Morgan).

Slightly taller are two varieties of tiny French peas or petit pois: Burpee's PETIT PROVENCAL and Vermont Bean Seed's DARVON.

A new development in garden peas is the semi-leafless NOVELLA. Growing 20–28" high, this bush-type pea offers built-in support through its many strong tendrils. When planted in wide rows and beds (a high-yield method for all peas, by the way), NOVELLA's tendrils will interlace and so hold the plant up without trellising. And because the pods are held near the top of the plant, picking is easier.

Seeds for the NOVELLA pea are carried by Jung, Park, Cook's Garden, Johnny's, Jung, and Gurney's. LACY LADY is a 20", similar variety from Vermont Bean Seed, as is the 28" 'LEAFLESS' PEA TWIGGY from Thompson & Morgan and the 18" CURLY from Stokes.

At the other end of the scale are taller garden peas for poles and trellises. Growing over 5' high, TALL TELE-PHONE (or ALDERMAN) from Vermont Bean Seed and Stokes will put those pea pods within reach.

Johnny's, however, describes their MULTISTAR as "considerably better" than TALL TELEPHONE. A late-maturing variety, the vines will grow 3 ½–4 ½' high, or 5–6' high in fertile soil.

In the 3' range are ALASKA, LINCOLN, and ALMOTA peas (Vermont Bean Seed), MIRAGREEN (Jung), AR-GONA petit pois (Johnny's), and TRIO (Thompson & Morgan).

If you're new to gardening, be sure to add some legume inoculant to your shopping list when you're buying your pea and bean seeds. Inexpensive and simple to use, the inoculant adds live nitrogen-fixing bacteria to your soil to improve the growth and yield of your plants. Look for it in almost any garden center or seed catalogue.

Snow, Snap, and Sugar Peas

Instead of or in addition to your regular garden peas, consider growing some of the edible-podded varieties. Snow or sugar peas have flat, crisp pods and are a classic addition to a stir-fry. Snap peas have thicker pods; both the pods and plump peas are delicious.

SUGAR SNAP is a tall snap pea growing 5' or more. Available from most seed companies, it's an all-time AAS Award Vegetable winner. Another tall snap pea is MAMMOTH MELTING SUGAR from Mellinger's, Gurney's, and Burpee; it will grow 4' high.

On the shorter end for snap peas, Park has SUGAR POP, at 18" high.

For a tall snow pea, try NORLI from Shepherd's. Its 4–5' vines are best on a trellis or other support. Also at 4' is the attractive CAROUBY DE MAUSSANE from Cook's Garden.

For raised beds and planters, there's the shorter SNOW-BIRD snow pea. This variety will grow 18" tall; seeds are available from Burpee. LITTLE SWEETIE, from Stokes, is even a bit shorter.

Cucumbers

Cucumbers are another crop that can be trained up a fence or trellis to an accessible height, or grown in planter boxes or containers, to which a small trellis can be added. In fact, for producing a crop of long, straight cukes, training the vines to some support is recommended.

Bush-type cucumbers are ideal for growing in containers. Try BUSH CHAMPION (Burpee), BUSH CROP (Vermont Bean Seed and Gurney's), SPACEMASTER, ARKANSAS LITTLE LEAF, and BUSH BABY (Stokes), or BUSH PICKLE (Jung and Stokes) for compact plants.

SALAD BUSH HYBRID is an All-America Selections Winner that's great for planters, hanging baskets, and small-space gardens (Park, Burpee, Vermont Bean Seed, Jung, and Shepherd's).

For pickling cukes look to PICKLEBUSH with 2' vines (Burpee), BUSH PICKLE (Park), and HYBRID BUSH PICKLE (Gurney's). There's even a cucumber for the indoor gardener. FEMBABY F1 HYBRID, available from Thompson & Morgan, will grow on any windowsill except a north-facing one.

Sweet Peppers

Peppers make a useful and delicious addition to your garden, and also provide a wonderful splash of color. Peppers are now available in a rainbow of shades: creamy white, yellow, gold, orange, red, green, lilac, purple, and chocolate brown. For a wide range of colors, check the catalogues from Park, Johnny's, Burpee, and especially, Stokes.

There are several varieties of sweet peppers that are particularly good for growing in containers, thanks to their compact size. Try Park's POT HYBRID, which grows only 10–12" high yet produces a big crop of medium-sized fruits. It can even be grown in a hanging basket.

ITALIAN GOLD, from Stokes, is also recommended for containers, as are three green-to-red peppers from Johnny's: ACE, LIPSTICK, and CHERRYTIME, plus SWEET CHOCOLATE.

Thompson & Morgan suggests REDSKIN F1 HYBRID as an early sweet pepper originally bred for patio container growing.

Remember, if you want to boost the taste and nutrition of your peppers, let the green fruits ripen to a mature red. They'll be at their sweetest and higher in vitamins A and C too.

Hot Peppers

Not to be outdone, hot peppers are also available in compact sizes just right for pots or patio containers. Two hot peppers suitable for con-

The Super Cayenne Hybrid pepper.

tainer culture are both AAS winners: SUPER CAYENNE HYBRID and SUPER CHILI HYBRID.

Seeds for the former are sold by Jung, Thompson & Morgan, and Park, while the latter is available from Jung, Park, Gurney's, Shepherd's, and Vermont Bean Seed. With their abundance of green and red fruits, these peppers are attractive ornamentals that can go indoors, too.

THAI HOT is another pepper that is as beautiful as it is hot! The bushy plants are covered with cone-shaped red and green peppers and are excellent for containers, hanging baskets, and as houseplants. THAI HOT is carried by Cook's Garden and Park.

Bush Beans: Green and Yellow

Like peas, beans should be carefully chosen with regard to harvesting: you need to be able to reach the pods. Although I haven't yet found a green or yellow bean specifically recommended for container growing, there are some options. Whatever type you select, be sure to use the legume inoculant as you did for the peas.

A few beans are described in the seed catalogues as being short and/or bushy and thus worthy of consideration for growing in pots. (I've even heard of beans being grown in window boxes.) Other snap beans are described as bearing their pods at the top of the plant, making them easier to see and pick. Another choice is to grow one or more of the various varieties of pole beans.

From Vermont Bean Seed come two shorter green bush beans. TOP CROP—described as very productive and of high quality—grows to 16", while DWARF KENTUCKY WONDER BUSH, for string or shell beans, is suggested for growing in a small area.

Other shorter bush beans include BLUE LAKE 274 at 16" and BUSH KENTUCKY WONDER 125, only 12–15" high; both are from Park. If you're interested in growing French filet beans, or haricots verts, Cook's Garden FINAUD is also a short plant. Another French bean is FLAGEOLET "CHEVRIER VERT" from Shepherd's, which grows to a compact 14".

HONEY GOLD from Stokes is an early bushy, short yellow wax bean. Or try PENCIL POD BLACK WAX (EAST-

ERN BUTTER WAX) from Jung, which grows 16" high and is very productive.

Another choice might be Gurney's IMPROVED GOLD-EN WAX for a plant with a compact growth habit.

For easy picking, DERBY comes highly recommended by several seed companies. An AAS Winner, this green bean produces large crops on an 18" bush. The pods are said to slip off easily from the stem, making this variety a good choice for the gardener with stiff hands or impaired fine motor control. Seed for DERBY is carried by Stokes, Gurney's, Jung, Vermont Bean Seed, Park, Burpee, and Thompson & Morgan.

Also suggested for easier picking are EZ PICK (Park and Johnny's), a Blue Lake type of bean whose pods also separate from the plant without effort, and REMUS MR. This latter green bush bean is described in the Park catalogue as having the "most astonishing plant habit," namely that the pods are in clusters and hang from the top of the plant. Not only is picking simplified, but the pods are kept cleaner, too.

The Derby green bean.

Bush Beans: Lima, Shell, and Soy

Lima beans that should be considered for containers or planter boxes are the dwarf FORDHOOK 242 BUSH lima (Vermont Bean Seed), and the 18" EARLY THOROGREEN BUSH (Gurney's).

Burpee, who introduced the famous FORDHOOK® limas named for their seed farm, offers BABY FORDHOOK® lima as a compact grower only 14" high.

For shelling or drying beans, the NAVY PEA bean has a small, semi-vining plant; RED MEXICAN and RED PEANUT beans grow to just 14"; and BLACK TURTLE SOUP beans are produced on a dwarf bush plant. Seeds for all these varieties can be found in the Vermont Bean Seed catalogue.

As the name implies, Park's DWARF HORTICULTURAL TAYLOR STRAIN (OCTOBER BEAN) produces its crop on a short plant.

Another dwarf bush bean is SOYBEAN EDIBLE EARLY HAKUCHO, also from Park. It only grows 12" high, is a strong producer, and matures early enough to be grown in Northern gardens.

Pole Beans

For producing accessible, space-saving crops, pole beans are a fine addition to the garden. Bean towers (see page 99) are a great way to handle their vertical growth. Just make sure that your harvest doesn't grow out of reach: SCARLET RUNNER, for instance, can grow over 10' tall!

The Vermont Bean Seed catalogue—not surprisingly—carries a very large selection of pole beans, 20 varieties in all. Green, yellow, lima, and shell beans are all available from this company as climbing vines.

Next in number of varieties offered is Thompson & Morgan, with an even dozen. Other catalogues carry pole beans too, in fewer numbers. Names to look for include KENTUCKY BLUE, an AAS Winner; KENTUCKY WONDER, an old variety; KENTUCKY WONDER WAX; ROMANO ITALIAN, another old variety; and KING OF THE GARDEN lima.

Eggplant

Eggplant is a handsome garden plant, with its purple flowers and glossy fruit—and where would ratatouille be without it!

New for 1993 is BAMBINO, a true genetic baby vegetable. The pretty plants only grow 12" high, so it's a perfect choice for containers. BAMBINO bears an early crop of purple fruit that are about the size of big walnuts. Look for it in the Burpee, Shepherd's, Gurney's, and Stokes catalogues.

Park suggests EARLY BIRD HYBRID for a container-grown eggplant. This plant has a compact size and bears long oval fruit.

PIROUETTE, from Johnny's, produces egg-shaped fruit in a size between BAMBINO and EARLY BIRD HYBRID. It too is good for containers.

Cook's Garden offers two eggplants for growing in pots. OSTEREI is a hybrid white eggplant bearing small oval fruits, while SLIM JIM produces baby-type lavender to purple fruits.

Cabbage

Cabbages can grow quite large and take up a fair amount of garden space, but even this vegetable is available in varieties suitable for container and small-space growing.

Dating back to the early 1800s is the heirloom cabbage EARLY JERSEY WAKEFIELD. This pointed-head cabbage is very sweet and tender, and produces heads weighing 2–3 lbs. Johnny's recommends this variety for containers, as well as PRIMAX, another early cabbage weighing in at 2–4 lbs. Also carrying seeds for EARLY JERSEY WAKEFIELD are Vermont Bean Seed, Thompson & Morgan, Cook's Garden, and Mellinger's.

Thompson & Morgan suggests MINICOLE F1. HYBRID cabbage for very close plantings, small gardens, and containers. Its small- to medium-sized heads are ready for eating in the summer and fall.

Three other varieties are also notable for their compact size: EARLIANA (Burpee), HYBRID STONEHEAD (Gurney's), and STONEHEAD IMPROVED (Vermont Bean Seed).

Why not try a red cabbage, too? LASSO from Johnny's is another compact grower, with heads weighing 2–4 lbs.

Other Cole Crops

Cabbage, broccoli, cauliflower, Brussels sprouts, and other similar plants make up the cole family. Although small-size plants in this group are harder to come by, there are a few varieties suggested for container growing.

Of the dozen or so seed catalogues I researched, the only broccoli described as "compact" was WALTHAM, from Mellinger's. It bears medium to large heads that hold well before flowering.

For cauliflower, Park's offers WHITE CORONA HYBRID. The single-serving heads are only 3–4" across and are "just right" for smaller garden spaces and containers.

CARGILL EARLY MATURING VARIETY is a mini-cauliflower available from Thompson & Morgan. This quick producer can be grown as closely as 6" x 6" apart.

Also from Thompson & Morgan is a dwarf type of Brussels sprouts called PEER GYNT F1. HYBRID. Again, its small-size plants are ideal for the closer quarters of a planter box or other container. The high quality sprouts are produced in abundance.

While not a dwarf, the Brussels sprouts JADE CROSS HYBRID is a smaller plant growing about 18–24" tall. This

AAS Winner is especially recommended for short-season areas. Seed can be purchased from Jung.

Melons

One of the great delights of summer, fresh melons from the garden simply have no equal. Whether you plant cantaloupe, watermelon, or both, these delicious fruits deserve a spot in your garden. By selecting short-vined or bushy types, melons can be grown in planter boxes, raised beds, or containers, making them easier to reach for cultivation and harvest.

Sweet Bush Hybrid melon from Burpee.

For choices in cantaloupes (muskmelons), Burpee describes their SWEET BUSH HYBRID as "ideal for the small garden or container growing."

Stokes and Park both suggest the new bush cantaloupe MUSKETEER for containers, too, as the plants grow only 2–3' across. MINNESOTA MIDGET from Gurney's is another compact grower, producing early, 4" melons.

Watermelons recommended for small spaces include BUSH SUGAR BABY (Burpee and Gurney's); BUSH BABY II HYBRID (Park); SUGAR BUSH (Vermont Bean Seed); SUGAR BABY (Shepherd's and Stokes); EXTRA EARLY SUGAR BABY (Jung); and GARDEN BABY HYBRID (Jung, Vermont Bean Seed, and Johnny's). These all produce round, "icebox size" watermelons on compact plants.

There's even a yellow watermelon to consider. YELLOW DOLL HYBRID is a very early AAS Winner melon available from Vermont Bean Seed and Jung. Its fruit is also round and sized just right for refrigerator storage. Jung even suggests training its smaller-than-usual vines up a trellis where garden space is at a premium.

Onions and Shallots

For very small spaces, try growing some summer "mini" onions. Baby pearl onions are fine fresh, pickled, or baked, and can be left to grow larger, too. Johnny's has two nice varieties, SNOW BABY and PURPLETTE. Cooks' Garden also carries PURPLETTE, along with POMPEII.

An Israeli baby onion, EARLY AVIV, is available from Shepherd's. Its white bulbs are produced very early, and can be harvested as small as ¾" in diameter.

Several other "mini" onions can be found in the Stokes and Park catalogues.

French shallots are easy to grow and can be cultivated outdoors in containers, or forced indoors in pots or tubs during the winter for fresh green onions. Johnny's carries the true French, pink-tinged shallot.

Beets

As with carrots, "baby"-type beets are a good bet for planting in containers. Since they're bred to be small, these beets will hold their optimum size without becoming woody or pithy if you can't harvest them all right away.

LITTLE BALL® is one of the true baby beets, with its dark red 3" roots. Seeds are offered by Park and Burpee; the latter also offers this beet as a seed tape.

From Shepherd's comes KLEINE BOL, a very tender Dutch variety producing round little beets. Other names in baby beets include SPINEL from Thompson & Morgan, LITTLE MINI BALL from Stokes, and PRONTO from Vermont Bean Seed, another Dutch variety.

Johnny's specifically suggests FORMANOVA for growing in containers. This cylindrical red beet, about 6" long, can be planted closer together than other types of beets. Seeds are also offered by Cook's Garden.

Did you know that most beet seeds are really little clusters of four to five individual buds? This means that once the sprouts are up, you'll need to thin them—not the easiest of tasks, especially if you have impaired fine motor control.

There are, however, two ways to avoid thinning your beets. You can take advantage of Burpee's seed tape, which comes in five varieties (or make your own tape). Or, you can plant beets that contain only one seed bud, so only one sprout per seed is produced. Look for MONOPOLY from Shepherd's and Thompson & Morgan, and MONOGRAM, also from Thompson & Morgan, for this type of beet.

Okra

Okra, a crop probably more familiar to Southern gardeners than to Northern, produces one of the key ingredients in gumbo. Its pretty flowers look like those of the hibiscus, to which it is related. Northern gardeners can have a good crop of okra too, for if a growing season is long enough for sweet corn, it's long enough for okra.

BLONDY, an AAS Winner, is described as an early dwarf okra. Harvesting the pods is easy as their whitish green color stands out against the foliage. Mellinger's and Gurney's carry seeds for this okra.

For closer planting in a limited space, Park recommends LEE—"the first base-branching okra"—and CANDELABRA BRANCHING. The latter has the added benefit of bearing spineless pods.

Summer Squash

It's hard to imagine a garden without some sort of summer squash in it. These plants, however, tend to be space hogs, taking up a sizeable amount of garden area. Luckily, breeders have worked to produce smaller, bushier types of squash that are suitable for growing in the confines of raised beds and containers. Here are some varieties to look for.

GOLDBAR HYBRID is a true bush-type yellow summer squash. An early, high-yielding squash of fine quality, it's offered by Jung and Vermont Bean Seed.

Another compact grower is an AAS Winner, SUN DROPS HYBRID. This new class of summer squash produces pale yellow, small oval fruits. Seeds can be bought from Jung and Park.

The Sunburst Yellow Hybrid squash.

BUTTER SWAN HYBRID, a smooth crookneck from Park, grows to a bushy plant about 3–4' across.

Also described as compact are HYBRID CRESCENT, from Gurney's; DIXIE HYBRID, from Park; and SUNBURST YELLOW HYBRID, from Park and Shepherd's. This latter is an AAS Winner too, producing beautiful little bright yellow and green, scalloped-shaped fruits.

For zucchini, try GREEN MAGIC II, which Park describes as the "first space-saving, compact bush zucchini." Or, plant BURPEE HYBRID ZUCCHINI for big yields on a bush-like, compact plant.

With its vines spreading only 30", HYBRID JACKPOT ZUCCHINI from Gurney's is another one to consider, as is ZUCCHINI SELECT from Stokes.

There's even a yellow zucchini for growing in limited spaces, GOLD RUSH. This AAS Winner hybrid is sold by Park, Thompson & Morgan, and Gurney's.

From the Middle East comes CLARIMORE LEBANESE ZUCCHINI, with the same compact, bushy habit. Seeds for this special pastel green squash are available from Shepherd's. Stokes offers COUSA, a Lebanese zucchini, with a similar growth habit.

Perhaps the amount of room a squash takes up is of less concern than those annoying prickles that irritate your skin every time you reach into the plant to pick a zucchini. If so, get some seeds for SPINELESS BEAUTY HYBRID from Gurney's, Thompson & Morgan, Park, or Stokes. The latter company says this variety is the "only green zucchini that offers spineless stems and petioles." The dark green fruits are produced generously and are of a very fine flavor.

Cream of the Crop hybrid squash.

Instead of growing your summer squash in a container, you can grow selected varieties vertically, on a trellis, fence, or poles. If this growing method would make the plants and fruits more accessible for you, try LONG GREEN STRIPED (Thompson & Morgan); the Italian heirloom ZUCCETTA RAMPICANTE (Shepherd's); or TROMBONCINO (Cook's Garden).

Winter Squash

It's wonderful to have some hard-shelled squash in storage for those long winter months; however, the vigorous vining plants can take over a summer garden. Opt instead for some of these varieties.

The AAS Winner CREAM OF THE CROP HYBRID (Thompson & Morgan, Park, Jung, and Johnny's) is a white acorn squash. Its compact, bushy plants are well-suited for smaller spaces.

For a bush buttercup there's ALL SEASONS HYBRID, an orange squash from Park, Gurney's, and Jung.

Semi-bush or bush-type plants, or those with compact vines, include TABLE QUEEN (Gurney's and Jung); EARLY ACORN HYBRID (Burpee and Gurney's); BURPEE'S BUT- TERBUSH; TABLE GOLD (Jung); EARLY BUTTERNUT HYBRID (Park); TABLE KING BUSH ACORN (Vermont Bean Seed); and AAS Winner SWEET MAMA HYBRID (Vermont Bean Seed and Park).

Potatoes

Newly offered by Park and Mellinger's in their 1993 cata- logues, minituber seed potatoes are a fascinating development in potato breeding. These certified, miniature tubers are only ½" to 1½" in diameter, yet each will produce 3–4 lbs. of full- sized potatoes. Instead of cutting up a large seed potato and then curing or treating the cut surface before planting, you simply plant the whole little potato.

Both companies offer YELLOW FINN, DESIREE, and ALL BLUE as minituber seed potatoes. Park also carries DARK RED NORLAND, DONNA, and RED GOLD varie- ties, as well. For ease in handling and planting—to say noth- ing of a great color variety—these little potatoes might be just the ticket! (For tips on planting, refer back to pages 6 and 44.)

Sweet Potatoes

Long a favored Southern crop, sweet potatoes can easily be grown in Northern gardens too as long as they have plenty of sun, warmth, and well-drained soil. Sweet potatoes are sold as plants, or slips; note that they can't be shipped to Califor- nia, Alaska, or outside the continental United States.

Two varieties of sweet potatoes are especially recom- mended for growing in limited spaces, thanks to their com- pact, bushy habits. If you've ever sprouted a sweet potato tuber in water, you know that the vining types are capable of very vigorous growth.

BUSH PORTO RICO boasts a copper-colored skin and reddish-orange flesh. Great for baking, this delicious sweet po- tato is available from Burpee, Vermont Bean Seed, and Gur- ney.

With its dark green and purple foliage and stems, VAR-DAMAN is both decorative and useful. This sweet potato has a gold skin with deep orange flesh, and produces heavily. Plants can be purchased from Burpee, Vermont Bean Seed, Gurney, and Park.

Pumpkins

Like sweet potatoes, pumpkins are known for producing long, rambling vines. There is one short-vine variety, BUSHKIN {vp}, from Burpee. It bears 1 to 3 bright orange, 10–lb. pumpkins on vines that spread 6'. BUSHKIN might still be too big for a patio container or tub, but could work well in a large planter box.

Turnips

As with several other vegetables discussed above, baby turnips are your best bet for growing in containers as their small size lends them to this type of cultivation.

Tokyo Cross hybrid turnip.

New for 1993 is a Japanese turnip from Shepherd's called MARKET EXPRESS. This hybrid variety bears an early crop of one-inch pearly white turnips that are very uniform in size. Sweet and mild enough to eat raw, these baby turnips are easy to grow.

Another turnip to consider is TOKYO CROSS HYBRID. While this vegetable will grow 6" across, it can be harvested at only 2". The roots of the AAS Winner turnip are smooth, pure white, and delicious. Seeds are available from Burpee, Gurney's, and Thompson & Morgan.

Other Vegetables

It may be inconceivable to you to plant your garden without including parsnips or rutabaga, collards, celery, or leeks. Rest assured that just because these and a few other vegetables weren't discussed individually in this chapter, it doesn't mean that you can't grow them.

As noted in the Introduction to this chapter, when I researched the seed catalogues I sought specific recommendations from the companies themselves. What I looked for was that a plant was either bred especially for container growing or was otherwise particularly suited for it; or that a plant was a good candidate for growing vertically on a trellis; or that it had some adaptation making it easier to plant; or it was available in a dwarf, "mini," or baby form. These are the vegetables that I selected for this section.

When no mention was made of a particular vegetable—parsnips, say—it simply means that I didn't find any varieties that specifically met the above criteria. So, if you want to grow parsnips in a container, raised bed, or planter box, please do. First check Chapters One and Two for information on how deep a bed the plant will need, then study your catalogues or go to the local garden center to select a variety to grow.

HERBS

Herbs are a marvelous addition to a vegetable or flower garden, or in a special garden all by themselves. Many excellent books are available on their cultivation, care, and use. You'll also find in these books some fascinating historical material tracing herbal lore through the centuries.

A nice selection of herbs—both seeds and plants—can be found in the Burpee, Vermont Bean Seed, Cook's Garden, Shepherd's, Stokes, Nichols, Mellinger's, Johnny's, and Thompson & Morgan catalogues. One wonderful place to visit and from which to buy herb seeds and plants is Caprilands Herb Farm in Coventry, Connecticut.

Most herbs are not large growers and can thus be included in any container garden. One notable exception is angelica, with its evocative botanical name of *Angelica archangelica:* this herb grows 6' tall! Otherwise, herbs tend to range from low-growing creepers up to about 3' high. Many are also good as indoor pot plants or in a window box.

There are two varieties of herbs in particular that are of special interest to the container gardener. First is FERNLEAF dill, a 1992 AAS Winner. While common dill grows 3' tall, FERNLEAF measures only 18", making it an ideal choice for containers. The dark green leaves of this attractive, base-branching dill are finely cut, giving it a fern-like appearance. Seeds are available from Vermont Bean Seed, Johnny's, Stokes, Burpee, and Jung.

Second is a pretty little basil, SPICY GLOBE. Smallest of the basils, it grows in a compact mound about 6" high and wide. The tiny leaves are bright green and aromatic. SPICY GLOBE is useful both as an indoor pot plant, and in patio containers or window boxes, where it can be interplanted with flowers for a pleasing effect. Johnny's, Shepherd's, Stokes, Cook's Garden, Thompson & Morgan, and Vermont Bean Seed all carry this herb.

Of course fresh herbs are unequalled in cooking, but even if you don't make full use of their culinary or medicinal properties, do plant some herbs. Just having their varied forms, colors, and fragrances near you can do wonders for the soul.

FLOWERS

Introduction

An absolute wealth of annual and perennial flowers and bulbs is available for growing in window boxes, in pots, in tubs, barrels, and other large containers, and, of course, in a ground-level bed. Since I couldn't possibly list every choice you have in flowers, I've selectively narrowed the list, including both some tried-and-true old favorites, and some new and interesting varieties.

For gardening with a physical disability, there are a few things to keep in mind when choosing what flowers you want to plant. You can, certainly, grow whatever pleases you if you're determined to do so. But generally speaking, you'll do best to select flowers that won't put undue demands on either your time or your energy.

For starters, use these questions to help you evaluate potential choices. Consider how much maintenance will be required to keep your flowers looking good:

- Will they demand frequent watering, or can they withstand some dryness?

- Will they wilt in the summer sun, or can they take the heat?

- Will regular deadheading (that is, removing dead flowers) be needed to improve their appearance?

- Do they need to be pinched back often to keep a nice bushy shape?

- Will they grow out of reach?

- Will you have to contend with thorns or prickers?

- Must they be pruned?

- Are they exotics that will be more susceptible to pests, diseases, and winter damage, instead of hardier native plants?

- Will they have to be divided?

- Will they need to be lifted in the fall, stored, and then replanted in the spring?

If you answer "Yes" to all or most of these questions, be prepared for some work! Otherwise, decide what you *are* willing and able to do to care for your plants; it may mean choosing flowers that require little or no attention. Flowers that are considered easy to grow are certainly a plus too, and, for container gardening, flowers that are bred to be especially suited to this type of culture are recommended.

Besides the care required, you'll also need to think about what type of environment your flowers prefer, and what you have to offer. Full sun, light shade, or deep shade; plenty of water, or a drier situation; sandy, clay, or poor soil; hot winds; salt spray, and similar factors must all be taken into consideration. The more closely you can match your growing conditions with what your plants need, the greater your chances for success will be. Remember, though, that if you're gardening in containers you'll already have control over much of your flowers' environment.

THE AESTHETICS OF FLOWER SELECTION

To truly get the most out of your plantings, consider the flowers and the plants they grow on from an aesthetic standpoint. Color, shape, texture, and fragrance all appeal to our senses, while how the flowers are presented can lend importance and definition to your garden. Selecting the various flowers you want to plant together in a container or bed thus becomes an adventure in personal expression and creativity.

A Theme or Focus

First, decide if you'd like a theme for your flower garden— it really does make it more fun! An excellent book to consult for sixteen different and interesting gardens is *Theme Gardens* by Barbara Damrosch. In it she describes plantings as diverse as a medieval paradise garden, a winter garden, and a garden of love, with all sorts of plant specifics and historical background included for each garden. Even if your own garden consists of one window box, you can still get some wonderful ideas from this book.

Other possibilities for a theme or focus include a cutting garden of flowers for bouquets, an everlasting garden of flowers for drying, and a wildflower garden. Your flower choices could echo plants you knew as a child, or feature some of the newest varieties on the market. Or, the flowers you grow may simply happen to be your very favorites.

Color

In terms of a flower's sensory appeal, color is probably the first thing that comes to mind. Use it as an artist would by deciding what effect you want to create with your flowers, as illustrated by a spin around a color wheel. Here are four colorful ways you can achieve these various effects.

First, harmonious colors are ones that are closely related: blue and green, red and purple, orange and yellow. Picture scarlet and violet tulips planted together, and you can see how they combine for a pleasing display.

Complementary colors are opposites: green and red, purple and yellow, blue and orange. Think of the little yellow-and-purple faces of Johnny-jump-ups, or how right violets and dandelions look together in the spring.

Coolness seems to come from blue, purple, and green, and warmth from red, orange, and yellow. Massed plantings of marigolds would be an easy way to achieve this latter color scheme.

Finally, monochromatic colors are the various dark-to-light shades of any one color. Here the effect might come from a bed planted in shades of pink, from the palest tint to the brightest hue.

Silver, as from dusty miller, lamb's ears, and artemisia, can make a wonderful accent color, as can the judicious use of white. Or, combine the white and silver in a flower bed that will glow like a pearl in the moonlight.

Unless you happen to like the effect of what Jim Crockett calls "clowns' pants," don't plant a bed or border with single varieties of many flowers. Instead, plant them in *groups* of color, with three or more of one kind.

Color: Annuals, Perennials, Bulbs

As one last point regarding flower colors, remember that annuals will provide you with a whole season's worth of color, with most blooming up until frost. They offer a great variety in colors, sizes, and flower shapes, with the most popular annuals widely available as plants. They are, by and large, easy to grow; many can be sown as seeds right where they're to bloom.

Annuals can be combined with great success with perennials, herbs, and even vegetables, and can help bridge any gaps between the perennials' blooming periods. About the only drawbacks to annual flowers are that they generally need to be deadheaded to look their best and keep the blooms up, and, of course, unless they self-seed (which some varieties will), they'll be gone come frost.

Perennials, on the other hand, can be with you for many years; with peonies, even a century is quite possible. It's a pleasure to mark a season's progress as the various plants come into glorious bloom, then retire from the stage in anticipation of next year's show.

This very characteristic of seasonal flowering, however, means that if your bed or border is composed solely of perennials, you must plan carefully so that one type of plant will succeed another as they come in and out of bloom. (And if you include biennials in your design, remember that they're on a two-year schedule, producing leaves the first, and flowers and seeds the second.) Without advance planning, the garden that was so beautiful in May will probably look rather ragtag in July.

Care must be taken with perennials in other regards as well. Some popular varieties—like iris—need to periodically have their roots divided, which can be a tough chore. Others, particularly those with woody stems, may require pruning. Also, some perennials are prey to certain insect pests (as columbines with leaf miners, for instance).

Finally, perennials can have problems overwintering in unprotected raised beds and planter boxes, particularly those exposed to a cold northerly wind. Temperature extremes can cause great damage to their roots.

Don't let any potential disadvantages scare you off from growing perennials and biennials, though. Some of your most colorful and rewarding choices in flowers come from these groups!

Bulbs also offer the gardener great rewards in beauty. Dramatic effect, brilliance of color, fragrance, and sheer variety combine to make this group so popular. And, since many can be left in place to grow on and multiply, they can be an undemanding choice. Like perennials, however, their season will come and go. Planning is necessary, then, to maintain a succession of blooms.

Shape

Shape refers to the form both of the flowers and of the plant on which they grow, and is an important aesthetic consideration when planning your flower garden. Generally speaking, the more variety you can achieve with your plants, the more interesting your garden will be.

Flowering plants vary in height from a low 3" alyssum, to a 1' dahlia, to a 30" zinnia, to a 4' cosmos, and on up to a giant 12' sunflower, with every size in between. Whether you're putting in annuals, perennials, or a mixture of both, you'll need to plant according to height. Usually this means putting taller plants in the back of the bed, and the shorter ones in front.

Follow this plan *too* strictly, however, and the effect will become somewhat military, with rows of plants marching in proper formation. Aim instead for a more flowing design:

bring some of the medium-height plants up front now and then, with the taller plants still behind them. Jim Crockett aptly uses the words "undulate" and "waves" to suggest the gardener's goal in planting a border or bed.

As you plan for a variety of heights, visualize the shape or form of the plant. Is it bushy like a chrysanthemum, or does it grow as a tall spike, like a delphinium or gladiolus? Does it have the frond-like leaves of a lily, or the feathery foliage of a marigold, or the rounded leaves of a nasturtium? Will it grow in a neat mound like a primrose, or cascade luxuriantly like an ivy-leaf geranium?

Finally, think about the shape of the flower itself. There's the tiny forget-me-not and the huge moonflower; daisy and bell and pinwheel shapes; simple poppies and complex columbines; single impatiens and double begonias; and on, and on. Or perhaps, like the coleus, the leaves, and not the flowers, are the attraction.

Texture

Texture is often overlooked when selecting flowering plants, yet it too is aesthetically important, from both a tactile and a visual standpoint. Again, a mix of textures is key. Look for smooth leaves and furry; silk-like flowers and papery; finely cut foliage and large, simple leaves; velvety blooms and fuzzy. Enjoy the differences!

Fragrance

Having been almost bred out of many flowers in favor of larger blooms and more exotic colors, fragrance is making something of a comeback as gardeners are demanding the return of "old-fashioned," perfumed flowers. A sweet fragrance is a delight to the senses, one that should be accounted for in every planting of flowers, no matter how small.

Fragrant flowers include alyssum, mignonette, sweet pea, stock, candytuft, heliotrope, carnation, peony, rose, dianthus, hyacinth, lily, daffodil, wallflower, tuberose, and violet, among others. Be sure the variety you select is described as fragrant, for not every type from this list is sweet-smelling. For scented roses, look especially for older varieties. Barbara Damrosch recommends MME. HARDY, MRS. JOHN LAING, LA REINE VICTORIA, common moss rose, and BLANC DOUBLE DE COUBERT as nicely fragrant.

Particularly evocative are the night-scented flowers. These only release their fragrance in the late afternoon or evening, a time well-suited to contemplation and romance. Some of the flowers to look for are nicotiana (night-flowering tobacco), moonflower, dame's rocket, four o'clocks, fairy lily, and night-scented stock.

You might take a tip from our Colonial ancestors and plant your fragrant flowers right under a window, so that their sweet scents will waft into your home when the window is open. Or, fill a window box with fragrant blooms.

All this business of maintenance, blooming seasons, and aesthetics may seem like too much fuss for some simple flowers. I assure you, none of it is absolutely required, but, I also assure you, that if these issues are at least considered when you choose and set out your flowers, the time invested will be wisely spent. Once you've selected your flowers, refer back to Chapter Two for specifics on how to plant up your container, hanging basket, or window box.

A FEW GOOD FLOWERS

Sources and Selections

The lists of flowers that follow include both general suggestions and some specific recommendations garnered from three catalogues, ones that carry a nice array of flower seeds (and sometimes, plants and bulbs): Park Seed, Stokes, and Burpee. There are, of course, many, many fine sources for flower seeds, but since together these three companies cover a few hundred choices, I think they're an excellent place to begin.

I've divided the flowers into groups as being particularly good for containers, window boxes, and hanging baskets; naturally there is some overlap. While a lot of these plants are available at your local nursery, many of the specific varieties will probably need to be grown from seed.

As you choose the flowers with which to fill your container, hanging basket, or window box, remember that vegetables and herbs can be combined with them for a very pleasing effect. A tomato in a half whiskey barrel can be ringed with marigolds and nasturtiums; oregano can spill over the edge of a hanging basket; parsley and leaf lettuce can join the dwarf calendulas in a window box.

There are also a number of foliage plants—many of which are familiar as houseplants—that make excellent choices for adding to a container, hanging basket, or window box. Many are good as trailing specimens, others lend a touch of color, and still others provide contrast with interestingly-shaped leaves.

Spider plants, pothos, caladium, dracaena, ivies, ferns, and grasses are just a sampling of the various plants that can provide color and contrast to your flowers. A few specific varieties of other foliage plants that are particularly recommended for container growing can be found after the lists of flowers.

As long as they're compatible in their light and moisture requirements, the possibilities for combining various types of plants are practically endless. See page 54 for more ideas on mixed plantings.

Flowers for Containers

achimenes (*Achimenes*): part shade or shade, bulbs/ white, pink, red, violet, and blue flowers in singles and doubles with a long blooming period; plant 3–5 bulbs in a 10" container; can also be grown from seed—Burpee and Park

African daisy, Cape marigold (*Dimorphotheca*): sun, annual/ STARSHINE is "excellent" for large containers; mounded 1' plants spread to 18" in diameter; the daisy-like flowers come in pinks and white; it loves heat and sun—Park

ageratum, dwarf (*Ageratum*): sun or part shade, annual/ fuzzy-looking flowers in white and shades of blue; compact 8" mounds make it a good border plant; easy to grow

alyssum, sweet: sun or part shade, annual/ tiny white and pastel sweet-smelling flowers cover 3–4" low-growing, spreading plants; good in cool weather; trim dead flowers for almost continuous bloom

aster, dwarf (*Aster*): sun, annual/ 6" POT 'N PATIO MIXED in white, blue, pink, red, will bloom indoors in sunny window—Burpee; Stokes recommends RIBBON, COMET, MINI LADY, DWARF SPIDER, and CONTRASTER types in mixed colors; DWARF COMET is 8" in mixed colors and new from Park

begonia, fibrous (*Begonia*): part shade, shade, or sun, annual/ 5–10" plants are seldom damaged by pests, rain, wind; pastel flowers with bronze or green foliage bloom continuously; can go indoors as winter pot plant; has fine seeds

begonia, tuberous (*Begonia tuberosa*): part shade, annual/ big, gorgeous mixed single and bicolor blooms are spectacular in containers; lift tubers before frost to re-plant following year; easy to grow from seed but it's fine, dust-like; also sold as tubers

blazing star, gayfeather (*Liatris*): sun or part shade, perennial/ SPICATA KOBOLD's 18" plants bear spikes of rose-purple flowers from midsummer into fall; nice cut flower for Zones 3–10–Park and Stokes

bulbs: Hardy bulbs for forcing indoors include hyacinths, daffodils, and tulips, plus the smaller ones like crocuses and grape hyacinths. Select varieties that are especially recommended for forcing, either as indicated in a catalogue or suggested at the nursery

bush violet, dwarf (*Browallia americana*): part shade, annual/ 8–10" tall with blue and white star-like flowers and bright green foliage—Park

buttercup (*Ranunculus*): sun, perennial/ beautiful double and semi-double flowers in rich, bright mixed shades resemble peonies or roses, with fern-like foliage; 8–10" plants are hardy south of Washington, D.C.; grow from seed or bulbs

calla (*Zantedeschia*): sun or part shade, tender bulbs/ waxy flowers in yellow, pink, white, and lavender; for large containers; lift bulbs in fall to replant in spring—Burpee and Park

canna, dwarf: sun, annual/ TROPICAL ROSE, an AAS Winner, is for large containers; it grows 2 ½–3' with big rose flowers and tropical-looking foliage; hardy Zones 8–10, otherwise lift and store rhizomes over winter—Burpee and Park; other dwarf cannas from 18" to about 30" in mixed colors—Park

carnation, dwarf (*Dianthus*): sun, annual/ DWARF FRA-
GRANCE is 15" with very stiff stems for cutting; it's quite fragrant and comes in mixed colors—Stokes

Chinese orchid, hardy (*Bletilla*): part shade, perennial,
bulbs/ 12" high and easy to grow; lavender and white flowers
resemble cattleya orchids; Zones 5–9–Park

chrysanthemum, dwarf: sun, perennial/ AUTUMN GLORY
HYBRID grows 6–8" high and spreads 18–24" without pinch-
ing; the double and semi-double flowers are in mixed colors—
Park

cockscomb (*Celosia cristata*): sun, annual/ TREASURE
CHEST is 8" with velvety crested flower heads in bright colors—Park

columbine, dwarf (*Aquilegia*): part shade or sun, perennial/
MUSIC DWARF hybrid is wind tolerant in bicolors and
white—Stokes

cosmos, dwarf (*Cosmos*): sun, annual/ SONATA MIXED
has a great profusion of single flowers in shades of pink, red,
and white; the bushy plants are 20–24" tall and very easy to
grow—Burpee and Park

Dahlberg daisy (*Thymophylla tenuiloba*): sun, annual/ single
daisy-like flowers in bright yellow with fern-like foliage; 8"
high—Park

dahlia (*Dahlia*): sun, annual, seeds or tender tubers/ lovely
flowers in every color but blue, in single and bicolors and various flower forms; shorter varieties are 8–14" high; easy to
grow from seed; bulbs can winter over in warmer areas and
elsewhere be dug and stored for spring re-planting

daylily (*Hemerocallis*): sun or part shade, perennial/ STELLA
DE ORO's 2' mounded plants with bright yellow flowers are
gorgeous in containers; requires little maintenance

flowering tobacco (*Nicotiana*): sun or part shade, annual/
DOMINO SERIES hybrid is 12" tall; the mostly pastel flowers
are quite fragrant; it's highly recommended by Stokes for containers as well as NICKI SERIES at 20" for larger containers;
METRO™ SERIES hybrid is 12" high and drought tolerant;
its flowers are mostly in pastels—Burpee

garden pinks (*Dianthus*): sun, annual/ PRINCESS and
MAGIC CHARMS hybrids are 6" in mixed colors: Stokes;

award-winning PARFAIT HYBRID's flowers are rose and pink with eyes—Park

gazania (*Gazania*): sun, annual/ the big daisy-like flowers in bright colors are easy to grow, and tolerate drought and heat; they grow 6–10" high

geranium (*Pelargonium*): sun, annual/ very popular flowers come in a wide range of types and colors for summer-long bloom

heliotrope, dwarf (*Valeriana officinalis*): sun, annual/ the bushy 8" plants bear large heads of deep purple, delightfully fragrant flowers; it can also be used as a winter houseplant

impatiens (*Impatiens*): part shade and shade, annual/ singles, doubles, and New Guinea type in various colors and bi-colors; this widely grown flower requires little or no maintenance

iris, Japanese (*Iris kaempferi*): sun or part shade, perennial/ showy flowers in white, pink, blues, and purples are "excellent" in containers for early summer bloom; they're 2 ½–3' tall and are for Zones 4–9, with a winter mulch in colder areas—Park

larkspur (*Delphinium*): sun, perennial/ MAGIC FOUNTAIN MIX is 24–28" tall and wind tolerant with no staking needed; flowers are in various blues, lavender, white, and pink—Stokes and Park

lily, fairy, rain lily (*Zephyranthes*): sun or part shade, tender bulbs/ plant 10–12 bulbs in an 8" pot for white and pink crocus-like flowers—Burpee

lily, magic (*Lycoris squamigera*): sun or part shade, hardy bulb/ fragrant, lily-like flowers for Zones 5–8

lily, dwarf Oriental (*Lilium*): sun, perennial, hardy bulbs/ gorgeous flowers in mixed colors are hardy and easy to grow; STRAWBERRY SHORTCAKE is 18–24" high with big strawberry-colored, fragrant flowers—Park

lisianthus, dwarf (*Eustoma*): sun, half-hardy perennial/ LISA grows 6–8" tall with attractive foliage and large, exotic-looking dark blue flowers; doesn't require staking; pelleted seed—Park

lobelia, edging (*Lobelia Erinus*): sun or part shade, annual/ plants grow 5–8" tall with flowers in white, rose, purples, and an intense blue; likes cool weather

lupine, dwarf (*Lupinus*): sun or part shade, perennial/ GALLERY is an 18" Russell-type lupine; the sturdy plants have flowers in mixed colors—Stokes; MINARETTE, at 20", doesn't need staking and comes in a wide color mix; for Zones 4–7–Park

marigold (*Tagetes*): sun, annual/ African and French types come in bright shades of yellow, orange, red; many shorter varieties grow only 8" and 10" tall; a very popular and trouble-free plant

monkey flower (*Mimulus*): sun, annual/ MYSTIC is a 10" hybrid that prefers cool spring weather; its flowers are in shades of red, orange, yellow, and ivory—Park

morning glory, dwarf (*Ipomoea*): sun, annual/ VARIEGATED LEAVED has variegated foliage and flowers in mixed colors; tolerates drought; grows about 5" high and spreads 8"—Park; DWARF PICOTEE MIXED is a bushy 12" with flowers in mixed colors and green and white foliage—Stokes

moss rose (*Portulaca*): sun, annual/ the 5" SUNDIAL MIXED hybrid has bright colors and is highly recommended by Stokes for containers

nasturtium (*Tropaeolum*): sun, annual/ very easy to grow and tolerant of drought and poor soils; bush types grow about 8–12" high; fragrant blooms are in shades of yellow, orange, red; leaves and flowers are edible

pansy (*Viola*): part shade or sun, annual/ a popular flower in solid and mixed colors, both brights and pastels, either plain or with faces; good for cooler spring or fall weather although some have heat tolerance

periwinkle (*Vinca*): sun or part shade, annual/ pastel flowers and shiny green leaves are on compact plants; it's drought and heat tolerant and seldom bothered by diseases or insects

petunia (*Petunia*): sun, annual/ this very popular flower comes in many colors and bicolors in singles and doubles; remove dead blooms for continuous flowering

phlox, annual (*Phlox drummondii*): sun, annual/ dwarf varieties grow 6–8" tall with flowers in pastel colors

pincushion flower (*Scabiosa*): sun or part shade, perennial/ BUTTERFLY BLUE™ is a 12" compact plant that's covered with lavender-blue flowers spring to fall; it's attractive to butterflies and trouble-free—Park

pot marigold (*Calendula officinatis*): sun, annual/ DWARF GEM MIXED is 12" in shades of yellow and orange—Burpee

pot of gold (*Coreopsis*): sun, perennial/ MOONBEAM's creamy yellow flowers are produced all summer; it grows 1 ½– 2' with fern-like foliage; easy-to-grow award winner—Park

rose, miniature (*Rosa*): sun, perennial/ perfect little roses grow 12–20" high in a variety of colors

salvia, dwarf (*Salvia*): sun or part shade, annual/ features spikes of bright red flowers

Shasta daisy, dwarf (*Chrysanthemum x superbum*): sun, perennial/ SNOW LADY is an AAS Winner featuring white and yellow flowers in the classic daisy shape; blooms all summer on 10" plants that are 12" across; "outstanding" in containers—Park

snapdragon, dwarf (*Chaenorrhi*): sun or part shade, annual/ plants grow 5–12" high with bright-colored flower spikes

statice, dwarf (*Limonium*): sun, annual/ PETITE BOUQUET MIXED is a special 12" midget strain in shades of yellow, blue, rose, and white—Stokes and Park

stock (*Matthiola*): sun, annual/ MIDGET SERIES grows 8–10" tall with flower spikes in red and white—Park

sunflower, dwarf (*Helianthus*): sun, annual/ SUNSPOT is only 1 ½–2' high but has large flower heads; it's very easy to grow—Burpee

Swan River daisy (*Brachycome iberidifolia*): sun, annual/ profuse star-like flowers in white and shades of blue with black or yellow centers; grows to 9" with fern-like foliage—Park

sweet pea, dwarf (*Lathyrus*): sun, annual/ BURPEE'S BIJOU MIXED at 15" is bushy and spreading; distinctive flowers are mostly pastels; SNOOPEA MIXED at 16" has no tendrils so it's non-climbing;it comes in mixed colors—Stokes twinspur (*Diascia barberae*): sun or part shade, annual/ BAR-BARAE PINK QUEEN has clusters of pink flowers with yellow throats; grows 9–12" high—Park

violet (*Viola*): part shade, perennial/CUTY is 6" high with purple and white pansy-like flowers; they bloom in early spring and are longer-lived than pansies; "ideal" for containers"—Park

wishbone flower (*Torenia*): shade or part shade, annual/ CLOWN MIXED is an AAS Winner called "the next impatiens"; it grows 8" high and has rose, white, violet, and blue flowers—Burpee

zinnia (*Zinnia*): sun, annual/ this popular flower comes in a wide range of single and bicolors, in various flower shapes; it's drought and heat tolerant; cutting will encourage more blooms; the shorter zinnias are 6" to 1'; PINWHEEL SERIES at 12" is mildew resistant for locations with humid summers—Burpee

zinnia, African (*Melampodium*): sun, annual/ SHOWSTAR is a 10" dwarf with yellow daisy-like flowers; it's "outstanding" in dry locations and mildew-tolerant—Stokes

Flowers for Hanging Baskets

achimenes: [see above]

alyssum: [see above]; BASKET SERIES is especially for hanging baskets in mixed pastel colors—Stokes

begonia, fibrous: [see above]; especially for baskets is HANGING BASKET TYPE in pink or white—Stokes

begonia, tuberous: [see above]; especially for baskets are HANGING GIANT DOUBLE HYBRIDS in mixed colors—Burpee—and HANGING SENSATIONS HYBRID in mixed colors and ILLUMINATION PINK—Park

black-eyed-Susan vine (*Thunbergia*): sun, annual/ SUSIE MIXED is wonderful in hanging baskets and will bloom all winter indoors; the easy-to-grow vine has simple flowers in white, yellow, and orange, many with black eyes—Park and Burpee; Stokes carries the similar ALATA and ALATA SUZIE MIXED

bush violet: [see above]; HANGING BASKET GROUP in blues and white is 14" high—Park

cape primrose (*Streptocarpus*): part shade, perennial/ BLUE ANGEL is an "ideal" plant for bloom all year round, indoors or out—Park

Dahlberg daisy: [see above—"unsurpassed in baskets"]

falling stars (*Campanula isophylla*): part shade, perennial/ profuse star-shaped blue or white flowers all but hide the bushy plant—Park

fuchsia (*Fuchsia*): part shade, perennial/ lovely in baskets with single and double flowers in white, pink, red, magenta, and purple solids and bicolors

geranium (*Pelargonium*): [see above]; ivy geraniums have long, cascading stems; recommended for baskets are SUM-MER SHOWERS in mixed colors and BREAKAWAY HY-BRID in salmon or red—Park and Stokes

impatiens: [see above]; recommended for baskets are DAZ-ZLER HYBRID SERIES in a wide range of colors—Burpee—and SUPER ELFIN® HYBRID SERIES, again in many colors—Burpee and Stokes

lobelia: [see above]; trailing lobelias are especially good in baskets; FOUNTAIN SERIES—Park—and COLOR CAS-CADE MIX—Stokes—come in shades of blue, purple, pink, rose, and white

marigold: [see above]; the dwarf French types are best for hanging baskets

monkey flower: [see above]

morning glory: [see above]; DWARF PICOTEE MIXED is also good for baskets

nasturtium: [see above]; cascading types are especially attractive in hanging baskets; WHIRLYBIRD comes in mixed colors—Stokes and Park; SEMI-TALL DOUBLE GLEAM MIXED, an AAS Winner, is a trailing type in mixed colors; EMPRESS OF INDIA boasts lovely dark red single blooms—Stokes

nolana (*Nolana*): sun, perennial/ SKY BLUE is a spreading plant producing quantities of morning glory-like flowers in sky blue with white throats; it's easy to grow and likes a dry location—Stokes

pansy: [see above]

periwinkle (Vinca): [see above]; Park recommends MAGIC CARPET especially for baskets; it's long-lasting, with flowers in pink, rose, and salmon

petunia: [see above]; for hanging baskets Burpee and Stokes recommend DREAMS SERIES and SUPERCASCADE SERIES, both in mixed colors; CLOUD SERIES in mixed colors is also "excellent" for baskets—Stokes; COUNTDOWN HYBRID grows very fast and comes in a wide range of colors—Park

pot of gold: [see above]

rose, miniature: [see above]; cascading types are beautiful in baskets; RED CASCADE is an award winner that's "superb" in hanging baskets—Park

Spanish daisy (*Erigeron*): sun, perennial/ hundreds of little white daisy-like flowers cover the cascading plant—Stokes

vervain (*Verbena*): sun, annual/ IMAGINATION is a double award winner; it has a spreading habit and lacy foliage, with intense bluish-violet flowers—Park

zinnia: [see above]; LINEARIS is a compact, spreading plant that's very heat tolerant; the white, yellow, and orange flowers cover the plant—Park

Flowers for Window Boxes

achimenes: [see above]
ageratum: [see above]
alyssum, sweet: [see above]
begonia, fibrous: [see above]
begonia, tuberous: [see above]; Stokes notes that NON STOP SERIES begonias—in mixed colors—are "perhaps the number one choice for window boxes in Europe"

black-eyed-Susan vine: [see above]

bulbs, spring: sun, perennial/ try the smaller bulbs like crocus and grape hyacinth, or shorter forms of tulips, hyacinths, and daffodils

buttercup: [see above]

cockscomb: [see above]

falling stars: [see above]

forget-me-not (*Myosotis*): sun or part shade, annual/ a dainty, old-fashioned flower in a lovely shade of blue

garden pinks: [see above]

geranium: [see above]; both standard and ivy geraniums are ideal for sunny window boxes

impatiens: [see above]

lobelia: [see above]

marigold: [see above]; rock garden marigolds are mound-shaped 8" plants that are attractive in window boxes; the fern-like foliage is fully covered with small flowers; LULU has yellow flowers and LITTLE GIANT has orange—Stokes; the dwarf French types are also good choices

morning glory: [see above]

moss rose: [see above]

nasturtium: [see above]; both the mounded and cascading types are wonderful in a sunny window box

pansy: [see above]

petunia: [see above]

pot marigold: [see above]

rose, miniature: [see above]

Shasta daisy: [see above]

stock: [see above]

sweet pea: [see above]

Transvaal daisy (Gerbera Tamesonii): sun or part shade, perennial/ HAPPIPOT MIXED is "outstanding" for window boxes; the plants grow one foot high with large daisy-like flowers in shades of red, pink, orange, yellow, and cream; they make excellent cut flowers—Burpee

twinspur: [see above]

verbena: [see above]

violet: [see above]

Foliage Plants for Containers, Baskets, and Boxes

asparagus fern (Asparagus densiflorus): good light but not strong direct sun, perennial/ used by florists, it's easy to grow from large seeds; Asparagus densiflorus MYERS has light green fronds covered with fine foliage—Park

coleus: part shade, annual/ grown for its colorful foliage; DWARF RAINBOW TYPE hybrid is "ideal" for containers—Stokes; WIZARD SERIES resists flowering; 10" plants don't need pinching—Burpee; recommended for hanging baskets are SCARLET PONCHO in red with a chartreuse margin and MILKY WAY MIX in nine blended colors—Stokes; FAIRWAY SERIES is a dwarf coleus with a neat habit in mixed colors—Park

dusty miller (*Cineraria*): sun, annual/ an easy-to-grow, heat and drought tolerant plant prized for its silver and white leaves; gives color and texture contrast to other plants; grows 8–12" high; several varieties are available with SILVERDUST and SILVER LACE featuring very finely cut leaves

fleece flower (*Polygonum captitatum*): sun, perennial/"an ideal creeping plant" for hanging baskets; it forms a mat of red and green leaves, with small pink clover-like flowers—Stokes

ice plant (*Mesembryanthemum*): part shade, annual/ the succulent foliage looks frosted—Stokes

kale, flowering (*Brassica oleracea*): sun, annual: FRIZZY HYBRID is "outstanding" in containers; has green foliage with pink and white; it likes cool weather and is frost tolerant; grows 8" high and 12" across—Park

ORNAMENTAL SHRUBS AND TREES

Introduction

It may come as a surprise that shrubs and trees can be grown—quite successfully—in containers. Plants that are either slow-growing types or dwarf varieties best suit this kind of culture. Since the container itself will help keep growth in check, however, a more rapid grower needn't be ruled out entirely; judicious pruning will also help limit its size.

While your potted shrub or tree may not be around as long as a hundreds-of-years-old bonsai, your plant should provide many years of enjoyment.

Shrubs and Trees for Containers

Listed below are 25 examples of shrubs and trees that are especially suited to growing in a container. Included are many familiar ones that are widely grown throughout the country as landscape plants. Your local nursery or garden center will have varieties that are hardy for your area.

Others on the list may be unfamiliar and will, I hope, spark your interest. Still others are more frequently grown as vines or bushy plants, but can be trained as standards; i.e. the plant is pruned to one erect main stem so that it resembles a small tree.

There are, of course, many more shrubs and trees that are particularly good as container specimens. Besides a nursery, catalogues can be another source of information and inspiration for these potted plants. Wayside Gardens and White Flower Farm, to name two, have fine selections of trees and shrubs.

- **azalea (*Rhododendron*):** A popular, pretty flowering shrub. Most are evergreen, some deciduous. May need indoor protection in winter.

- **bougainvillea (*Bougainvillea*):** An evergreen woody vine with brilliant flowers. Some varieties grow to tree-like forms in containers. Not cold hardy.

- **camellia (*Camellia*):** An attractive evergreen shrub known for its flowers and glossy foliage; there are a number of varieties. Hardy to about 25°F.

- **crab apple (*Malus*):** Lovely pink, red, or white flowers in spring followed by reddish fruits in fall. The deciduous tree has many varieties, some more attractive or hardier than others.

- **crape myrtle (*Lagerstroemia indica*):** Summer-flowering, deciduous tree. Showy crepe-like flowers in white, pink, or lavender bloom a long time. Most varieties are hardy to about 0°F.

- **dwarf Alberta spruce (*Picea glauca* 'Conica'):** A hardy evergreen tree only growing about one inch per year. Its conical shape and fine, thick foliage make it look like a Christmas tree.

- **English or common boxwood (*Buxus sempervirens*):** An evergreen shrub or small tree densely covered with small, glossy green leaves. Needs winter protection in the North. Popular for hedges, training into formal shapes, and in elegant plantings. The variety "Suffruticosa" is a slow-growing dwarf that's especially good in containers.

• **fuchsia (Fuchsia):** A deciduous or evergreen plant widely grown in hanging baskets for its beautiful flowers. Can be trained as a standard. Only hardy to about 32°F.

• **geranium (Pelargonium):** Beloved pot plant, it gains new formality grown as a standard. Plain and variegated leaves, flowers in many colors. Not cold-hardy.

• **glossy privet (Ligustrum lucidum):** Beautiful glossy evergreen foliage, white flowers, blue fruit. Easy to train into shapes. Hardy to about 20°F.

• **hibiscus, shrub althea, rose of Sharon (Hibiscus syriacus):** There are many named varieties of this hardy deciduous shrub. Flowers are single or double, and large. Pruning can be advisable.

• **holly (Ilex):** Chinese holly (I. cornuta) is cold-hardy and slow-growing. Evergreen leaves are very glossy, berries bright red. English holly (I. aquifolium) also has glossy evergreen leaves and red or yellow berries. Some varieties have attractive variegated leaves. Hardy to about New York City.

• **hydrangea (Hydrangea macropylla):** A hardy, deciduous shrub popular for its big flower clusters that are blue in acid soil and pink in alkaline.

• **Japanese maple (Acer palmatum):** A deciduous, slow-growing, and graceful tree that's hardy in colder climates. Leaves are often finely cut, turning red in fall.

• **juniper (Juniperus):** A hardy evergreen shrub in a wide variety of forms. Can be slow-growing. Some have striking colors, or a cascading form, or are easily trained into shapes.

• **Mugho pine (Pinus mugo):** This short evergreen tree is quite variable in form. Ideal for containers, it also makes an excellent bonsai specimen. Very hardy. Japanese black pine (Pinus thunbergiana): A slow-growing evergreen tree popular for bonsai training. Very hardy.

- **patio rose (*Rosa*):** Jackson & Perkins term for hybrid shrubs 2–4' tall. Flowers are pink, red, yellow, white. Excellent for containers.

- **rhododendron (*Rhododendron*):** Most of these handsome flowering shrubs are evergreen. Smaller types are easier to grow in containers. Some need winter protection.

- **rosemary (*Rosmarinus officinalis*):** Evergreen herb cultivated for centuries. Needle-like leaves used in cooking. Can be trained as a standard. Not cold-hardy.

- **Sago palm (*Cycas revoluta*):** An ancient, prehistoric-type plant. Dramatic and very slow growing. Protect indoors in winter. Lady palm (*Raphis excelsa*): A shorter, fan-leaved palm growing in bamboo-like clumps. Not cold-hardy.

- **sour gum, pepperidge, black gum (*Nyssa sylvatica*):** A pyramid-shaped deciduous tree with drooping branches. Lustrous leaves turn brilliant orange and red in autumn. Very ornamental and hardy everywhere.

- **southern magnolia, bull bay (*Magnolia grandiflora*):** An elegant evergreen shrub with large, fragrant flowers. There are several varieties; smaller, slower-growing forms can stay potted for years. With shelter, hardy to about Philadelphia.

- **sweet bay (*Laurus nobilis*):** Bushy when unpruned, but often sheared to a formal tree shape. Leaves (bay) are used in cooking. An evergreen, it's hardy to about Washington, D.C.

- **tree rose (*Rosa*):** Roses take on new elegance in a tree shape. Jackson & Perkins carries 24 varieties of standard tree roses (36" stem) including classics like PEACE, MISTER LINCOLN, and TROPICANA, and 6 varieties each of patio size (24" stem) and miniature tree roses (18" stem).

- **Washington thorn, hawthorn (*Crataegus phaenopyrum*):** A thorny, deciduous tree of graceful habit. White flowers are followed by red berries, then bright orange-red leaves in fall. Quite hardy.

- **wisteria (*Wisteria*):** A deciduous, woody vine loved for its pendant clusters of fragrant blossoms. Can be trained as a small tree with an umbrella-shaped top. Hardy in cold weather.

FRUIT TREES, VINES, AND BUSHES

Introduction

I hope you've had the opportunity to enjoy really fresh fruit, right off the tree or vine. If you have, I won't need to persuade you to consider planting a few berry bushes or fruit trees—you already know that the flavor and quality of just-picked fruit are unsurpassed. And, if you've priced those little half-pints of "fresh" berries the supermarkets offer in the summer, you'll be pleasantly surprised to find that you can purchase a berry *bush* for nearly the same cost!

Catalogue Sources

Once again I've combed the catalogues to find varieties especially suited to the gardener with a physical disability. Berry bushes that are thornless or that don't need staking, fruits that adapt well to container growing, and dwarf and miniature fruit trees top the list for plants that are easy to care for and harvest, and accessible in height.

I haven't gone into specifics on price as there are several options available: plants purchased singly or in multiples; plants that will need a pollinator; plants that come in one- and two-year sizes. And, of course, it's possible to find various items on sale, too.

But since raspberry and blackberry plants, for instance, average out at about $2.00 to $3.00 apiece, you can be assured that putting in a berry patch needn't break your budget. Fruit trees, of course, will run you a little more—say, $20.00—but will easily repay their initial cost in fruit.

Be sure to check the catalogues, your local garden center, or Extension Service for recommended planting zones for the fruits you're interested in. These hardiness zones will guide you in your selections so that winters won't be too cold or summers too hot for a particular variety of fruit bush or tree. If you don't know your planting zone, check the map in the Appendix.

The following suggestions come from companies that have been in the fruit business for decades, or even generations. Let their recommendations help you make your own decisions and choices.

FRUIT VINES AND BUSHES

Introduction

Red and black raspberries and blackberries are among the most expensive fruits in the stores—when they're available. Red raspberries especially are quite fragile, which drives the price up and the quality down.

Yet, neither these berries nor any of the others described in this section are difficult to grow in the home garden. The fruits will provide you with delicious, nutritious choices for eating fresh, in baked desserts, and for jams and jellies. Do consider giving them a try, or adding one of the following easier-to-manage varieties if you already have berry bushes in your garden.

Red Raspberries

Let's start with the fruit many consider to be the very essence of summer: the red raspberry. TITAN JUMBO is from Stark and is described as being practically thornless, with large-size berries.

Another red raspberry with big fruit—up to one inch long—is MAMMOTH. It has thornless canes and is available from Gurney's and Burpee. Also thornless is the hardy CANBY, from Mellinger's and Gurney's.

An Easy-Care Raspberry Bed

HERITAGE is a favorite and widely available everbearing red raspberry (Gurney's, Miller, Burpee, Stark, Mellinger's, Park, and Jung.) It bears fruit on one-year canes which don't require pruning. Instead, mow the canes down after frost; they'll be back next year ready to bear sweet, juicy berries.

In *Tips for the Lazy Gardener,* Linda Tilgner further describes this easy way of handling everbearing raspberries. Mow all those canes down in the fall, she says, even the new ones that would normally produce next summer's crop. The plants will come up more vigorous, with a (probably earlier) fall crop at their tips.

The Heritage red raspberry.

The gardener is thus saved the tiresome, prickly work of cutting out this summer's bearing canes. And, as Tilgner points out, it's much more pleasant to harvest berries in the coolness of fall rather than in summer's heat. If you're skeptical, she says, try this method on just half of your bed.

When setting out your raspberries, by the way, never plant them more than one row wide. If you do, it won't be long before they've grown together and berry picking will become an unpleasant task.

To support the canes, drive posts at 6' intervals on either side of the raspberry bed. String two courses of wire between the posts, one at about knee level and the other chest-high. Then, be sure to promptly remove any suckers that try to grow outside of the row.

Black Raspberries and Boysenberries
A black raspberry, BRISTOL, is offered by Stark. While not thornless, it does have upright canes that don't require staking.

A thornless boysenberry from Gurney's boasts purplish-red berries and is self-pollinating. The 8–10' trailing canes will need to be trellised for support. Stark's boysenberry is also thornless and has large berries.

Blackberries

Several varieties of thornless blackberries are available. Both Gurney's and Park carry BLACK SATIN, which bears early and heavily. It's semi-erect and quite hardy, but does need a pollinator.

HULL is another thornless blackberry, described by Burpee as heavy-bearing, self-pollinating, and the hardiest thorn-free.

Developed by W.H. Perron and Co. of Quebec, Canada, the PERRON thornless blackberry ripens in mid-July through late October. Find this variety in the Park catalogue.

THORNFREE is self-pollinating, quite hardy, and has the advantage of not suckering (Miller, Stark, and Mellinger's).

Other thornless blackberries from Stark include
NAVAHO ERECT THORNLESS, an upright, non-trailing
plant, and CHESTER THORNLESS. This latter blackberry is
a newer USDA introduction and is described as the hardiest
choice for the Upper Midwest. Both these blackberries are
self-pollinating, but neither can be shipped to California.

EBONY KING blackberry, from Gurney's, isn't thornless
but does have upright 3–4' canes that don't require support.

Strawberries

One of the most popular summer fruits is, of course, the
strawberry. If you're putting in a conventional strawberry be-
dor planting a jar, barrel, or pyramid, there are many excellent varieties from which to choose.

Strawberry plants are widely available from catalogues
and the local nursery or garden center. There's even one with
pretty pink (instead of white) flowers called PINK PANDA,
available from Park. For especially easy growing, though, you
might want to give alpine strawberries a try.

A relatively recent introduction to the United States, the
alpines are popular with European gardeners. Alpine strawberries are small—about one inch long—with a marvelous, intense fragrance and taste. Since they bear all summer long,
you'll be able to pick a handful of these gems every few days.

The plants themselves are attractive, forming bushy, compact mounds. They make a pretty edging plant, and do wonderfully in containers and window boxes. And because these
perennials don't put out runners, alpine strawberries relieve
gardeners of the chore of repositioning and training them.

Burpee offers plants of a red alpine strawberry called
RUEGEN IMPROVED; Shepherd's carries RUEGEN. For
seeds, Park has a red, MIGNONETTE, and a yellow, PINE-
APPLE CRUSH.

Another red alpine is ALEXANDRIA, a standard European variety. Seeds for this strawberry are available through
the Thompson & Morgan and Johnny's catalogues. FRAISES
DES BOIS MIXED, also from Thompson & Morgan, are
seeds for a mixture of red and yellow alpines.

Blueberries

Blueberry bushes are also readily available, both locally
and from catalogues. Regular high-bush types—some of
which can grow 6–7' tall—may be too tall if you're gardening

from a wheelchair, although there are some blueberries in the 4–6' range. Thanks to the talents of plant breeders at three universities, however, shorter blueberries are now available at very accessible heights.

NORTHBLUE, developed by the University of Minnesota, is a dwarf or "half-high" blueberry growing only about 2' tall. The plants are very hardy, and each can yield 4–7 lbs. of fruit of an "exceptionally good" flavor. Plants are carried by Miller, Jung, and Gurney's.

Another small blueberry, NORTHCOUNTRY, is also from the plant breeding experts at the University of Minnesota. This blueberry grows 2' high and spreads to 3 ½'. The berries, said to have the flavor of wild ones, ripen mid-season. Both NORTHBLUE and NORTHCOUNTRY (available from Miller) can take temperatures to -35°F.

NORTHSKY is yet another blueberry to come from this university. It too is very hardy, withstanding temperatures to -40°F. The plant, with its flavorful, sky-blue berries, only grows 18" high, making it a fine choice for growing in tubs. NORTHSKY blueberry can be purchased from Miller.

Not to be outdone, the University of Wisconsin has developed the FRIENDSHIP blueberry. The decorative plant grows about 2' tall, with leaves that turn bright orange-red in the fall. It also has a flavor that's compared to wild blueberries. FRIENDSHIP, available from Jung, adapts well to colder areas.

Standing a little taller, at 3–4', is NORTHLAND, developed at Michigan State University. The variety is a hybrid cross between native lowbush and highbush types. Quite hardy, this blueberry produces fine quality, very large fruits. Plants can be purchased through the Jung catalogue.

Finally, Gurney's carries a unique little blueberry called DWARF TOPHAT. At only 9–12" high, it's just the right size for a container or pot. This blueberry is cold-hardy, easy to grow, doesn't need a pollinator, and bears full-sized fruit.

Gooseberries

A popular fruit in Great Britain, gooseberries are firm green-and-white striped globes that turn pinkish-red when mature. Gooseberries make a wonderful choice for pies and preserves. Park offers a newer variety called CARELESS. The spineless plants will grow 3–4' tall and wide; older branches should be pruned occasionally.

Described as "nearly" and "practically" thornless are Gurney's WELCOME gooseberry and Miller's PIXWELL. The former grows 4–5' high and is self-pollinating; the latter is very hardy and has easy-to-pick berries. See the Jung and Stark catalogues, too, for PIXWELL.

Easy-Care Gooseberry Bushes

You might take a tip from British gardeners and try pruning and training gooseberries to a single stem. If you already have the thick, prickly kind of bushes, this method would eliminate some painful moments at pruning and harvesting time. Mary Chaplin, author of *Gardening for the Physically Handicapped and Elderly*, describes how to do it.

In the fall, take a hardwood cutting about 8" long and remove all the buds except 3. Plant the cutting so that about 5" of its length is in the soil, then add some sharp sand around its base.

Next year, when the cutting has rooted, transplant it to a permanent site. Now let the cutting grow on a single stem, removing any side growth just as you would with a tomato plant. When the cutting has grown to the right height to reach easily, let the head of the bush develop.

While the bush does need staking, you won't need to bend to harvest the fruit. Red currants can also be trained this way.

Jostaberries

Cross a gooseberry with a black currant and you'll have a jostaberry (say, "yost-a-berry"). The large, tangy fruits are almost black and loaded with vitamin C; use them in preserves and pies.

A thornless, self-pollinating plant from Gurney's will bear 10–15 lbs. of fruit. Miller sells a very cold-hardy, self-pollinating jostaberry that does well in most soil types. It is a vigorous grower, however, up to 8' high and 6' wide, which may put it out of reach unless the plant is kept pruned. Jung says their thornless jostaberry will grow 4–6' tall; Stark, about 6'.

Easy-Care Black Currant Bushes

If you already have black currants in your garden, here's a tip that might make harvesting easier. Mary Chaplin tells of a British gardener who planted black currant bushes along a garden pathway. Working from her wheelchair, the gardener used long pruners to remove a whole stem of fruiting wood and then brought the branch indoors to pick off the fruit.

Not only does this method simplify harvesting, but, as Chaplin notes, black currants like having the fruiting wood cut out once the berries are harvested.

Because they can spread white pine blister rust—a fungal disease that can decimate pine forests—gooseberries, currants, and jostaberries cannot be shipped to certain areas. These may include Vermont, New Hampshire, Maine, Massachusetts, Connecticut, New Jersey, Delaware, West Virginia, North Carolina, Hawaii, Puerto Rico, and Canada. Check with the company, nursery, or your local Extension Service before ordering or purchasing.

Figs

Northern gardeners may think figs too exotic a fruit to grow in their areas, but with the right variety and some winter protection, it's entirely possible to enjoy your own fresh, delicious figs.

The very hardy BROWN TURKEY fig from Stark and Miller can be grown in a large tub, then stored in an unheated garage or cellar during the winter. Self-pollinating, it's everbearing and will yield its first year. This fig can't be shipped to California, however.

Park offers the ITALIAN HONEY fig, a slow grower but prolific producer. From Maryland south, it's hardy outdoors in the open ground; farther north, it makes a fine container plant. This variety can't be shipped to Arizona.

Two figs can be found in the Burpee catalogue: PETER'S HONEY and VERN'S BROWN TURKEY. The former is self-pollinating and bears the first year after planting. In Zones 6–7, give it winter protection; in Zones 7–9, no protection is needed. The latter fig will bear two crops.

Burpee suggests that Northern gardeners grow their figs outdoors in a container over the summer. Then in winter either bring the plant in to a greenhouse or sun room, or else wrap it in burlap, stuffed with leaves like a protective blanket, and leave it outside.

Other hardy outdoor figs for planting in tubs and moving indoors for the winter can be found in the Gurney's and Mellinger's catalogues. Just be sure all of these figs are provided protection before the temperature hits 10°F.

Of course, this by no means covers all the soft fruits available to the home gardener. The plants suggested above do have much to recommend them in terms of easier growing methods and harvesting. However, other fruits might be equally good choices for you. Think about what you can and cannot do in terms of bending, reaching, etc., then decide if there's a way to match that plant's growth habits with your capabilities.

FRUIT TREES

Introduction

It wasn't long ago that fruit trees came in one size—big. Now there are standard, semi-dwarf, dwarf, and miniature trees to offer a choice to every gardener. Even more alternatives are possible when fruit trees trained to various shapes—cordon, espalier, fan, and dwarf pyramid—are included, as previously described in Chapter Three.

Fruit trees aren't terribly fussy in their requirements. Given plenty of sun and moderately fertile soil, along with adequate water, fertilizer, pest control, and pruning, these trees will reward the home gardener with plenty of good, fresh fruit.

Dwarfs and Miniatures

Especially recommended for the gardener with a disability are the dwarf and miniature fruit trees. Whether you're sitting or standing, it's very tiring to work with your arms up in the air, caring for a tree that's just too tall for you. These small trees will put their branches and fruit within reach, making pruning and harvesting more of a pleasure and less of a chore.

A miniature fruit tree will grow only about 6–8' high, with some in the 5' range. A dwarf tree grows about 8–10' tall, although some cherries can be a bit shorter. Contrast this with the height of a semi-dwarf at 12–15' and that of a standard fruit tree at 18–25', and it's clear why the shorter trees are your best bet.

Dr. Suman Singha of the University of Connecticut is a respected pomologist; that is, a horticulturalist who specializes in the study of fruit growing. When I asked him about selecting dwarf fruit trees, he told me that "dwarf trees [as opposed to semi-dwarf trees] are definitely superior" "from the standpoint of accessibility for care and harvesting by individuals with disabilities."

The only drawback is that the rootstocks of dwarf trees tend to be shallow rooted. This problem, however, is easily surmounted. Support the trees, advises Dr. Singha, with a stake or a wire trellis to keep the roots anchored in the ground.

Finally, keep in mind the fact that even if a variety is listed as self-pollinating, you'll often get a heavier yield of fruit if the tree is *cross*-pollinated. The idea is that if more than one fruit tree is in bloom in your yard, more bees will be attracted, and thus more pollination can take place. And this, of course, can mean a bigger harvest of fruit for you.

Sources for Trees

Naturally, there's more than one source for small fruit trees. I decided to focus, however, on two companies in particular: Stark Bro's Nursery of Louisiana, Missouri, and Miller Nurseries of Canandaigua, New York. They've both been in operation for well over a century, have a wide selection of different varieties of trees, and pay careful attention to producing superior stock.

At the end of this section I've included a few other catalogue sources for fruit trees. You'll recognize these names from the references above on vegetables, herbs, and soft fruits, making it easier to combine an order from one or two sources for all your seed and plant needs.

Your local nursery will almost certainly carry fruit trees suitable for your growing area. Also check with your Agricultural Extension office as they can offer excellent advice on what will grow best where you live.

Whether you decide to buy from Stark, Miller, or from someone else, I'd suggest taking a look at the various catalogues before you order your trees. You'll get some good ideas as to what's available in the dwarf and miniature fruit tree market, specific descriptions of the fruits, information on cross- and self-pollinating varieties, and guidance for making your selections.

VARIETIES OF FRUIT TREES

Miniature Fruit Trees

These are an exciting development for the gardener with a physical disability, since Stark's miniature fruit trees only grow from 4' to about 6–8' tall. This makes them largely accessible from either a standing or sitting position, for both adults and children.

Stark suggests growing these genetically dwarf trees in 18–24" planters, or out in the yard. For Zones 4–6, however, the company recommends growing the trees in planters and then moving them to an unheated, sheltered area or garage, to give them adequate protection in winter.

The Goldenglo™ apricot from Stark®.

The company offers these varieties of miniature trees for taste-of-summer fruits: HONEYGLO™ nectarine, SENSA-TION™ peach, and GOLDENGLO™ apricot. All are self-pollinating. And, just for Southern gardeners, there's GARDEN SUN peach and NECTAR BABE nectarine. These miniatures will grow 4–5' high, and will pollinate each other.

Miniature apple trees—which are kept small by a special rootstock—are available too. "Patio-size" GOLDEN DELICIOUS STARKSPUR® and JON-A-RED® are self-pollinating; ROYAL GALA® can be pollinated by either of these two.

Stark states that all of their miniature fruit trees will begin bearing as early as the second summer after planting.

Dwarf Fruit Trees: Apples and Pears

Apples are probably everyone's first pick for a home orchard, and quite a selection is available from Stark. Since they include both older and newer varieties, from WINESAP to GRANNY SMITH, GRIMES GOLDEN to LODI, you're likely to find at least one favorite here. Some of these dwarf apples are self-pollinating; others need pollinators.

Miller offers a fine array of standard, hybrid, and antique apples, calling it in fact "the world's largest selection." The smallest apple trees they offer are semi-dwarfs, which they term no-ladder® trees. Since they grow 10–12' tall, they'll only be partially accessible for harvesting from a wheelchair. With some assistance from an apple picker, the gardener who can stand may be able to reach the fruit without too much difficulty.

The Big Red Delicious Compspur apple from Miller.

A dozen varieties of dwarf pear trees are offered by Stark, from BARTLETT and COMICE to the "newer" Asian pears. They'll do best when they're cross-pollinated with other pear types.

Nine varieties of dwarf pears are available from Miller, including favorites like SECKEL and BEURRE BOSC. A nice choice might be Miller's 3–in-1 dwarf pear, with BARTLETT, D'ANJOU, and CLAPPS FAVORITE grafted on a single, self-pollinating tree. Note that pears must have two varieties for cross-pollination.

For something more unusual, try Miller's dwarf Asian pears SHINSEIKI, CHOJURO, and HOSUI. The first two are not self-fruitful; HOSUI is, but CHOJURO is recommended as a pollinator. These three Asian pears have also been grafted onto one dwarf rootstock, for an ornamental and self-pollinating fruit tree.

Dwarf Fruit Trees: Peaches and Plums

The Garden Gold peach from Miller.

Peaches, a great summer favorite, are available as dwarfs from Stark in 11 varieties. Choose from among popular names like ELBERTA and REDHAVEN, or a cold-hardy variety like RELIANCE. These trees are self-pollinating. Dwarf peaches will bear in their second year, with full production by the fourth or fifth.

ELBERTA, HALE HAVEN, and the super-hardy FINGERLAKES are among the dozen dwarf peaches offered by Miller. They'll usually bear the next year after they're planted, yielding about a half-bushel of fruit per tree. The winter-hardy GARDEN GOLD peach will grow 5–5 ½' tall but can be pruned to an even shorter height for container gardening. All these peaches are self-pollinating.

If you're looking for a dwarf plum, Miller has those too, in eight varieties. Familiar names include SANTA ROSA, GREEN GAGE, and STANLEY. Some are self-fruitful, while others need one or two different pollinators.

Stark also carries dwarf plums: STANLEY PRUNE-PLUM, BLUE RIBBON™ PRUNE-PLUM, STARK-ING® DELICIOUS™, and REDHEART. The plums will start bearing 3–4 years after planting. The first two are self-pollinating; the other two need a pollinator.

Dwarf Fruit Trees: Nectarines and Apricots

Stark's dwarf nectarines are CRIMSON GOLD, MERI-CREST, and SUNGLO. The trees bear in 2 years and are self-pollinating. This description also fits their dwarf apricots, which include WILSON DELICIOUS, EARLI-ORANGE, GOLDCOT, and SWEETHEART™.

Miller carries MERICREST too, as well as another hardy dwarf nectarine, NECTACREST. When planted in a tub, GARDEN BEAUTY only grows 5' high, making it a fine choice for containers. All three nectarines are self-pollinating.

Miller's dwarf apricots—MOONGOLD, SUNGOLD, MOORPARK, and SUPER HARDY CHINESE—will usually start bearing fruit the second year after planting. Some of these apricots need pollinators, while some are self-fruitful but produce their biggest crops with a pollinator.

Dwarf Fruit Trees: Cherries and Other Fruits

Miller offers three dwarf varieties of cherries. NORTH STAR, a sour (tart) pie cherry, is a self-pollinating tree that will grow 7–9' tall. This very hardy cherry is a cross between a Siberian one and the English MORELLO.

Even the ever-popular BING cherry is now available from Miller as the X-TRA DWARFED BING. Growing just 5' high in a container, this attractive tree needs no pollinator. Also self-pollinating is the sweet cherry COMPAC STELLA.

NORTH STAR is also carried by Stark, as their sole dwarf cherry. Stark lists its height as a bit shorter, at 6–9'.

Three unusual dwarf trees from Stark are FLAVOR DELIGHT APRIUM®, FLAVOR QUEEN PLUOT®, and FLAVOR SUPREME PLUOT®. The APRIUM is a cross of 75 percent apricot and 25 percent plum. It can be pollinated with the FLAVOR SUPREME PLUOT® or any apricot.

The PLUOT is bred from plums and apricots, and needs the APRIUM or any Japanese plum as a pollinator. Plant breeder Floyd Zaiger of California developed these fruit crosses, described as being uniquely flavored and very sweet.

Stark also sells jumbo varieties of various fruits. Since most of them are offered as dwarf trees, they might make a good growing project for children, who of course are fascinated by such things as a $2\frac{1}{2}$ lb. apple!

For one final fruit, consider Miller's dwarf orange quince. Self-pollinating, it can be grown either as a bush or a tree.

The Compac Stella cherry.

DWARF CITRUS TREES

A Taste of Sunshine

Dwarf citrus trees not only produce edible fruit but with their evergreen leaves and sweet-smelling flowers, they're very decorative as well. Naturally they enjoy a lot of sun. In warmer climates they can be planted right in the ground. Where it gets cold, plant them in tubs to be moved indoors for the winter.

Gurney's carries five dwarf citrus, ranging in height from about 2–4' tall. Varieties include a lime, lemon, banana, fig, and OTAHEITE orange. Available from Mellinger's are a lime, lemon, grapefruit (Citrus paradisi), orange (Citrus sinensis), DANCY tangerine, and KARA Mandarin orange. Your local nursery may have these and other dwarf citrus—like the calamondin orange—as well.

ADDITIONAL CATALOGUE SOURCES

Choices Abound

Dwarf apple trees are also available through the Gurney's catalogue, with both newer and older varieties featured. Pears, peaches, apricots, cherries, and plums are carried in dwarf sizes, too.

Jung's dwarf fruit trees include antique and new varieties of apples, pears, peaches, a cherry, and a plum.

The smallest apple and pear trees in the Mellinger's catalogue are semi-dwarfs, but peaches, apricots, plums, a cherry, and a quince are all available as dwarfs.

Burpee's smallest apples, cherries, and pears are also semi-dwarfs.

Park offers RED SUNSET nectarine, a genetically dwarf tree that at 5' tall is ideal for containers. The tree is self-fertile and will produce its second year.

DOING YOUR RESEARCH

Some Final Thoughts

I hope you're now seriously considering growing your own fruit; however, let me conclude with just a word of caution. Any gardener who rushes out and buys the first available fruit tree, sticks it in the ground, and then stands next to the tree with a bushel basket in hand waiting to collect all the fruit is bound for disappointment.

Growing fruit trees, particularly, is something of a long-term proposition, requiring forethought and a certain commitment of time and energy. It is very important, then, that you do your own research before purchasing and planting.

Besides considering a plant's basic requirements of proper light, soil, and water, ask the following questions.

- Is the fruit tree or bush self-pollinating or will it need a pollinator?

- How high and wide will it be at maturity?

- Is the plant the right selection for my hardiness zone?

- Am I willing and able to do the necessary pruning?

- How long will I have to wait before the vine, bush, or tree bears fruit? (It could be a few years.)

- Is the plant suitable for container growing?

If you're choosing a fruit tree or bush from a catalogue and you can't find all the information you need in the text, call or write the horticulturist the company almost assuredly has on staff to handle customers' questions. If you buy from the local garden center or nursery, again, talk to the resident horticulturist. Finally, don't hesitate to contact your Extension Service office for advice on growing various kinds of fruit. They can also send you a list, prepared by the United States Department of Agriculture, describing what fruits will do best in your state.

With all that said, may your experiences growing fruit be productive and delicious!

CHAPTER SIX

Plant Pests
and Diseases

Introduction

"If you plant it, they will come" is the gardener's version of that famous line from the movie *Field of Dreams*. In this case, however, "they" refers not to a throng of baseball fans but to a visitation of a different sort. Bugs and slugs, marauding birds, thieving animals—in a word, pests.

Let's face it: you're not going to have a garden without something coming along to munch on your plants and crops. How you handle the situation is, I think, determined on how you view your—and that slimy slug's—place in the world.

Take, for instance, the gardener who feels that the only good bug is a dead bug, especially the one that was so bold as to take a bite out of a prized cabbage or rosebush. Equipped with an arsenal of toxic chemical weapons, this gardener declares war on any flying, crawling, or four-legged intruder in the garden. But as pests are eradicated, so too are a variety of other creatures, some of them beneficial, who actually could have helped in the quest for a successful garden. Even the gardener, perhaps, might prove to be a "chemical casualty" someday, when it's discovered that those sprays and powders were more dangerous than anyone thought.

This all-out approach to pest control may temporarily tip the scales in the gardener's favor. In the long run, though, the cost may be too great (remember DDT?).

At the other end of the scale is the gardener who thinks the only way to be "at one" with nature is to ignore the cabbage loopers who've decimated the broccoli, or the birds who yearly make off with the best of the raspberries. The garden may be a shambles, but no bug was bothered in the process!

GARDENING ORGANICALLY

Somewhere between these two extremes lies the concept of organic gardening. Once associated with granola, long hair, and the whole counterculture movement, organic gardening has now found a respectable niche as an idea whose time has come.

Simply put, gardening organically means working with—not against—nature. The organic gardener uses natural controls and preventatives to encourage a healthy balance between productivity and a certain degree of inevitable loss in the garden.

Various types of insects and birds, for instance, are welcomed to the garden, to dispose of those varieties whose presence there is most *unwelcome*. Barriers such as floating row covers, fences, and humane traps are used to deter pests. And when sprays and powders *are* used on the plants—sometimes as a last resort—they're of botanical origin, with no poisons allowed.

Noted gardening author Barbara Damrosch describes the organic approach this way. You first identify what is eating your plants, and then decide on an acceptable "level of damage," as well as whether solving the problem will prove more costly than the damage itself. Finally, you select a plan of attack, targeting the pests yet sparing the beneficial insects.

Since a few pests and some damage is inevitable in the garden, aim for *control*, not extermination or elimination. You and your garden will both be the better for it.

WARNING!! For the gardener with a physical disability who is elderly and/or on medication, there's even more reason to approach the various insecticides, pesticides, fungicides, and herbicides with a great deal of caution. Your situation makes you more susceptible to a toxic or allergic reaction when using these products. Moreover, pesticides can aggravate asthma and other respiratory diseases in both children and adults. Get approval from your doctor before trying out the powders and sprays!

INSECT PESTS AND HOW TO DEAL WITH THEM

Beneficial Insects

You'll need to know who you're dealing with, so arm yourself with a good field guide or two, and start identifying your insect visitors. Study a gardening reference book or a book on garden pests, to see if that bug is considered a gardener's friend or foe. Then take steps to encourage the insect either to stay or to depart.

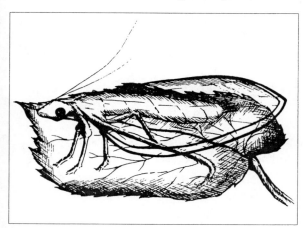

Green lacewing.

If you're stumped by an insect, talk to your gardening neighbors: they probably know all the local bugs. Your County Agricultural Extension Agent can also help you with specific identifications and controls. There are a number of beneficial insects that are natural enemies of garden pests. Here are a few of the best.

• Green lacewing: An excellent all-purpose predator. The larvae will eat quantities of aphids, whiteflies, mealybugs, mites, the eggs of many insects, and more.

• Lady beetles (lady bugs): Aphids are a favorite food of both larvae and adults, but they'll also eat other pests as well.

• Trichogramma wasp: The larvae devour insect pest eggs, including cabbage loopers, cutworms, corn earworms, codling moths, webworms, and many more. One variety (*Trichogramma minutum*) will attack pests in trees. The adults are harmless.

• Praying mantis: Young ones eat soft-bodied insects like aphids, while older ones favor tent caterpillars, beetles, and more. These large insects are quite interesting to watch, especially for children.

• Spiders: Not true insects, but often considered in this group. Many are useful in the garden, catching insect pests in their webs (although beneficial insects can be caught, too). Also fascinating to watch.

Count yourself fortunate if you already have these predators at work in your garden. Otherwise, to establish a new population, packages of certain beneficial insects can be purchased for release in your garden and yard. Your local garden center may carry them, or try Gardens Alive! and other gardening supply catalogues.

Encourage these insects to stay by providing water, shelter, and nectar-producing flowers. Many of the annual and perennial herbs, and wildflowers like goldenrod, Queen Anne's lace, yarrow, and asters are attractive to the beneficial insects. Consider establishing a "wild patch" in your yard where they can reproduce and overwinter without being disturbed.

Birds

Now turn to your field guide on birds, and see who's at home in your yard and garden. For many people, bird-watching is of course a very satisfying hobby. After learning the identities of various birds, you as a gardener might delve deeper into this avian study and find out which insect pests are preferred by which birds.

Carried a step further, you may even find yourself creating habitats suited to certain specific species, to encourage them to remain in your area. The fact that many birds can easily consume 1000 insects *in a day* should provide all the incentive you need!

While entire books are available on the subject of attracting and keeping birds in your yard, what birds require, in brief, are three things: water, shelter, and food. The Garden Club of America has selected the following trees and shrubs as among the most useful for food, nesting, and shelter. Check to see which are already growing on your property, and which could be added.

Note that some of these are also very suitable for container growing, including the hollies, cotoneaster, crab apple, magnolia, and dogwoods.

- highbush blueberry (*Vaccinium corymbosum*)

- red cedar (*Juniperus virginiana*)

- pin or fire cherry (*Prunus pensylvanica*)

- red chokeberry (*Aronia arbutifolia*)
- cornelian cherry (*Cornus mas*)
- early cotoneaster (*Cotoneaster adpressa praecox*)
- Japanese flowering crab apple (*Malus floribunda*)
- white flowering dogwood (*Cornus florida*)
- shrub dogwoods (*Cornus alba siberica*)
- scarlet firethorn (*Pyracantha coccinea*)
- hawthorn, Washington thorn (*Crataegus phaenopyrum*)
- Canada hemlock (*Tsuga canadensis*)
- American holly (*Ilex opaca*)
- Chinese holly (*Ilex cornuta*)
- English holly (*Ilex aquifolium*)
- Japanese holly (*Ilex crenata*)
- star magnolia (*Magnolia stellata*)
- Russian mulberry (*Morus alba, M. a. tatarica*)
- white pine (*Pinus strobus*)
- pokeweed (*Phytolacca americana*)
- Russian olive (*Elaeagnus angustifolia*)
- shadbush, serviceberry (*Amelanchier canadensis*)
- skimmia, reeves (*Skimmia reevesiana*)
- viburnum, European cranberry (*Viburnum opulus*)

A combination of different heights and sizes of plants and trees is very appealing to birds, and will help you attract a greater variety. If your yard and garden areas include a selection of flowering and seed-producing plants, ground covers, bushes, shrubs, and trees, birds of many types will be able to find the habitats they prefer.

Providing fresh water via a protected birdbath, putting up nesting boxes, and offering a reliable source of food during the winter months will further meet their needs.

Bacteria and Parasites

Besides beneficial insects, other biological controls include bacteria and parasites which feed upon insect pests. Discovered in 1901, the bacterium *Bacillus thuringiensis*, or Bt, has proved to be a powerful weapon against the destruction caused by various caterpillars and corn borers. Bt is applied as a spray or powder, and is so safe that even the strictest organic gardener would approve its use.

As for parasites, beneficial types of nematodes will prey upon insects having a larval stage in the ground, or that crawl upon the soil. Japanese beetle grubs, cutworms, borers, cabbage root maggots, and white grubs are among the many pests attacked by nematodes.

Barriers

Floating row covers can be an excellent, simple way to deter a number of insect pests. Made of a soft, filmy polypropylene fabric, row covers are laid right on top of the plants. As they grow, the plants lift the cover up with them. Cabbage worms, Colorado potato beetles, cucumber beetles, squash bugs, flea beetles, and many others cannot penetrate this barrier to damage your crops, yet sun, water, and air pass easily through.

Row covers come in a slightly heavier weight that offers spring and fall light frost protection, and a lighter weight that transmits sunlight but only allows a small increase in temperature. Some covers need to be placed over wire hoops; others need only have their edges secured with soil or U-shaped pins. Depending on the type, the covers will need to be removed either during hot weather or at blossom time, for pollination.

Besides keeping out insects, row covers also provide protection from wind and small animals, and capture warmth, which can mean earlier and bigger yields. The covers are inexpensive and will last a season or two, or more. Catalogue sources include Gardens Alive!, Johnny's, Gardener's Supply, and Shepherd's.

Homemade Controls

If you feel the insect pests are getting out of hand, investigate your options. Always begin with the safest, least toxic choice, then move up the toxicity ladder if the situation seems to be getting desperate.

For more information on sprays and powders, I'd suggest reading through the Gardens Alive! catalogue, which advertises itself as carrying "environmentally responsible, organic products for a healthy garden," and various titles from Rodale Press, including *The Organic Gardener's Handbook of Natural Insect and Disease Control,* edited by Barbara W. Ellis and Fern Marshall Bradley.

Applications of a basic dishwashing soap-and-water spray are helpful with some insects, like aphids. Small potted plants can also be turned upside down (hold the soil in place with your hands) and swished about in a bucket of soapy water. Rinse well after this treatment. Even a strong spray of plain water can be enough to dislodge some pests.

Homemade sprays of ground garlic and chile peppers in water, with a few drops of liquid soap added, can be effective. Some gardeners have even experimented with pulverizing insect pests with water in a blender, then spraying the concoction on plants affected with the same pests. Although this is probably not for the faint-hearted, it has had its successes.

Commercial Sprays and Powders

It's gratifying to see that gardening catalogues are becoming "greener" in their approach to insect pest control. While many still offer the take-no-prisoners type of sprays and powders, showing up alongside these potent chemicals are more earth-friendly alternatives. The following include some of these options.

Diatomaceous earth is a powdery substance made of the fossilized remains of diatoms, single-cell creatures of the ocean. It's very useful against slugs, Mexican bean beetles, aphids, and many other pests, including indoor ones. Diatomaceous earth won't harm the environment.

Widely used botanical insecticides include pyrethrum and rotenone. Pyrethrum, derived from a type of chrysanthemum, is considered safe and is nonpersistent. Rotenone is derived from a tropical plant, is of very low toxicity, and is also nonpersistent.

The Safer® line of insecticidal soaps and other products is formulated to help control many destructive insects on a wide variety of plants, both indoors and out. As the name implies, they're a better choice than toxic chemicals.

The Dustin-Mizer is one popular choice for applying various types of powders. Widely available through gardening catalogues (at around $28.00), this duster is considered "easy-to-use." It does, however, require a two-handed operation: one to hold the duster and the other to turn the crank. The powder is blown out through a 15"–long tube, which allows you to reach in among the plants. An optional nozzle attachment (about $6.00) helps to dust underneath the leaves. A

New Jersey gardener reports that he also uses his Dustin-Mizer—from his wheelchair—to apply limestone.

On a safety note, even if your powder or spray is a botanical, organic one, always wear goggles and gloves, and follow directions exactly.

Various Other Insect Controls

• Hand-pick the offending bugs. Squash them, step on them, or pop them in a can of soapy water to drown. You can always wear gloves! Kids are often less squeamish about insects than adults are, so enlist their help, too. Catching cabbage butterflies with a butterfly net, for instance, is a time-honored pursuit. Other kids frankly enjoy smushing insects—just make sure they go after the offending ones. (I once saw our golden retriever carefully pull a 3" tomato hornworm off a plant and kill it. Perhaps our pets are an untapped resource in pest control!)

• Learn to recognize natural controls. If that tomato hornworm has white eggs attached to its back, you can leave it alone. Those are the eggs of a parasitic wasp, and will soon do the hornworm in, with no help required from you.

• Select plant varieties that have been bred to be resistant to certain damaging insects. WALTHAM butternut squash, for example, has been bred to resist the squash vine borer. Specific varieties of tomatoes and certain other plants are also bred to resist various diseases.

• Foil cutworms by placing a 2"–wide collar of cardboard, thin metal, tar paper, plastic, or other material around the base of a young and tender plant.

• A garden toad is a valuable ally against insect pests. Encourage one to stay by providing shelter in a cool, moist spot. Commercial toad houses are available, or try an upside-down clay pot with a piece knocked out for a "door."

• If you see bats flitting about at night, remember that, like birds, they too consume enormous numbers of insects.

• Overplant your crops if you have the space. If pests make off with part of your harvest, you'll still have some left. If they don't, you'll have plenty to share.

• Take a tip from British gardeners and make root maggot mats to act as a barrier to the egg-laying flies. Using 12" squares of carpeting material or tar paper, make a small hole in the center, then slit the material from the hole to one edge. Slip the mat around the young plant's stem and tape the slit together with waterproof tape. As the plant grows, it will easily enlarge the hole. The mats will protect cabbages, broccoli, and cauliflower, and will deter cutworms, too.

• As corn silk begins to brown, apply a drop of mineral oil to the tip of each ear to take care of corn borers. Repeat every 5–6 days for 3 or so times. Added bonus: the silk will come off easily when you harvest the ears.

• Various traps will lure insects to their deaths. Red spheres coated with a sticky substance (like Tangle-Trap) are widely used to control apple maggots, while yellow sticky traps will catch small insects like aphids and whiteflies. Other traps depend on sex lures, using pheromones to catch insects on a sticky surface. Codling moths and peach borers are among those trapped with sex lures.

• Use your pocketknife to dig squash vine borers out of their entry hole in a squash stem. Cover the slit stem with a layer of moist soil.

• Practice good garden hygiene: keep debris in the composter and out of the garden; destroy any diseased plants.

• Discourage slugs and snails by eliminating the cool, dark, moist hiding places they like: a piece of board, flower pot, or debris lying around the garden. Surround individual plants, a bed, or the whole garden with a barrier their soft bodies can't cross. Try lime, wood ashes, crushed egg shells, cinders, sharp sand, or other similar materials.

• Or, tack strips of copper sheeting to boards and surround the plant or bed—snails and slugs won't cross it.

• Or, set out shallow bowls of stale beer. The slimy critters climb in for a drink, and drown. If this method works for you and you want a steady supply of brew to fill the bowls, visit your neighborhood liquor store. When a rented keg is returned, there's usually some flat beer left inside, which the staff may be happy to let you have.

• Take a different approach and *create* hiding places for them to stay under at night, like a cabbage leaf or a shingle. The next morning, uncover and dispose of them.

• Try companion planting—many gardeners swear by it. The idea is that certain plants repel certain insect pests. If the companion, then, is planted next to a crop that's attractive to a pest, it will deter that insect. You may want to investigate this further, but for starters, here are some combinations to try.

—tomatoes: French marigolds deter nematodes

—cabbage: chamomile, dill, mint (keep contained), rosemary, sage, thyme repel cabbageworm moths (and thus the caterpillars)

—beans: marigolds, rosemary, summer savory deter Mexican bean beetles

—carrots: rosemary, sage repel carrot flies

—potatoes: horseradish deters potato bugs

—squash: nasturtiums deter aphids, squash bugs

—cucumbers: tansy repels striped cucumber beetles

Tansy repels striped cucumber beetles.

Or you can simply intersperse French marigolds, onions, garlic, chives, nasturtiums, and tansy among your plants, as these deter a wide variety of insect pests. They also break up crops that are planted in large blocks, which are especially inviting to pests.

• For a different spin on companion planting, grow trap crops. Since certain plants will *attract* various pests, these are planted near a crop that needs protection. The insects are free to devour the trap crop, and with any luck they'll leave your other plants alone. Try a border of borage, for instance, to entice striped and spotted cucumber beetles away from your cukes.

This is just a sampling of some of the ways that insect pests can be controlled in the garden. For more ideas and information, read up on the subject, talk to local organic gardeners, and try some experimenting yourself. You can also subscribe to *Organic Gardening* magazine for the latest in organic techniques. Sometime you may find yourself writing in to share with fellow gardeners your *own* ideas for natural insect controls!

AVIAN AND ANIMAL PESTS, AND HOW TO DEAL WITH THEM

Scare Tactics

As welcome as birds in general may be as insect-eaters, it's another matter entirely when some species visit your garden to feast upon the seeds and crops. Four-legged friends who stop by to nibble on your plants can be equally undesirable guests. Try the following methods to frighten them away.

- Scare off nuisance birds with realistic plastic owls and rubber snakes set up in strategic spots.

- Hang aluminum pie plates to blow and rattle in the breeze.

- Sprinkle human or dog hair around the edge of the garden.

- Make a scarecrow. (Even if it turns out not to work, creating one is a fun and creative project to do with the kids.)

- Capitalize on the fear small birds have of big ones. My brother once cut out of tin a large silhouette of a raptor in flight. Painted black and suspended from a very long pole, it "flew" protectively over the corn plot.

• If you can get lion dung from a local zoo, spread it around the edge of the garden—it's a *great* deterrent!

• Dried blood (a fertilizer available at garden centers) sprinkled around the garden's perimeter will scare off some pests. Reapply after watering or rain.

• Frighten birds away with strips of reflective red and silver tape that flash in the sunlight. Hang them in fruit trees or near plantings. Catalogue sources include Brookstone, Gardener's Supply, and Jackson & Perkins.

• The family feline can be an invaluable ally in catching mice and shrews; its mere presence can also frighten off larger animals like rabbits and squirrels. A dog is handy too for chasing pests away.

Protecting Seeds and Sprouts

The old saying "One for the blackbird, one for the crow, one for the cutworm, and one to grow" reminds us that it's good insurance to sow more seeds than absolutely needed. It's also much easier than having to re-plant! Here are some more ideas to help protect what you plant.

• Lay down lengths of black plastic, slit holes in it, and plant seeds through the openings, to deter birds.

• Once the seeds have germinated, lay wire or plastic netting or mesh over the seed beds to protect newly-emerged sprouts.

• Spread a loose mulch of hay or straw over the seedlings.

• To guard the sprouts, make row covers of aluminum fly screen stapled to a portable wood frame.

• Build a mesh or wire frame to lay over a raised bed, to keep rabbits and birds out. Or try a tunnel of hardware cloth.

Protecting Crops

Don't resign yourself to losing your beautiful crops and plants! Fight back with some of these ideas.

• Ripe corn is one crop in particular that birds seem to find irresistible. Slipping a paper bag over each ear after it's pollinated will foil any bird—or squirrel. Use a twist-tie or string to hold the bag in place.

• Raccoons are perhaps the biggest threat to corn: they've been known to wipe out a whole planting in a single night. Tune a transistor radio to an all-night talk show and leave it—protected in a plastic bag—out in the garden, or scatter mothballs around the perimeter of the corn patch (keep these away from children).

• Alternately, surround the bed with pumpkins and squash, and interlace the vines to form a sort of fence. Presumably the raccoons don't like the prickles and won't go through the vines. This old trick, said to be of Native American origin, could prove to be very effective—as long as *you* can get into the corn patch at harvest time!

• Set up cage traps such as Havaheart™, which come in small, medium, and large sizes. After you've made a catch, take a drive and release the animal—carefully—far from your home.

• A 3' chicken wire fence will keep some pests out, including neighborhood dogs and cats.

• Attach a piece of chicken wire to the top of the fence, letting it hang over the outer edge by about 2'. Animals who try to grab it to climb over the fence will be left swaying back and forth on the floppy wire.

• Surround the garden with an electric fence, or add a strand to the top of another fence. Its mild current is a very effective way to keep pests out, but you may end up with a few dead birds, too. *Warning:* check with your doctor first if you wear a pacemaker or other heart device!

• To keep burrowing animals like woodchucks out of a raised bed, excavate the site, then line the bottom of the bed with fine-mesh chicken wire before replacing the soil.

• For a ground-level garden, you'll need to extend a fence to run one foot underground—and ideally one foot horizontally too—to keep out burrowing pests.

• If deer are jumping over the garden fence, spread a standard 4' width of chicken wire on the ground around the outside of the fence. Lay it out rather loosely and the deer will avoid stepping on the springy surface. Stakes or U-shaped staples (as cut from an old coat hanger) will hold the wire in place.

• Cover ripening berries with tobacco netting or plastic mesh bird netting.

• Plant some of the bushes, shrubs, and trees recommended above to attract birds. Given the choice, they'll probably go after the wild berries and leave yours alone.

There are, of course, many other tricks and techniques for protecting your garden from bird and animal pests. Every one won't be appropriate for every situation, but all have worked at one time or another. Talk to fellow gardeners, read, and experiment to see what ideas are most successful for keeping unwanted visitors out of *your* garden.

PLANT DISEASES

Disease-Resistant Plants

Besides insect, bird, and animal pests, plant diseases are the bane of gardeners. Here the best line of defense is a strong offense: use as many *disease-resistant* varieties of plants as you can. This information is provided in every seed catalogue along with the plant's description, or noted on a label if plants are purchased.

For example, certain varieties of tomatoes have been bred for resistance to various diseases, including fusarium wilt, verticillium wilt, tobacco mosaic virus, and nematodes. If you know any of these to be a problem in your area—or if you just want to avoid trouble—look for identifying letters after the variety's name. BEEFMASTER VFN, then, means that this tomato is resistant to verticillium wilt, fusarium wilt, and nematodes.

Other times a variety's disease resistance will be spelled out in the catalogue text itself. Catalogues that cater to the commercial grower as well as the home gardener (like Stokes and Johnny's) provide even more information on a greater number of plant diseases, along with the varieties bred to resist them.

The following are some of the more common plant diseases that can wreak havoc with specific vegetables. Check for a variety's resistance to these diseases in particular.

- **beans, snap:** powdery mildew, mosaic, root rot
- **cabbage:** virus yellows
- **cantaloupe (muskmelon):** fusarium wilt, powdery mildew
- **cucumbers:** mosaic, powdery mildew, downy mildew, scab, anthracnose
- **spinach:** downy mildew, mosaic, blight, blue mold
- **tomatoes:** verticillium wilt, fusarium wilt, tobacco mosaic virus, alternaria.

Certain flowers can be affected by various diseases, too. Zinnias, phlox, and lilacs, for instance, are susceptible to mildew. Among roses, black spot is a common disease, although some varieties are more vulnerable to it than others. Wilt can strike asters and clematis, while rust can damage hollyhocks.

Fruits aren't immune to diseases, either. Scab, fireblight, anthracnose, powdery mildew, leaf curl, brown rot, and cedar rust are just some of the diseases that can plague fruit trees, bushes, and vines.

Thankfully, plant researchers work to breed more disease-resistant varieties of plants each year. They also study different control methods, to give gardeners additional help when plant diseases do strike. These are just two of the many good reasons to stay abreast of horticultural developments, by studying several seed catalogues each year and by subscribing to a gardening magazine or two.

Preventing Diseases

The good news is that since climate has a great deal to do with plant diseases, not every disease occurs in every area. What may be a problem for you in your New England garden, for instance, may not be a concern at all in your sister's garden on the West Coast—she'll have to contend with her own plant diseases. Your gardening neighbors can tip you off on any diseases that are especially troublesome where you live.

There are certain situations, however, that favor the outbreak and spread of plant diseases. While some, like a week of solid rain, are beyond the gardener's control, others can be

the result of poor gardening practices. These conditions may
lead to fungus and viral diseases among your plants:

- Plants are too wet, for too long.
- Water splashes onto plants.
- Plants are handled when wet.
- Plants are spaced too closely together.
- Insect pests—especially aphids—aren't controlled.
- The garden is full of weeds.
- Soil drains poorly.
- The same crop is grown in the same space every year.
- Debris is left in the garden.

Now let's look at some of the ways to help *prevent* diseases
striking your garden. Remember that starting with disease-resistant varieties is your single best way to avoid losing plants
to disease!

• Water early in the day so foliage can dry off. Fungal
spores need wet conditions to germinate, so don't provide
opportunities.

• Use mulch to combat splashing, which can spread fungus diseases. Mulch also helps plants maintain a uniform
moisture supply, which reduces stress and thus makes a
plant less susceptible to attack by diseases.

• Stay out of a wet garden until the foliage dries. This is
especially important with bush beans as touching wet
leaves can spread anthracnose, a fungus disease.

• Allow plants enough "breathing room" so air can circulate.

• Work at controlling insect pests, which can spread disease.

• Keep the garden reasonably weed-free. Weeds can harbor both diseases and insects.

• Add *lots* of organic matter to lighten the soil and allow
for good drainage: this helps prevent fungus diseases.
Also, fertile soil produces plants that are strong and vigorous, and so better resistant to disease.

• Rotate crops so that the same crop or one from the
same family doesn't grow in the same spot each year. Al-

though not always possible, the garden site itself should ideally be moved every few years.

• Keep the garden clean of debris. Either compost vegetation or turn it into the soil. Promptly remove and throw out or burn any diseased plants and the soil in which they're rooted (*don't* compost them!). Identify the disease if you can, but quick action in removing the sick plant is preferable to time spent poring over a reference book figuring out what you're dealing with. You could lose your whole crop in the process of trying to identify the culprit!

Controlling Diseases

There aren't always simple answers to treating a diseased plant. Often the only recourse is to destroy the plant and hope for the best with the ones that remain.

There are, of course, commercially available sprays and powders formulated to combat specific fungus and viral diseases, particularly those that affect fruit trees and vines. For instance, sulphur in a powdered form has been used for centuries as an effective, non-toxic fungicide. Others, though, like Bordeaux Mixture, are very effective but quite poisonous.

The staff horticulturalist at a reputable garden center, or your Agricultural Extension Agent, can help you decide what—if any—course of action is best and safest to take should disease strike your garden.

CHAPTER SEVEN

Children and Gardening

Introduction

Children and gardening seem made for each other. It's a creative, physical activity that involves their whole body and all the senses; produces exciting results that can be eaten, smelled, or otherwise enjoyed; can be done indoors or out at any time of the year; promotes self-esteem and well-being;

can be engaged in alone or with friends or family; teaches about nature and ecology; and, lets them get permissibly dirty! Moreover, a child who comes to love gardening is likely to carry this interest into adulthood, making for a satisfying hobby or even a career.

For this chapter I'm switching my focus a bit, by talking *about* kids and gardening. I'm going to assume that a parent, relative, friend, or teacher is reading this, for the simple reason that a child can begin to participate in some of these activities while only two or three years old. An older child can, of course, read the chapter for himself.

If you are already a gardener, you have a head start on interesting your young son or daughter in growing and caring for plants. If you haven't gardened before, participating in these activities with your child can open up new worlds for you both.

A child is both pleased and eager to do whatever Mom and Dad—or siblings—are doing. Working together in the garden can bond a family in a unique way, and open the door to increased sharing and caring among its members.

Whatever gardening projects you decide to undertake, don't be too particular as to methods and results, especially with a young child. Remember that *process* is usually more important than *product*. That is, learning and doing tend to be more helpful to a child's development than concentrating on a final product. Be there as a guide, then, but let him learn from his mistakes and experiments.

Success in some form is important, however, so do choose dependable, easy-to-grow varieties of plants, or, for the smallest children, seeds that germinate quickly. *Hos successus alit: possunt, quia posse videntur,* as the Roman poet Virgil put it 2000 years ago. "These success encourages: they can because they think they can." He wasn't referring to either kids or to gardening, but the point holds true nonetheless!

WHY GARDEN?

Benefits for Your Child

If you are the parent of a child with a physical disability, you in particular know how important self-esteem issues are in the life of your child. Having a visible physical disability immediately sets that child off from his peers; if equipment like a

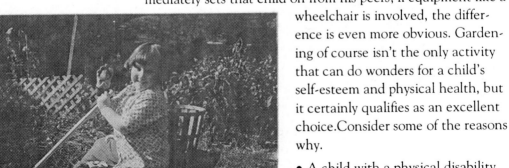

wheelchair is involved, the difference is even more obvious. Gardening of course isn't the only activity that can do wonders for a child's self-esteem and physical health, but it certainly qualifies as an excellent choice.Consider some of the reasons why.

• A child with a physical disability has had more than her share of medical attention, treatments, therapies, and hospitalizations. Gardening can move her focus and concern away from the medical arena and redirect it to the more natural environment of the plant kingdom. The stress related to medical treatment may well be lessened by this change in the direction of her energies.

• A child with a physical disability may not have all of the freedom and independence of movement so associated with childhood. Caring for plants can help her reverse a dependency on adults and others by giving her a sense of responsibility and mastery over some part of her world.

• A child with a physical disability may have missed out on some of the sensory experiences of early childhood that are critically important to development. Lack of mobility, hospitalizations, etc. may have interfered with a child's ability to explore her environment first-hand. By involving the mind, body, and all the senses, gardening can help make up for some of these missed or delayed experiences.

• A child with a physical disability may need extra encouragement to be physically active, whether to strengthen weakened muscles or to maintain muscle tone. Gardening provides the opportunity for either mild or more strenuous outdoor physical activity. Both fine and gross motor skills, and hand-eye coordination, can be improved and developed.

• A child with a physical disability may have diminished self-confidence and self-esteem. Seeing a gardening project through from planting to harvest reinforces a child's sense of accomplishment. It provides positive outlets for her in-born needs to nurture, for her creativity, and for her independence.

• A child with a physical disability, because of a feeling of "apartness," may need help at developing good social relations. Becoming involved with others in growing and caring for plants fosters social skills and inter-active communication, all within the base of a pleasurable activity.

GARDENING SAFELY

Protecting Your Child

To help ensure that your child's outdoor gardening experiences are both safe and fun, see that he's prepared with sunscreen, a hat, gloves, sunglasses, and appropriate clothing. Naturally you'll need to follow your everyday, indoor procedures too. From fastening the safety belt on a wheelchair to wearing protective headgear, take the required steps to safeguard your child.

Avoid letting your child work in the heat of the day, and remember that short sessions are best—stop *before* he gets tired. Always have plenty of drinking water on hand, and watch for signs of over-exertion. Be especially vigilant concerning skin breakdown and pressure sores. Heat and perspiration may make this problem worse if braces or tool cuffs are rubbing against the skin.

If your child is ambulatory, you may need to insist that shoes be worn outdoors, or at least while gardening. Nails, glass, and bits of rusty metal have a way of working themselves up to the surface of the ground, especially if the homesite has been occupied for many years. The resulting threat to tender feet would make footwear a requirement.

For the child who has little or no sensation in the lower legs yet can crawl, protection is also advised. Long pants, shoes, and socks will shield the skin, but if this clothing is too much to wear in hot weather, try knee pads for at least partial protection. Child-size gloves (see page 130) will of course guard the hands.

Make sure vaccinations are up-to-date, as tetanus can be contracted from working with any garden soil. Ask your health-care provider if a booster is indicated for your child. And, since sunlight can cause adverse reactions with some medications, talk with your pharmacist about any possible interactions.

If occupational, physical, or other therapists are involved in your youngster's care, let them know about your plans to garden. They can suggest specific ways for you to help your child strengthen muscles and improve skills while he's having fun in the garden. Finally, *check with your doctor* for any additional health and safety recommendations!

Poisons and Hazardous Materials

Safety is absolutely essential where any poisonous or potentially poisonous materials are involved. Fertilizers, pesticides, and the like must always be stored *in their original containers* and kept out of a child's reach. Add "Mr. Yuk" stickers and emphasize the fact that your child is not to touch these items, period! Ideally, you won't be using these chemicals in your garden to begin with.

Toxic Plants

Also critically important to teach a child is this safety rule: Never put *any part* of *any plant* in your mouth unless a grown-up says it's okay! Things are not always what they seem in the garden, as one part of a plant may be edible while another part is hazardous if ingested.

Potatoes and rhubarb, for example, are good garden crops, but their vines and leaves, respectively, are poisonous to eat. Likewise, consuming any part of an eggplant other than the fruit can cause a toxic reaction, as can ingesting tomato vines.

The following list includes some of the other more common indoor and outdoor plants that have toxic parts. Depending on the plant, and how much and what part is ingested, symptoms can range from gastrointestinal upset and skin irritations on up to heart irregularities and even death.

If you're unsure about the toxicity of other plants not mentioned here, check your library for books on poisonous plants, or talk to your doctor or poison control center.

While toddlers at that everything-in-the-mouth stage are considered most at risk for accidental poisoning, a parent can't assume that even an older child is beyond consuming something that's potentially hazardous.

It's up to adults to learn what harmful plants grow wild locally, what houseplants are toxic, and what garden plants pose a threat. Then, either remove these plants, grow another type or variety, or locate them well out of reach.

Should it happen that your child does eat a part of a plant—even a small amount—that you either know is hazardous or aren't sure about, call your local poison control hotline immediately. Be prepared to name or describe the plant ingested, then follow their instructions.

Toxins affect each person differently, so even a small amount of toxin could cause a serious reaction. (Conversely,

many plants that are listed as hazardous are only dangerous if
consumed in very large amounts. However, even plants that
are considered non-toxic can, in certain individuals, cause an
unexpected reaction.)

BULBS

amaryllis

crocus, autumn

daffodil

hyacinth

iris (underground rhizome)

narcissus

tiger lily

LEAVES, STEMS, FLOWERS, AND BERRIES

azalea

bittersweet

bleeding heart

boxwood

burning bush (euonymus)

buttercup

caladium

Carolina yellow jessamine

castor bean

cherry laurel

Christmas rose

cyclamen

daphne

delphinium

dieffenbachia (dumb cane)

elephant ears

English ivy

foxglove

golden chain

holly

Jack-in-the-pulpit

jasmine

Jerusalem cherry

lantana

larkspur

lily-of-the-valley

mistletoe

monkshood

morning glory

mountain laurel

mushrooms (non-edible)

nightshade

oleander

philodendron

pokeberry

privet

rhododendron

rosary pea (rosary bean)

sweet pea

wisteria

yew

Note: Poinsettia has long been thought to be potentially fatal
if eaten. Poison experts now agree, however, that the plant's
toxicity has been overstated: if consumed in large amounts,
minor gastrointestinal symptoms are the possible results.

SEEDS

apple seeds (large amounts)
pear seeds
kernels (inside the pits) of peaches, plums, and wildcherries
seeds used for planting that have been chemically treated

Other Safety Measures

- Even though your garden and yard may be fenced in, never leave a young child unattended outdoors.
- Know basic first aid procedures and keep appropriate supplies handy for treating minor wounds.

- Watch for insect and tick bites, and allergic skin reactions to plants.

- Teach your child to recognize poison ivy and stinging nettle. If you yourself need help in identifying these plants, get a knowledgeable friend or neighbor to assist you.

- Put a fence or other barricade around any sharp-thorned bushes that might be brushed against or run into.

- Use tall stakes instead of short ones for plant supports, which can be run into and possibly cause eye injuries. Even better than vertical stakes are the rounded supports that encircle a plant, as described in Chapter Three.

- Periodically check for splinters on wood-handled tools, wood-framed raised beds, and wooden containers.

- Never leave a child unattended near water, whether in a pond, pool, bucket, or other container. Drowning can occur in just one inch of water.

- Look out for areas of rough terrain, protruding sticks or stones, or spots that can become slippery from water, dew, or mud, particularly if your child has mobility problems.

- After gardening, be sure your child washes her hands thoroughly.

GARDENING OUTDOORS

A Variety of Benefits

Does your child know where her fruits and vegetables come from? Many kids, particularly from urban areas, don't. By growing their own edibles children quickly learn that there's more to food sources than cans, boxes, and cello bags at the grocery store.

There can be an agreeable side benefit, too: your child may actually come to enjoy eating vegetables, a scenario most parents would applaud with relief. Even broccoli may take on a new appeal if she's grown it herself!

Much of the advice for adults on setting up the garden, selecting tools, choosing what to grow, and so on that is covered in previous chapters is also applicable to children. I've tried to keep repetition to a minimum, so refer back to the appropriate section when you need more detailed information.

Just as in the last chapters, you'll find included here the specific names of the various vegetables and fruits discussed, plus the company or companies that sell these seeds and plants. So you can study their catalogues for yourself, company addresses can be found in the Appendix. Again, costs for seeds range from about $1–2.00 a packet; sources are accurate for 1993.

THE GROUND-LEVEL GARDEN

Some Gardening Basics

As discussed in Chapter One, accessing the garden will be your first priority. Perhaps your family already has an established garden in the backyard; now your child with a disability wants to garden, too. This makeover will require careful planning, and, depending on the garden's size, may well need more than one season to implement. You could start by adapting one section or corner of the garden. Then, as her interests and abilities grow, expand that spot to include more areas that are easily accessible to her.

Like an adult, the child who uses a wheelchair will need safe and secure paths to get in, around, and out of the garden.

If rough terrain lies between the house and the garden, a path or ramp may be required here as well.

Vegetables and flowers grouped in short rows or small blocks will be easier for your child to reach from either a standing or seated position. For crawling or kneeling, a soft, thick mulch may be adequate; otherwise, an old blanket or something similar laid down between the rows or beds will protect tender skin. For sitting, try a small folding chair, a beach chair, or one of the scoots or trikes mentioned on pages 123–24.

OTHER TYPES OF GARDENS

Ground-Level Alternatives

There are several alternatives, however, to trying to make a standard, ground-level garden accessible. Choices include a variety of containers, boxes, planters, A-frame stands, pyramids, tables, trellises, and other methods of growing that will probably be easier for you to construct or provide, and for your child to use. For details, refer back to the appropriate chapter.

Raised Beds

Raised beds, also described in detail in Chapter Two, are yet another option. For access from a child's wheelchair, they'll need to be about 1½' high. To determine width, measure your child's reach from armpit to fingertips, both with and without tools in hand. Bear in mind that a young child may have difficulty manipulating a longer-handled tool like a hoe, so to avoid awkward reaching, keep the beds on the narrow side.

Containers

Let your child make his own decision in choosing the type of container that will hold his seeds and plants. If a standard flowerpot is selected, he can have fun decorating a clean, new clay pot with acrylic paints before starting his garden.

Moving up in size and planting potential are big crocks and half whiskey barrels. Since they're accessible from either a seated or standing position, these can make a good choice for a child's garden.

Rachael's first garden, at age three, was in a half whiskey barrel. The two yellow pear tomatoes we planted ultimately grew too tall for her to reach unassisted, but Rachael was very proud of her plants and plied friends and neighbors with handfuls of tomatoes. No sooner had the vines gone into the composter in October than she was ready—despite the frost—to plant up her barrel again!

Window boxes are another option for a child's garden, as their narrow width can be just right for little hands. If your child can't easily reach the window box in its conventional location, set it on sawhorses or a bench instead. Provide for drainage and air circulation by putting a few small boards or bricks underneath the box, to raise it up a bit.

Strawberry jars are an interesting way to grow berries, flowers, herbs, or a combination of plants. Like any container, you can locate it in either a higher or lower position to suit your child's needs.

A table garden can be arranged on an old child-size or larger card table, or on a wooden frame. Use either an assortment of plant containers, several window boxes, or build one box to fit the size of the table top. Again, elevating the box(es) a little will allow for water to drain and air to circu-

late. Or, instead of a container on the table top, your child could simply plant right into a bag of commercial growing medium, slitting the plastic to insert plants or seeds.

A table garden may not be appropriate, however, if your child has limited upper body strength and mobility and would be gardening from a seated position. The table must be high enough to allow space for the knees, which in turn means that your child would have to work with his arms and hands raised. For some children, this position will simply be too fatiguing. The same holds true with the A-frame garden described below.

Vertical Growing

Vertical growing on a trellis or fence (see Chapter Three) can put a wide variety of flowers and vegetables within your child's easy reach. A planter box with a vertical frame attached is handsome and simple enough to build. Stakes, or a homemade or purchased trellis can be added to a large container or barrel to train the plants upward. Wheeled vertical gardens in square, rectangular, and column shapes can be used and re-used for years.

Another type of upwards growing is the popular child's tepee. Choose a spot that gets morning or afternoon sun, as full sun will make the interior of the tepee too hot. Then lash three to six bamboo poles, plastic pipes, or wooden stakes together at the top.

Spread the poles out and push the ends into the ground to form a circular tepee shape. Plant seeds or set in plants around the perimeter, and train them to climb up the poles until you've created a leafy green hideaway. Soft hay or a "sitting stone" inside the tepee will complete the project.

Pole beans are the classic choice for covering a tepee, but scarlet runner beans have the added bonus of pretty, hummingbird-attracting flowers. Other choices in annual vines include morning glory, climbing nasturtium, and vegetables like cucumbers and melons.

Or, for a perennial vine, try one of these: grapes, clematis, honeysuckle, wisteria, trumpet vine, Virginia creeper, or star jasmine. Until a perennial vine is established, you may want to mix annual vines with it to fill out the space.

This tepee design, of course, may not be suitable for your child. A more accessible design for a child who walks with braces or uses a wheelchair might be a sunflower "house." Plant tall-growing sunflowers like MAMMOTH in a circle about 18" apart, and stake each one with a long pole. Leaving

a 2–3' gap between two of the sunflowers will create the "doorway."

Then, at a height a little above your child's head, start winding twine about the sunflowers and stakes and continue around the circumference two or three times, to help secure the plants. It won't take long until the sunflowers are taller than your youngster, their heads waving above his as he stands or sits in the middle of his "house."

Structures to Build

Other garden possibilities to build—or have built—are the two- and five-step planter boxes described in Chapter One. Even a scaled-down version should remain accessible for several years as your child grows, thus off-setting the initial cost of materials and labor.

Another fine choice for the child with a disability is the A-frame stand with a planting box (see also page 48). This design has much to recommend it. For instance, the open construction allows a child in a wheelchair to pull right up to the planting box with his knees underneath it. This eliminates the awkward reaching that can come from sitting either face-on or sideways next to a very large container.

The A-frame stand, accessible from both sides, can be built higher or lower to suit your child's height. If he uses crutches or a walker, he'll be able to use the frame itself as a support to lean on and/or hold on to. The good-sized growing area can be expanded even further by adding hanging baskets to the top of the stand.

Combination Gardening Areas

For multi-sensory stimulation, additional opportunities for fine and gross motor skill development, and for just plain fun, consider combining a gardening area with a play area. The creative possibilities for designing such a spot are limited only by your and your child's imagination, and, of course, the family finances. Note, though, that a basic garden/play area needn't be expensive to construct; that it can be used by the child's siblings, too; and that the area can be expanded as resources permit.

Organic elements such as sand and water are naturals for combining with a garden. Sand boxes, wading pools, and sand/water tables, for example, can be constructed or placed alongside raised beds, planter boxes, or a container garden. Just as digging in the earth can heighten sensory awareness, playing with water and sand also provides a wonderful tactile experience. For soothing sounds and visual delight, bubbling and spraying fountains have great appeal to these senses, as well.

If your child has spent some time doing fine motor activities in his garden, having an adjoining play area for gross motor activities will let him readily engage in a different type of play. Logs for climbing, playhouses, swings, a paved area for toy vehicles, and so on offer a chance to exercise the large muscle groups. The chance for imaginative play and positive social interactions can be other important benefits from this type of garden/play environment.

Also, if your child's garden doesn't already include them, add plantings of brightly colored flowers, plants with interesting shapes and textures, and fragrant flowers to the play area. These will stimulate the senses of touch, smell, and sight. Look for some suitable choices in plants later in this chapter and in Chapter Five.

The Sensory Garden

Horticultural therapist and author Bibby Moore describes this type of sense-stimulating garden as appropriate for, among others, young children with severe physical disabilities. Designed to appeal to the senses of sight, sound, touch, and smell, the therapeutic value of a sensory garden lies in a child's "being in a relationship with our living world."

Like the combined gardening/play area, the sensory garden includes a variety of elements. Bibby suggests the following plants and materials, grouped in raised planters, to create this garden.

- For sight: large flowers in shades of red, orange, yellow, and white, which are easier for a sight-impaired child to see than blues and purples.

- For sound: pine trees, grasses, and bamboo, which rustle in the wind; walkway materials that create a variety of sounds when stepped on; a fountain and pool.

- For touch: various mosses, sedums, grasses, and succulents; an area of sand, smooth pebbles, or pine bark, to retain the sun's warmth and to touch with hands and/or feet.

- For smell: various annual and perennial herbs and flowers, including scented geraniums.

TOOLS

Selecting and Maintaining

For the very young child, plastic gardening tools from the toy store, or a big spoon from the kitchen, may be perfectly adequate for creating all those holes the littlest gardeners like to dig. An older child will take pride in having her own real gardening tools, just like Mom's and Dad's. Until she's more sophisticated in her gardening skills, however, keep to the basics at first. Start with a trowel and/or shovel or spade, a rake, and a hoe, then round out the tool collection as you and she see fit.

Tools made of wood and steel are available from several catalogue sources, in several price ranges; also check your local garden center. Look for tools that are both lightweight and strong, and that are appropriate to her age, strength, and abilities. Items that are too heavy and awkward to use, or that break easily, will quickly dampen enthusiasm and can be dangerous for your child as well. If she has uncontrollable movements, it's especially important that tools be chosen for safety; here, plastic tools can be a good choice.

Depending on what type of gardening your youngster will be doing, you'll probably want to select either child-sized tools, hand tools, long-handled hand tools, or a combination of sizes. Then, to cushion the hands and provide an easier, more secure grip, add some padding to the handles. More information on buying and adapting garden tools is found in Chapter Four. Your child's occupational therapist can also suggest ways to make tools easier to use.

If your child's new tools aren't already brightly colored, paint some bands in red, yellow, or orange on their handles. Lightly sand the area first, wipe it with turpentine, then apply color using weather-resistant enamel paints. The tools will be much easier to see and find if they're left lying in the grass.

Teach your child how to care for her tools, and set a good example yourself. Wipe them clean after use, or use the sand-and-oil treatment described previously. Then put them back in their designated spots. Working together will help encourage your child to take responsibility for her tools.

Tool Safety

Where tools are concerned, everyone who works in the garden should know this basic safety rule: teach your child never to lay down a hoe, rake, or other tool with the blade or tines facing up. Point out the dangers of stepping on a sharp tool; of getting struck on the head when a long-handled tool is stepped upon; and of tripping and falling over a tool left carelessly on the ground.

KID-PLEASING PLANTS: THE SMALL AND THE LARGE

Some Special Varieties

Children delight in the very small, the very large, bright colors, and unusual shapes. Vegetables, fruits, flowers, and herbs have all these qualifications—and more—to offer. Encourage your child to choose what he wants to plant and care for. Here are some suggestions to get you both started, with details on these plants provided in Chapter Five.

Very Small Vegetables

Miniature or "baby" vegetables are fun to grow. Choices range from sweet corn, cherry tomatoes, lettuce, and carrots to pac choi, eggplant, beets, and turnips, all on small-size plants. Round little carrots and tomatoes, tiny ears of corn, and so on will delight a youngster and provide a delicious addition to meals and snacks.

Note that some vegetable seeds—like lettuce—are quite small; others—like carrots—are both tiny and slow to germinate. If these prove too frustrating for a very young child, or for one who has difficulty with fine motor control, consider the various aids to planting as described in Chapter Four. Slow-germinating seeds can also be mixed with quick-germinating radishes, for instance, that will keep up a child's interest while waiting for the other seeds to sprout.

Mini pumpkins are a special child-pleaser. The plants are full-size, but the pumpkins measure only 2" high and 3" across. JACK BE LITTLE was introduced a few years ago and is quite popular (Burpee, Johnny's, Mellinger's, Park, Gurney's, Jung, Vermont Bean Seed, Cook's Garden). Stokes describes SWEETIE PIE as an "improved JACK BE LITTLE." Shepherd's offers MUNCHKIN and suggests tying the vines to a fence, trellis, or bean poles for vertical growing.

Even white miniature pumpkins are available. Stokes and Shepherd's carry BABY BOO, whose creamy white little fruits are attractive next to the orange minis. They can also be trained to grow vertically. Both the white and the orange versions, by the way, are not only decorative but edible, too.

Dwarf and compact plants expand the list of possibilities for planting to in-

Sweetie Pie and Baby Boo Pumpkins from Stokes.

clude most other types of vegetables: peas and cucumbers, melons and beans, and so on. These plants are suitable for growing in containers, pots, or raised beds, to put them within your child's reach. A climber on a trellis or fence—if not allowed to grow too high—will accomplish the same goal.

Very Large Vegetables

On the other end of the scale are the giants. Kids love these huge vegetables, which are especially fascinating when a child has grown them herself. She may even like to enter a choice specimen or two in competition at a local or state fair. Not surprisingly, the very biggest growers will almost undoubtedly require adult assistance.

Seeds for seven huge vegetables (tomato, cucumber, marrow or squash, parsnip, carrot, cabbage, and pumpkin) are available through the Thompson & Morgan catalogue. These seeds are the results of the plant breeding efforts of Bernard Lavery, who holds twelve current world records for giant vegetables. His own growing instructions are provided with each seed purchase.

Thompson & Morgan also carries seeds for the Football Onion, LANCASTRIAN. With good growing conditions, this onion can weigh an average of 5 lbs. KELSAE SWEET GIANT, from Stokes, holds a world record for a 7 lb., 7 oz. onion, with 5 lbs. being an average weight.

For a super-size bell pepper, try BIG BERTHA hybrid (Gurney's, Mellinger's, Jung). The peppers, which turn red at maturity, grow 6–7" long and 4" wide.

As an unusual project your child might like to grow a bushel gourd. These big rounded gourds weigh 100 pounds, yet only weigh 1 pound when dried. Measuring up to 57" in circumference, a dried bushel gourd could be used for crafts projects, storing toys, or even as a planter. Seeds are available from Gurney's and Mellinger's.

Finally, what's summer without watermelon—at least according to the kids! How about growing a giant one and inviting the neighborhood to share in the feast?

Kelsae Sweet Giant from Stokes.

BLACK DIAMOND from Jung is almost round and often grows to 40–50 lbs. COBB GEM from Gurney's is oval-shaped and can grow up to 130 lbs. Topping both, however, is CAROLINA CROSS #183 from Burpee. This mammoth melon can readily grow over 200 lbs.!

Tomatoes

Even adults enjoy growing giant beefsteak tomatoes. For big tomatoes in the 1–2 lb. range, try BEEFMASTER VFN, WHOPPER VFNT HYBRID, and BRAGGER (Park); BEE-FEATER HYBRID VFN (Italian Beefsteak—Stokes); JUNG'S GIANT OXHEART; BURPEE'S SUPERSTEAK HYBRID and SUPER BEEFSTEAK vp VFN (Burpee and Jung); and SUPERSTEAK F1 HYBRID and BEEFSTEAK IMPROVED (Thompson & Morgan).

Also from Thompson & Morgan is MAGNUM, which they describe as a tomato excellent for competitions. Bernard Lavery's growing instructions are included with this variety.

One more huge tomato is DELICIOUS, from the Burpee catalogue. While most of the fruits weigh over 1 lb., this is the tomato variety that produced the world's biggest: a 7 lb., 12 oz. tomato grown in Oklahoma and listed in the *Guinness Book of World Records*.

Those Big Pumpkins

Perhaps the favorite vegetable to pursue in a big way is the pumpkin. There are several seed choices for growing these giants. BIG MAX, which has been around for years, produces pinkish orange fruits that can weigh 100 lbs. or more (Burpee, Gurney's). THE GREAT PUMPKIN from Shepherd's is of similar color and size.

Moving up in weight is PRIZEWINNER, a hybrid pumpkin with reddish-orange skin. It has the "classic pumpkin appearance," according to Burpee; Stokes and Jung carry it too. BIG MOON, a Vermont Bean Seed introduction also sold by Park, can weigh 200 lbs. or more. Its color is medium orange.

Biggest of all are pinkish gray TITAN and orange-skinned ATLANTIC GIANT. TITAN was developed by Bernard Lavery (see above), whose growing instructions are included

Big Max pumpkin.

with every order from Thompson & Morgan. One pumpkin he grew with this seed weighed 710 lbs.

Howard Dill of Nova Scotia developed ATLANTIC GIANT, carried by Vermont Bean Seed, Jung, Gurney's, Stokes, and Mellinger's. Without special attention, ATLANTIC GIANT will produce pumpkins weighing 200–300 lbs. However, a Canadian grower using this seed came up with a 755 lb. pumpkin—a true giant! If you buy seed from Gurney's, they'll also send you free tips on how to grow extra-huge pumpkins.

Howard Dill's name is linked with giant pumpkin-growing, an interest that has become quite competitive. Could your child's name be next on the list of record-holders?

KID-PLEASING PLANTS: COLORS, SHAPES, AND FORMS

Unusual Vegetables and Fruits

Here is a wide variety of plants sure to delight your child by the very fact of being unusual. Whether it's growing a purple pepper, planting strawberry popcorn, or harvesting spaghetti from the garden, these suggestions will spark his interest and creativity. Since very few of these plants are small-sized and thus not likely candidates for growing in pots, tubs, window boxes, or other containers, an adult may well need to help with the planting and care. The age and abilities of the child will naturally determine the degree of your participation.

A Little History

First is a pretty watermelon with an evocative name. MOON AND STARS was brought to the United States around the turn of the century, probably from Russia. The dark green 25 lb. melons are sprinkled with yellow moons on a field of little yellow stars. Even the foliage is decorated with stars, too. Seeds for this lovely old watermelon can be purchased from Shepherd's.

Or, how about planting Cinderella's pumpkin? ROUGE VIF D'ETAMPES, a French heirloom, was sold in the open markets of Paris during the 1800s. Described as the "true original model" for Cinderella's coach, this pumpkin is deeply lobed and flattened on top. The brilliant red-orange color is said to absolutely glow in the garden amidst its vigorous vines. ROUGE VIF D'ETAMPES is carried by Vermont Bean Seed, Cook's Garden, and Shepherd's.

Childhood Favorites

That beloved childhood staple, peanut butter, can be made right at home with peanuts your child grew himself. As long as you have a 4– to 5–month growing season and light, well-drained soil, you needn't be in Dixie to plant them, either. Try VIRGINIA JUMBO (Park, Burpee, Mellinger's), VALENCIA TENNESSEE RED (Park), EARLY SPANISH (Jung), or PRONTO (Park).

If your child is like most and loves spaghetti, he might want to grow his own by planting spaghetti squash in the garden. Its culture is like that of other vining-type squashes, with the fruits about 8–10" long and weighing 2–5 lbs. After baking the squash (a quick job in the microwave), cut it in half and fork out the tender, delicious strands of flesh that look and taste like spaghetti. Then just add your favorite sauce.

Seeds for the spaghetti squash can be found in the Jung,

Gurney's, Mellinger's, Johnny's, Stokes, Burpee, Vermont Bean Seed, and Thompson & Morgan catalogues. Burpee also carries a bigger spaghetti squash, PASTA HYBRID, that grows up to 12" long. TIVOLI, from Jung and Gurney's, is an AAS Winner with a bush habit. Good for limited space gardens, this spaghetti squash can be planted as close as 2' apart.

Another kid-pleaser, popcorn can be grown in the home garden, too, just like sweet corn. The wide range of choices includes PURDUE 410 HYBRID (Park); BURPEE'S PEPPY HYBRID; JAPANESE

Spaghetti squash.

HULLESS and SOUTH AMERICAN GIANT (Mellinger's); BABY RICE—no hulls, WHITE CLOUD HYBRID, and IOPOP 12 HYBRID (Jung); SOUTH AMERICAN YEL-LOW, HYBRID GIANT YELLOW, and JAPANESE WHITE and YELLOW HULLESS (Gurney's); TOM THUMB—3½' dwarf and ROBUST 20–70 (Johnny's); RO-BUST 10–84 HYBRID and WHITE CLOUD—hulless (Stokes); and ROBUST HYBRID and WHITE SNOW PUFF HYBRID (Vermont Bean Seed).

Out of the Ordinary

The husk tomato—also known as strawberry tomato, ground cherry, or cape gooseberry—is also fun for children to grow and harvest. The spreading plant bears golden berries enclosed in a paper-like husk that resembles a Japanese lantern. The fruits, whose flavor is quite sweet and unusual, can be eaten raw, made into various desserts or jam, or dried like raisins. Thompson & Morgan carries seeds, calling it golden berry; Johnny's and Jung carry GOLDIE.

Gourds are popular with children as they come in such a range of shapes and colors. Most of the catalogue sources carry seeds for decorative mixes of large and small gourds. Some varieties are good for crafts projects like dippers and birdhouses: try Jung, Mellinger's, Gurney's, Cook's Garden, Burpee, Park, and Vermont Bean Seed for these larger types. Gourds are very easy to grow and can be trained up a fence, tree, or trellis for within-reach harvesting.

ESPECIALLY FOR COLOR

Assorted Vegetables

One way to get a veritable kaleidoscope of color in the garden is to plant bell peppers. Shades of creamy white, yellow, gold, orange, red, green, lilac, purple, and chocolate brown planted together would make up a pretty crazy-quilt design. Look for assorted colored peppers in the Park, Johnny's, Burpee, and—especially—Stokes catalogues.

More color variety can be had from a radish with an appealing name. Oval-shaped EASTER EGG produces radishes in shades of white, pink, red, and purple. Seeds are available from most of the catalogue sources mentioned in this section.

Potatoes

Interesting colors are also possible from a somewhat un-likely source: the potato. DESIREE is a pretty blush-red with a cream interior (Mellinger's and Park); RED DALE is bright red with white flesh (Vermont Bean Seed and Johnny's); and CHERRIES JUBILEE is bright cherry pink outside and pale pink inside (Shepherd's).

For yellow potatoes, try YUKON GOLD or RUSSIAN BANANA, both carried by Vermont Bean Seed and Johnny's, or YELLOW FINN, in the Mellinger's, Vermont Bean Seed, Shepherd's, and Park catalogues. The latter vari-ety is described as looking and tasting as if it were already but-tered! For a striking contrast there's CARIBE, from Johnny's and Shepherd's, with its deep violet skin and white flesh.

Most unusual of all, however, is ALL BLUE. Not only is the skin of this potato bluish purple, but the flesh is, too! Sources for this surprising tuber include Park, Gurney's, and Mellinger's.

Some of these potatoes are available as minituber potato seed, which can be easier for children to plant. See page 190 for details.

Popcorn and Colored Corn

Are you ready for the *colored* popcorns? Not only are they edible, but they're wonderful choices for fall decorating. STRAWBERRY is an old favorite, with its strawberry-shaped, 2–3" ears and deep red kernels. Shepherd's, Vermont Bean Seed, Cook's Garden, Stokes, Jung, Johnny's, Mellinger's, and Gurney's all carry the seeds for this pretty corn.

Blue is a newer color in or-namental popcorn. MINI-ATURE BLUE POPCORN from Vermont Bean Seed has kernels of a medium to deep blue on a 2–4" ear. Shepherd's BABY BLUE is a deep "Colo-nial blue" color; ears are 3–4" long. For 1993 this company also offers PINK BO PEEP. Its soft mauve-pink blends nicely

Strawberry popcorn.

with the blue tones. For contrast add Jung's BLACK POP-CORN, which pops up white.

For multi-colored ears there's Indian or rainbow popcorn. Children love Indian corn because husking an ear reveals the beautiful "hidden treasure" inside—no two ears have quite the same colors or patterns. Try LITTLE INDIAN from Jung; CALICO POPCORN from Shepherd's; CUTIE POPS from Stokes; or POPCORN MINIATURE COLORED from Park. All bear small ears except CALICO, which is 6–8" long.

Regular ornamental (that is, non-popping) Indian corn is widely available. Choices include both miniature and standard size ears for attractive fall decorations.

FRUITS

Introduction

Does the child exist who doesn't love fruit in some form or another? If she can grow her own, so much the better! Just as for the adult gardener with a physical disability, fruits of special interest for a younger gardener would include those with thornless bushes, those requiring only easy care, and dwarf and miniature fruit trees.

Remember that small children like quick results, so check the nursery or catalogue to see if the bush, tree, or vine you're interested in will bear its first year. (When Rachael, then age 4, was told her MAMMOTH sunflower seeds had sprouted overnight, she immediately wanted a look. Why? To see if they were taller than her daddy yet.) An older child, who presumably has greater patience, might be more willing to invest his time in a longer-term fruit-growing project.

Descriptions of some suggested soft fruits and fruit trees can be found in Chapter Five. A few of special interest to children are repeated here.

Strawberries and Blueberries

Strawberries are almost universally popular with children, given their sweetness and appealingly bright red color. Planted at ground level, however, they can be difficult to reach for care and harvesting. In addition, the runners must be dealt with as they spread this way and that throughout the patch.

Alternatives to ground-level planting include raised beds, pyramids, and containers like barrels, hanging baskets, and strawberry jars (those with lips under the openings are easier to plant). Strawberries grown this way will be simpler to harvest. The runners, moreover, will now be in a more accessible position and so can make for an interesting experiment in plant propagation, rather than an awkward chore to be handled.

Instead of the standard white flowers, a newer variety of strawberry boasts blooms in that beloved little-girl color, pink. This perennial blooms throughout the summer and looks

lovely in a hanging basket, container, or window box. Called PINK PANDA and carried by Park, the plant produces small berries, has a spreading habit, and grows 6–8" tall.

As an alternative to standard strawberries, your child could try the alpines. Alpine strawberries form pretty, runnerless plants that are compact and bushy. They'll grow nicely in containers and window boxes, and will bear small fruits throughout the summer. Advise your child not to expect a taste identical to the strawberries he's used to: the alpines have their own distinct—and wonderful—flavor.

Alpine strawberries.

Blueberries are another good choice for children, with their fat little berries so good in pancakes, muffins, and pies, or right off the bush. At only 1½–2' tall, the blueberry bushes described in Chapter Five would make excellent choices for your youngster. Note especially DWARF TOPHAT, available through the Gurney's catalogue. It grows a tiny 9–12" high, making it an especially good candidate for planting in a container.

Fruit Trees

The Sensation™ peach from Stark®.

Dwarf and miniature fruit trees are your best bets if your child is interested in planting and caring for a fruit tree. Check the Stark Bro's Nursery catalogue for miniature peach, nectarine, and apricot trees. These genetically dwarf trees usually grow from 4' to about 6–8' high and can be planted either at ground level or in large planters.

Stark also offers 3 varieties of miniature apple trees, which grow about 6–9' tall. They too can be planted either in containers or in the ground.

Another genetically dwarf nectarine, RED SUNSET, can be purchased through the Park catalogue. At 5' high, it's just right for container growing.

The widely available dwarf fruit trees may be too tall for young children, as they grow about 8–10' high. With an adult involved in their care, however, they can certainly be considered. Stark carries dwarf trees that produce jumbo varieties of fruit, a feature likely to intrigue a youngster.

Finally, for something different—at least for Northern gardeners—consider dwarf citrus trees. Possibilities include lime, lemon, orange, banana, fig, calamondin orange, grapefruit, tangerine, and Mandarin orange. Plants are available both at local nurseries and through catalogues like Gurney's and Mellinger's.

FLOWERS

Introduction

The choices in this category are really limitless, so let your child decide what she'd like to plant. Look at the neighbors' flower beds when you're out for a walk or drive, and ask her what ones she likes best. Or, peruse a seed catalogue or the garden center seed display rack together and find out what catches her eye.

Of course, you'll need to determine if that particular plant is suitable for local growing conditions. If the plants are to be in containers, though, there's more flexibility in what your child can choose. With this type of gardening you have control over the planting medium, the amount of moisture a plant gets, and how much sunlight the plant receives, by moving the container to shade or sun.

For her first garden, you may want to guide your child toward choosing the following recommended flowers, as they're a good way to begin. All are annuals, which means that they will bloom the first year from seed. They'll provide a lot of color over a long period of time, usually until frost.

These flowers are also all sun-lovers and are simple to grow. Some are easy to start from seed: they'll both germinate and grow quickly, making them especially good for the youngest children. Others are easy to grow, but are best started as purchased plants from your local nursery or garden center since their seeds are very fine and/or slow to germinate.

Some of these suggested flowers have large seeds. These are less frustrating for very small hands to plant and are an enjoyable way to practice fine motor control. Then, after their blooming time is over, your child can harvest seeds for next year's planting.

Catalogues that offer especially large selections of flower seeds include Burpee, Stokes, and Park. Plants can be purchased at almost any garden center or nursery.

Especially for Beginners

Marigolds are a fine place to start for a child's garden. In shades of yellow, orange, and dark red, their cheerful blooms are as bright as the summer sun. Native to Mexico, marigolds are hardy, carefree growers that will bloom continuously until frost. Marigolds also make fine houseplants (just watch for red spider mites).

- seed germinates and grows quickly

Nasturtiums are one of the easiest flowers to grow. The fragrant blooms come in a nice mix of colors, including orange, red, gold, and yellow. The peppery-tasting petals can even be added to a salad. Nasturtiums come in both bedding and climbing types, and will flower happily in average soil.

- large seeds

Geraniums (*Pelargoniums*) have provided color and pleasure to generations of both windowsill and outdoor gardeners. Besides the classic red, geraniums are available in shades of pink, salmon, orange, white, rose, and lavender. Plant your geraniums in beds, pots, window boxes, and hanging baskets, then overwinter them indoors.

- buy plants

Another popular flower with all-season color is the **petunia.** Keep the dead flowers pinched off and they'll bloom until frost. Colors include white, pink, red, purple and all shades in between (even blue and yellow), in solids and bicolors.

- buy plants

Zinnias (*Zinnia*) come in even more colors than petunias. From the middle of summer until fall, zinnias will bloom again and again, especially if you cut them for flower arrangements. Flower sizes range from a petite 1" across to a giant 6".

- seed germinates and grows quickly

Four o'clocks, marvel of Peru, (*Mirabilis jalapa*) come in clear shades of white, yellow, and pink—some with stripes—and are nicely scented. They open in mid- to late afternoon (hence the name), attracting hummingbird moths.

- large seeds

Quick-growing **sunflowers** (*Helianthus*) provide seeds for snacks and for winter bird feeding. Types like MAMMOTH grow 12' and produce competition-size heads. SUNSPOT, a new type of sunflower, may be even better for kids to grow as its 18–24" height makes it a very accessible plant. Despite its shorter stature, SUNSPOT still produces good-sized, 10–12" flower heads. Jung and Burpee carry seeds for this variety,

while Shepherd's has BIG SMILE dwarf sunflowers. These grow just 12–18" high, with 5" faces. MUSIC BOX MIX, from Cook's Garden, is yet another short sunflower at 2½–3' tall, in mixed colors.

• large seeds

Cosmos will bloom in the summer and fall, and make nice cut flowers. Their colors are in the yellow, orange, and red group, or in white, pink, and red shades. Some types will grow 4' tall.

• seed germinates and grows quickly

For nighttime drama it's hard to beat the **moonflower:** the huge, fragrant white blooms open up in the evening while you watch! (Of course, if your young child is in bed at 8:00, he'll miss the show, but the blooms do stay open until the following morning.) Plant your moonflower by a porch or trellis as this strong climber can reach 15'.

• large seeds

Hand a preschooler a fistful of brightly-colored crayons and ask him to draw you some flowers: the result will probably look a lot like a SUNSHINE **gazania.** As Park puts it, this gazania is "famous for wild color combinations" since the big, daisy-like flowers each have as many as four or five bright colors. What child could resist that! Gazanias are tolerant of hot, dry locations.

• large seeds

HERBS

Introduction

Choices are myriad when it comes to selecting herbs. However, since most children are probably unfamiliar with these plants, you and your child may need to explore together some of the options for growing herbs. Gardening with herbs is also a wonderful opportunity to discover the historical roles these plants have played, as foods, medicines, dyes, and so on.

Like flowers and vegetables, the most popular, well-known herb varieties will be available as plants. For the lesser-known herbs, however, you'll probably need to grow them from seed.

As mentioned previously, check these catalogues for large selections of herb seeds: Mellinger's, Nichols, Burpee, Johnny's, Cook's Garden, Vermont Bean Seed, Shepherd's, Stokes, and Thompson & Morgan. Burpee also offers 8 common herbs in their special indoor growing sets called Seed 'n Start® Kits, plus 33 varieties as plants.

Most herbs are ideal for container growing, and for a pleasing arrangement, several plants can be grouped together in a single pot. Let your child be creative in selecting his containers. A gallon olive oil can, for instance, might hold oregano and basil. And remember the FERNLEAF dill and SPICY GLOBE basil for containers, as noted on pages 192–93.

The older child who cooks can begin with the herbs he uses in the kitchen: oregano, thyme, dill, chives, basil, rosemary, parsley, and sage, for instance. If he's only familiar with the little jars of dried herbs from the grocery store, the variety of plant shapes, leaf textures, flowers, and fresh flavors will doubtless come as quite a surprise.

Especially for Beginners

A very young child might do well starting with one of these three: mint, catnip, or lamb's ears. All are perennials, easy to grow, and like sun or a little shade. Each of these herbs has something of special interest to recommend them to children.

Ask your child if she would like to grow a plant that smells like that candy cane she had last Christmas, and you'll probably see her face light up. Mints (*Mentha*) are the source of a pleasing and refreshing taste that almost everyone enjoys.

The various mints are quite easy to grow—almost too easy, in fact. Unless their roots are contained, mints will spread very far, very fast. To keep them corralled, plant your mints in a container, or sink round or square flue tiles flush with the ground and use them as planters.

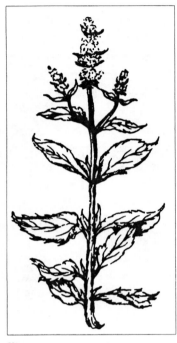

Mint.

Varieties of mints include peppermint and spearmint, plus various "flavored" mints like apple, orange, pineapple, and even chocolate! Add fresh leaves to lemonade, dry them to make hot mint tea, or just crush a leaf and sniff or chew.

Does your household include a cat or two? If so, they would certainly be delighted if your child planted them some catnip (*Nepeta cataria*). Even an adult cat will become kitten-like again if given a sprig of catnip or a toy made with the dried leaves.

Catnip will grow up to 3' high, but try to keep your cat from rolling on the young plants, or they'll never make it to this height. Humans can enjoy catnip, too, as a tea brewed from the leaves.

Lamb's ears (*Stachys lanata* or *S. byzantina*; also known as wooly betony) was once used medicinally but is now grown as a decorative or ornamental herb. The silver-gray leaves are delightful to touch. Fuzzy and soft, they do feel just like a baby animal's ear.

Catnip.

This rather low-growing plant sends up a flower stalk with small purple blooms, which some people prefer to cut off. Lamb's ears can be divided to increase your number of plants and will retain its silver color during the winter. Note that this plant is for touching, not tasting!

Lamb's ears.

THEME AND SPECIALTY GARDENS

Introduction

These theme and specialty gardens are some of my favorite gardening ideas for children, since they're an ideal way to reflect your child's individual tastes and interests. The gardens can be planted at ground level, in containers, or in raised beds. Some, like the pizza garden, can be grown to nice effect in a half whiskey barrel. Others, like the larger Halloween/harvest garden, will probably need to be grown in one corner of the ground-level garden. Chapter Five is the place to look for information on specific plants suitable for container growing.

20 Gardens

Here are some ideas to get you started, then let your child's imagination take over!

- *pizza garden:* plant tomatoes, onions, peppers, garlic, oregano, and basil

- *spaghetti garden:* plant all of the above, plus spaghetti squash

- *Chinese cuisine garden:* plant snowpeas, radishes, cucumbers, Chinese cabbage, pac choi, and other specialty vegetables

- *Mexican cuisine garden:* plant beans (pinto, kidney, black turtle, garbanzo), tomatoes, hot peppers, cumin, cilantro

- *Mediterranean cuisine garden:* plant tomatoes, eggplant, summer squash, peppers, onions

- *harvest/Halloween garden:* plant pumpkins, gourds, Indian corn, popcorn, sunflowers

- *Native American garden:* plant the Three Sisters: corn, beans, and squash

- *specialty garden:* plant six colors of peppers, four sizes of pumpkins, or an assortment of popcorn, for instance

- *edible flowers garden:* plant nasturtiums, calendulas, chives, Johnny-jump-ups, borage, signet marigold

- *miniature rose garden:* plant any that please

- *tea garden:* plant various mints, lemon balm, chamomile, cinnamon basil, anise hyssop

- *sharing garden* (for pets and wildlife): sunflowers, catnip, popcorn, birdhouse gourds, peanuts

- *herb garden:* plant any that please

- *color garden:* plant all in one color—yellow, say

- *touching garden:* plant lamb's ears, succulents, ferns, grasses, geraniums, mosses

- *scented garden:* plant carnations, scented geraniums, tuberose, heliotrope, mignonette, sweet peas, alyssum, nicotiana, stocks, four o'clocks, herbs

- *moon garden:* plant moonflowers, Madonna lily, white roses, artemisia, nicotiana, lamb's ears, night-scented stock

- *crafts garden:* plant flowers for drying (statice, strawflowers, etc.), artemesia (for wreaths), large gourds (for carving)

- *hummingbird garden:* plant bee balm (monarda), lobelia, salvia, trumpet vine, snapdragon, coral bells, cardinal flower, pineapple sage, scarlet runner bean

- *butterfly garden:* plant marigold, nasturtium, zinnia, salvia, buddleia, butterfly weed, yarrow, coreopsis, purple coneflower, cosmos, chives, lantana

EXTENDED GARDENING IDEAS

Introduction

Now that you and your child have planted his garden, have watered, weeded, fertilized, and spent time just watching it grow, think about how you can expand and extend the experience. Depending on his age and abilities, your child might like to try some of these ideas. Naturally, he'll come up with more of his own, too.

As a parent, you'll notice that these suggested activities involve reading and pre-reading, math, speech, fine and gross motor practice, sensory experiences, social development, and other skills. In the garden, fun and learning easily go hand in hand!

While the focus of this book is on outdoor gardening, I've included a few ideas from the wonderful array of *indoor* gardening projects that are available to your child, either to supplement or to substitute for a garden outdoors.

There are of course many more projects waiting to be "discovered." Some of these activities are appropriate for a child to do on his own; some are ideal for groups, with Mom or Dad, friends or siblings; and some are of equal interest for adults.

A Personal Experience

• Keep a diary or journal about his gardening experiences—dictated to and written down by you, if necessary. It can be illustrated with his own drawings and/or photographs, or with pictures cut from seed catalogues. Or, he could keep an oral diary on a tape recorder.

• See if there's a youth or junior garden club in your town, or a 4–H Club that's involved in gardening or farming. Your child might enjoy meeting with others his own age who share a common interest.

• Learn to identify the various visitors and residents of the garden and yard: birds, insects, butterflies, wildflowers, trees. Check the library or bookstore for good children's identification guide books.

• Grow personalized pumpkins. Choose a pumpkin that is growing well and still green. With a small knife, cut just through the pumpkin skin to "write" initials or a name. The scars will heal and the initials will grow as the pumpkin matures.

• Study the seed catalogues: read the descriptions; locate plant origins and hardiness zones on the map; compare weights and measurements of seed amounts; write out an order.

• Plant low-growers like alyssum, ageratum, dwarf marigolds in the shape of your child's initials or name; or plant in shapes like the U.S. flag, concentric circles, etc. (seed tapes make it even easier).

Sharing and Caring

• Bring extra produce to the local soup kitchen or homeless shelter, or give it to a family who is dealing with illness or unemployment.

• Have a harvest picnic and invite friends, family, and neighbors. Share and trade what everyone has grown.

• Sell extra produce at a roadside stand or at the local farmer's market.

• Harvest sunflower seeds for snacks and/or wild bird food.

• Have a neighborhood growing contest for the earliest tomato, biggest zucchini, or prettiest flowers.

• Harvest seeds for next year's crop, to keep and to share. Save only standard (that is, non-hybrid) seed, as hybrid seed will not produce plants true to the parent. However, if space permits, experiment to see what *does* happen when hybrid seed is planted.

• Look in the library for information on the Seed Savers Exchange, founded by Kent Whealy, and explore how people are working to save heirloom varieties of various plants (or write the SSE at RR3, Box 239, Decorah, IA 52101). Look in catalogues like Seeds Blum and Seeds of Change for heirloom seeds to plant. Discover the intriguing stories behind our common garden vegetables.

• Make your own seed tapes, as described in Chapter Four, for the family garden or as gifts.

Garden Investigations

• Measure fast-growers like beans every day and plot their progress on a simple chart.
• Have guessing games: How much does that giant zucchini weigh? How big around is the largest tomato? How many seeds are in the pumpkin? Then weigh, measure, and count to find out.

• Plant seeds in peat pellets, then water them. Time and measure their expansion as you watch the pellets swell.

• Create strange-looking squash, cucumbers, melons, gourds, eggplant, or pumpkins by growing them in Vegi-Forms. Fasten a reusable plastic mold around the young vegetable and watch it grow into an elf head, "pickle puss" head, or heart shape. Find them for $13.00 each in the Gurney's catalogue.

• Put young gourds, squash, cucumbers, watermelons—still attached to the vine—inside a glass bottle, to let them grow as novelties.

• Investigate companion planting and see whether it works for you. Examples include planting marigolds to discourage nematodes, basil with tomatoes to enhance their growth, or southernwood with cabbages to deter cabbage worms.

• Learn how to propagate various types of plants, through cuttings, layering, and so on.

How Does Your Garden Grow?

• Watch roots grow. Enfold bean or other large seeds in several layers of wet paper towels, and check their progress daily.

A root-viewing jar.

• Force a hyacinth bulb in a specially-designed clear glass vase, which will fill with roots.

• Sprinkle radish, lettuce, cress, or grass seeds on a wet sponge in a saucer of water. Fuzzy root hairs will appear quickly: look at them with a magnifying glass.

• Use a tall, straight-sided glass container you've lined with dark construction paper. Slide a few big seeds between the glass and the paper, then fill the jar with crumpled paper towels. Carefully water the towels so that finally the paper lining and the seeds are wet too. Slip a dark paper collar over the whole jar and set it on a sunny windowsill. Each day slide the collar up to see roots, stems, and leaves develop and grow. Add water as needed.

• Make a root-viewing box. Cut a large rectangle in the side of a milk carton and, from the inside, tape a piece of Plexiglas over the opening. Fill the carton with soil, then plant seeds of plants with easy-to-see roots, like squash or beans, and water them. Keep the carton in a sunny window. Through the "window" in the carton, watch the roots grow.

Creative Crafts and Activities

- Press or dry flowers, herbs, and various plant materials for craft use: note cards, arrangements, wreaths, catnip toys, Christmas tree ornaments.

- Make birdhouses, dippers, scoops, and other decorative objects from large gourds.

- Make block prints using firm fruits and vegetables. Cut them in half, brush on paint, and stamp them on kraft or tissue paper to make wrapping paper, or on notepaper to make greeting cards.

- Pick and arrange flowers in a vase. Include herbs, branches, and grasses for variety.

- Create a mosaic picture using a variety of small and large seeds.

- Create a collage using pictures from seed catalogues and old seed packets.

- Make animals, monsters, people, space creatures from oddly formed vegetables and fruits. Add parts of other vegetables, construction paper, crafts supplies, etc. to make their features.

- Make "egghead people." Cut the top off an empty eggshell and poke a tiny hole in the bottom for drainage. Draw a face on the shell, then fill it with soil. Plant grass or rye seeds, cover with more soil, and water. Set the shell on a base cut from the egg carton and put it in a sunny window. Green "hair" will sprout in a week.

- Or, use a paper or styrofoam cup, or a milk carton cut down to about 4" high. Cover the container with construction paper, then draw or paint a face on it. Fill the container with soil and plant grass seed for "hair."

Edibles and More

- Help prepare the harvest by husking corn, washing carrots, shelling peas, and so on. Let your child participate in any food preparation chores that are appropriate, up to and including cooking and serving the food.

- Toast pumpkin seeds for a snack.

- Dry apple slices for winter use, or string them to make a wreath.

• Make herb vinegars with fresh herbs, to keep or to give as gifts. Try these combinations, or make up your own: red wine vinegar and rosemary; white vinegar and dill; cider vinegar and tarragon, with a bit of garlic added; white vinegar and parsley, with summer savory, marjoram, and chives added. Purple basil will make a beautifully colored vinegar.

• Learn how to dry vegetables and fruits, either in the sun or with a commercial dryer. Make fruit leathers for winter snacks.

• Grow sprouts for salads and sandwiches. Park offers a half-dozen varieties. (*Caution:* Use only seeds designated for this purpose!)

• Grow mushrooms. Kits are available in many seed catalogues.

Indoor Gardens

• Set up your container garden indoors: plants grown on a sunny windowsill offer their own unique charm and interest. And, if you decide to install grow-lights for an indoor garden, you don't even need the sunshine.

• Try growing unusual plants. This sampling is from the Thompson & Morgan catalogue, all of which can be grown from seed.

—*Cycads* are palm-like living fossils from the days of the dinosaurs.

—*Venus fly traps* catch and dine on flies.

—Watch the leaflets of the *sensitive plant* fold up when touched.

—The *baobab*, or upside-down tree, is a curious and ancient plant.

—*Bananas* quickly grow large, decorative leaves.

• A giant amaryllis bulb puts on a lot of show for the money. With proper care it will last for years.

• Explore the world of cacti and succulents. Buy plants or start a collection from seed—Park carries several mixes. Forms vary widely, while many sport beautiful flowers. Beguiling names include bishop's cap, owl's eyes, hedgehog, fish hook, strawberry, pink pearl, and more.

• Train ivy, rosemary, jasmine, or other plants to grow as topiaries. Both simple and complex shapes are possible, including a circle, sphere, cone, spiral, or tepee. Check the Kinsman catalogue for wire topiary forms.

• An older child who is careful and patient can try bonsai. Begin with a pre-shaped little plant from the nursery, or start an appropriate plant from seed—try the Thompson & Morgan catalogue. Many books and special tools are available for this fascinating hobby.

• Experimenting with growing kitchen vegetables and fruits is fun and easy, and can produce surprising results. Here are some possibilities:

> avocado pit
> beet, carrot, turnip, and parsnip tops
> citrus (orange, grapefruit, lemon, lime, tangerine)
>   seeds
> coconut
> coffee beans (unroasted or green)
> dates (unpasteurized)
> fig seeds
> ginger root (fresh)
> grape seeds
> mango
> nuts of various kinds (in the shell)
> onion and garlic bulbs
> papaya
> pineapple top
> pomegranate seeds
> spice seeds (from the kitchen shelf)
> stone fruits (plum, peach, cherry, nectarine, apricot)
> sugar cane
> sweet and white potatoes (not treated with sprout-
>   inhibitor)

• Terrariums can be created from just about any clear glass container and can feature either woodland plants or small houseplants for a jungle-like effect. Use an aquarium tank to make a larger forest setting.

• Similarly, a desert dish garden can be formed in a wide, shallow bowl and planted with cacti. Add bits of stone or wood, or small figures for accents.

• Create a water garden in a 6–to–9"-deep bowl, using miniature water lilies.

A Final Note

I would enjoy hearing from you as to what gardening techniques worked in your situation (and what didn't). With enough feedback and new ideas, perhaps together we can create a sequel to this book! Please write to me with your suggestions and tips, in care of the publisher. Thank you, and may your time spent gardening be fruitful!

APPENDIX

Sources and Resources

All the catalogues referred to in this book are included below, with a few more added for good measure. This listing certainly isn't inclusive, however, as you'll discover once you get your name on a mailing list or two! Note that the majority of these companies offer a toll-free phone number for your convenience; many have a fax number as well.

CATALOGUES

Seeds, Plants, Bulbs, Bushes, Trees, Vines (and some tools)

W. Atlee Burpee Co., 300 Park Ave., Warminster, PA 18991–0001. (800) 888–1447; fax 215–674–4170

The Cook's Garden, P.O. Box 535, Londonderry, VT 05148. (802) 824–3400; fax 802–824–3027

Dutch Gardens, P.O. Box 200, Adelphia, NJ 07710. (908) 780–2713

Henry Field's Seed & Nursery Co., 415 North Burnett, Shenandoah, IA 51602. (605) 665–9391; fax 605–665–2601

Gurney's Seed & Nursery Co., 110 Capital Street, Yankton, SD 57079. (605) 665–1930; fax 605–665–9718

Harris Seeds, 60 Saginaw Drive, P.O. Box 22960, Rochester, NY 14692–2960. (716) 442–0100; fax 716–442–9386

Jackson & Perkins, 1 Rose Lane, Medford, OR 97501–0702. (800) 292–4769; fax 800–242–0329

Johnny's Selected Seeds, Foss Hill Road, Albion, ME 04910–9731. (207) 437–4301; fax 207–437–2165

J. W. Jung Seed & Nursery Co., 335 S. High Street, Randolph, WI 53957–0001. (800) 247–5864

Miller Nurseries, 5060 West Lake Road, Canandaigua, NY 14424. (800) 836–9630; fax 716–396–2154

Nichols Garden Nursery, 1190 North Pacific Highway, Albany, OR 97321–4598. (503) 928–9280

Park Seed Co., Cokesbury Rd., Greenwood, SC 29647–0001. (803) 223–7333; fax 803–941–4206

Pinetree Garden Seeds, Box 300, New Gloucester, ME 04260. (207) 926–3400

Seeds Blum, Idaho City Stage, Boise, ID 83706. (208) 342–0858; fax 208–338–5658

Seeds of Change, P.O. Box 15700, Santa Fe, NM 87506–5700. (505) 438–8080

Shepherd's Garden Seeds, Order Dept., 30 Irene Street, Torrington, CT 06790–6627. (203) 482–3638; fax 203–482–0532   (home office: SGS, 6116 Highway 9, Felton, CA 95018. (408) 335–6910; fax 408–335–2080)

R. H. Shumway's, P.O. Box 1, Graniteville, SC 29829–0001. (803) 663–9771

Spring Hill Nurseries, 625 North Galena Road, P.O. Box 1758, Peoria, IL 61656–1758. (800) 582–8527

Stark Bro's Nurseries & Orchards Co., P.O. Box 10, Louisiana, MO 63353–0010. (800) 325–4180; fax 314–754–5290

Stokes Seeds Inc., P.O. Box 548, Buffalo, NY 14240–0548. (716) 695–6980; fax 716–695–9649

Thompson & Morgan Inc., P.O. Box 1308, Jackson, NJ 08527–0308. (800) 274–7333; fax 908–363–9356

Van Bourgondien, P.O. Box 1000, 245 Farmingdale Road, Rt. 109, Babylon, NY 11702–0598. (800) 622–9997; fax 516–669–1228

Vermont Bean Seed Company, Computer Operations Center, Vaucluse, SC 29850–0150. (802) 273–3400 (home office: VBS, Garden Lane, Fair Haven, VT 05743)

The Vermont Wildflower Farm, P.O. Box 5, Route 7, Charlotte, VT 05445. (802) 425–3931; fax 802–425–3504

Wayside Gardens, 1 Garden Lane, Hodges, SC 29695–0001. (800) 845–1124; fax 800–457–9712

White Flower Farm, Route 63, Litchfield, CT 06759–0050. (203) 496–9600; fax 203–496–1418

Gardening Tools and Supplies

adaptAbility, P.O. Box 515, Colchester, CT 06415–0515.(800) 288–9941; fax 800–566–6678

Alsto's Handy Helpers, P.O. Box 1267, Galesburg, IL 61401. (800) 447–0048

Brookstone, 5 Vose Farm Road, Peterborough, NH 03458. (800) 926–7000

Dig This, 102–45 Bastion Square, Victoria, B.C. V8W 1J1 Canada. (604) 385–3212

Enrichments [Fred Sammons, Inc.], Department D-81, P.O. Box 471, Western Springs, IL 60558–0471. (800) 323–5547

Gardeners Eden, Mail Order Dept., P.O. Box 7307, San Francisco, CA 94120–7307. (800) 822–9600

Gardener's Supply Company, 128 Intervale Road, Burlington, VT 05401. (800) 444–6417; fax 802–660–4600

Gardens Alive!, 5100 Schenley Place, Lawrenceburg, IN 47025. (812) 537–8650; fax 812–537–5108

HearthSong, P.O. Box B, Sebastopol, CA 95473–0601. (800) 325–2502

Kinsman Company, Inc., River Road, Point Pleasant, PA 18950. (800) 733–5613; fax 215–297–0210

Langenbach, P.O. Box 453, Blairstown, NJ 07825–0453. (800) 362–1991

A. M. Leonard, Inc., 241 Fox Drive, P.O. Box 816, Piqua, OH 45356. (800) 543–8955; fax 800–433–0633

Mellinger's Inc., 2310 W. South Range Road, North Lima, OH 44452–9731. (216) 549–9861; fax 216–549–3716

The Natural Gardening Company, 217 Anselmo Avenue, San Anselmo, CA 94960–2822. (415) 456–5060; fax 415–721–0642

Walt Nicke's Garden Talk, 36 McLeod Lane, P.O. Box 433, Topsfield, MA 01983. (800) 822–4114

Plow & Hearth, 301 Madison Road, P.O. Box 830, Orange, VA 22960–0492. (800) 627–1712

Rubbermaid Incorporated, Specialty Products Division, Wooster, OH 44691–6000. (316) 221–2230

Smith & Hawken, 25 Corte Madera, Mill Valley, CA 94941. (415) 383–2000

Solutions, Dept. SLSP93, P.O. Box 6878, Portland, OR 97228–6878. (800) 342–9988; fax 503–643–1973

PRINTED MATERIALS

The following list provides complete bibliographic information on the books and booklets referred to in the text, as well as others that supplied, in varying degrees, useful information. Other sources of gardening ideas and information included various issues of *Organic Gardening* and *Better Homes and Gardens* magazines, and special-interest publications from *Family Circle* and *Woman's Day.*

Since every gardener needs a good reference book or two, I've also listed the titles of some general gardening books you may want to add to your bookshelf.

The Able Gardener: Overcoming Barriers of Age & Physical Limitations, Kathleen Yeomans, R.N., Pownal, VT: Storey Communications, Inc., 1992

Adaptive Garden Equipment: A Resource Manual for Patients, Families, and Professionals, Englewood, CO: Craig Hospital Horticultural Therapy Program, 1986

All About Vegetables (new expanded edition for gardeners of the 1990's), Walter L. Doty, writer & Anne Reilly, revision editor, San Ramon, CA: Ortho Books, 1973

The American Horticultural Society Illustrated Encyclopedia of Gardening: Vegetables, Mount Vernon, VA: The American Horticultural Society, 1974

Award-Winning Small-Space Gardens, written by Michael MacCaskey & edited by A. Cort Sinnes, San Francisco: Ortho Books, 1979

The Complete Book of Gardening, Michael Wright, ed., New York: Warner Books, 1978

The Complete Indoor Gardener, Michael Wright, ed., New York: Random House, 1974

Container Gardening for the Handicapped, Frank J. Schweller, Phoenix, AZ: Hand-D-Cap Publishing, 1989

Crockett's Victory Garden, James Underwood Crockett, Boston: Little, Brown & Company, 1977

"Designing Barrier-Free Areas," Debbie Krause, Ithaca, New York: Instructional Materials Service, Cornell University, n.d.

Gardening as Therapy: A Resource Manual for Development of Horticulture Therapy Programs for the Summer Season, Hortitherapy Committee, Vancouver, B.C., Canada: The Botanical Garden, The University of British Columbia, 1979 (also, manuals for the Spring Season, the Fall Season, and the Winter Season)

Gardening for the Handicapped, Betty Massingham, Aylesbury, England: Shire Publications, 1972

Gardening for the Physically Handicapped and the Elderly, Mary Chaplin, London: Batsford Press, 1978

Gardening in Containers, Ken Burke, project editor & Alvin Horton, editor, San Ramon, CA: Ortho Books, 1984

"Gardening in Raised Beds and Containers for the Elderly and Physically Handicapped," prepared by Paula Diane Relf, H.T.M., Blacksburg, VA: Virginia Cooperative Extension Service, rep. 1989

Gardening without Stress and Strain: Shortcuts for Less Active Gardeners, Jack Kramer, New York: Charles Scribner's Sons, 1973

Growing with Gardening: A Twelve-Month Guide for Therapy, Recreation, and Education, Bibby Moore, Chapel Hill, NC: The University of North Carolina Press, 1989

Grow It!: An Indoor/Outdoor Gardening Guide for Kids, Erika Markmann, New York: Random House, 1991

Horticultural Therapy at a Physical Rehabilitation Facility, the Horticultural Society Therapy Department Staff of the Chicago Horticultural Society, Eugene A. Rothert, Jr., and James R. Daubert, Glencoe, IL: Chicago Horticultural Society, 1981

Horticulture for the Disabled and Disadvantaged, Damon R. Olszowy, Springfield, IL.: Charles C. Thomas, 1978

Let's Grow!: 72 Gardening Adventures with Children, Linda Tilgner, Pownal, VT: Storey Communications, 1988

The Organic Gardener's Handbook of Natural Insect and Disease Control: A Complete, Problem-Solving Guide to Keeping Your Garden and Yard Healthy without Chemicals, Barbara W. Ellis & Fern Marshall Bradley, eds., Emmaus, PA: Rodale Press, 1992

Raised Bed Gardening: A Resource Manual for Patients, Families, and Professionals, Englewood, CO: Craig Hospital Horticultural Therapy Program, 1988

Reader's Digest Illustrated Guide to Gardening, Carroll C. Calkins, ed., Pleasantville, NY: Reader's Digest Assoc., 1978

Rodale's All-New Encyclopedia of Organic Gardening: The Indispensable Resource for Every Gardener (rev. ed.), Fern Marshall Bradley & Barbara W. Ellis, eds., Emmaus, PA: Rodale Press, 1992

Rodale's Illustrated Encyclopedia of Gardening and Landscaping Techniques, Barbara W. Ellis, ed., Emmaus, PA: Rodale Press, 1990

Source Book for the Disabled, Glorya Hale, ed., New York: Paddington Press, 1979

Square Foot Gardening: A New Way to Garden in Less Space with Less Work, Mel Bartholomew, Emmaus, PA: Rodale Press, 1983

Theme Gardens: How to Plan, Plant & Grow 16 Gloriously Different Gardens, Barbara Damrosch, New York: Workman Publishing, 1982

Tips for the Lazy Gardener, Linda Tilgner, Pownal, VT: Storey Communications, Inc., 1985

A FEW USEFUL ADDRESSES
AND MISCELLANEOUS HELPS

American Horticultural Therapy Association, 362A ChristopherAvenue, Gaithersburg, MD 20879. (301) 948–3010; (800) 634–1603; fax (301) 869–2397.
> Contact them about finding schools that offer courses in horticultural therapy; membership in AHTA and addresses of local chapters; membership in Friends of Horticultural Therapy (for backyard gardeners; quarterly newsletter); botanic gardens that offer internships in horticultural therapy—a few have special displays or areas set up as "enabling gardens" that you can visit.

American Society of Landscape Architects, 4401 Connecticut Avenue NW, Washington, DC 20008. (202) 686–2752; fax (202) 686–1001.
> Contact them about running a computer search to help find a landscape architect in your area who specializes in accessible design (there may be a nominal charge for the search).

GrowLab™ Indoor Gardens, National Gardening Association, Dept. 92, 180 Flynn Avenue, Burlington, VT 05401. (802) 863–1308; fax 802–863–5962.
> These attractive plant carts and stands (with lights, curriculum guides, and accessories) were created for classroom use for grades K-8. Often financed through a PTA/PTO fundraiser, the gardens can be used in a variety of classroom settings. Prices begin at around $350.00.

Stella® Cultura Pedestal Greenhouse, imported by A & B Andersson Import
Co., 3312 Crosby Street, Rockford, IL 61107. Phone and fax (815) 229–3388.
A unique pedestal garden of extruded aluminum, this handsome unit from
Sweden comes in four designs and can be used indoors or out. The growing
area, which is divided into 8 sections, has 32 detachable triangular pots; a soft
vinyl cover provides a greenhouse climate. With its rotating base, the garden
is easily accessible from a seated or standing position and is suitable for use by
both children and adults. Prices begin at around $1400.00.

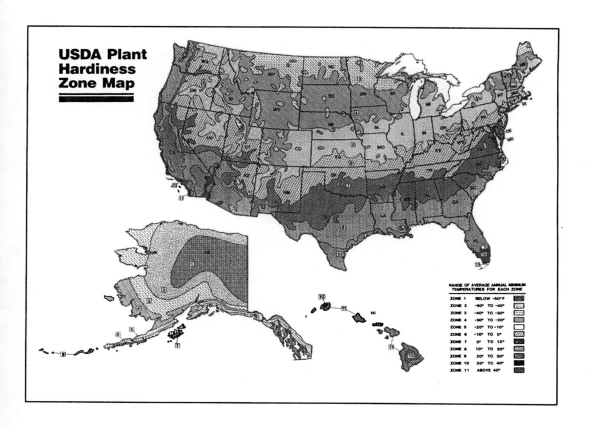

About the author:

An avid gardener and the mother of a child with spina bifida, Janeen R. Adil writes on gardening, disability, and children's topics for a variety of local and national publications. A New England native, Adil and her family are at present living in Quakertown, PA.

Index

A-frame planter stands, 48–49, 258
A-frames, 100, 102
All-America Selection (AAS), 169
Allan Blocks, 18
American Horticultural Therapy Association,
    292
American Society of Landscape Architects, 292
Animal pests, 239–42
Apple trees, 223, 224
Apricot trees, 223, 225
Aprons, 161
Arbors, 106
Arches, 106
Arts and crafts activities, 282
Augers, 146
Bacteria, and pest control, 233
Bags, for clean-up, 161
Barrels, 42–43
Baskets, hanging. See Hanging baskets
Baskets, wicker, 44
Bean towers, 99
Beans
    A-frames for, 100
    and pest control, 238
    cages for, 100
    harvesting, 163
    height of, 95
    poles for, 97
    teepees for, 96–97
    towers for, 99
    trellises for, 98
    varieties of, 182–84
Beets, 187
Belgian espalier, 111
Benches, gardening, 123–24
Biodegradable containers, 46, 61, 74
Birds
    helpful, 232–33
    nuisance, 239–242
Blackberries, 216–17
Blueberries, 217–18, 270
Bonsai, 284
Bouche-Thomas system, 113
Boysenberries, 216
Brick, for raised beds, 17
Broccoli, 185
Brussel sprouts, 185
Bulbs
    and container gardening, 53
    cold treatment of, 66

double-decker planting, 67
    forcing, 66, 67
    tools for planting, 145–46
    toxic, 252
Bushes. See Shrubs and bushes
Cabbages, 184–85, 238
Cacti, 283
Cages, 100
Cardboard boxes, 44
Carrots, 177–78, 238
Carts. See Wheelbarrows and carts
Catalogues, nursery, 287–88
Catnip, 276
Cauliflower, 185
Chard, 176
Cherry trees, 226
Children with disabilities
    A-frame gardens for, 258
    benefits of gardening for, 248–50, 254
    combination gardening areas for, 259
    container gardening for, 255–57
    creative gardening activities for, 282
    educational gardening activities for, 279–81
    food projects for, 282–83
    indoor gardens for, 283–85
    making gardens accessible for, 254–55
    raised bed gardening for, 255
    safety precautions for, 250–53
    sensory gardens for, 259–60
    theme and specialty gardens for, 277–78
    vertical gardening for, 257–58
Cinder blocks, 16–17, 43
Citrus trees, 226–27
Clay containers, 40–41
Climbing plants. See Vertical gardening
Companion planting, 26, 54–55, 238
Composters, 165–66
Composting
    benefits of, 164
    in a pot, 166–67
    worm composting, 166
Concrete
    containers made of, 43–44
    for raised beds, 16–17
Container gardens. See also Hanging baskets;
    Window boxes
    advantages of, 37–39
    air circulation for, 59–60
    cleaning, 58
    drainage of, 58–59

fertilizing, 64–65
for children, 255–56
growing bushes, shrubs, and trees in, 53–54
growing herbs and flowers in, 53, 200–206
growing vegetables in, 49–52
homemade, 47
maintaining, 65
materials for, 40–49
mixed plantings in, 54–55
planting, 60–61
removing plants from, 61
shelves for, 47–48
siting, 39–40
sizes of, 40
soil for, 56–58
stabilizing, 61–62
trellises for, 116
unusual types of, 84–85
vacation care of, 64
watering, 39–40, 62–64
Cordons, 109–10
Corn, 174–75, 240–41
Cosmos, 274
Crafts activities, 282
Crop rotation, 6, 244
Crowding, of plants, 23
Cucumbers
A-frames for, 100
and pest control, 238
fences for, 96
growing vertically, 96
towers for, 99
trellises for, 97
varieties of, 180
Currants, 219–20
Daffodils, 67
Deck planters. See Window boxes
Deer, 241
Desert dish garden, 284
Diatomaceous earth, 235
Dibbles, 137–39, 141
Digging tools, 131–33
Disease-resistant plants, 242–43
Diseases, soil-borne, 6
Double-digging, 19
Drainage, of pots and other containers, 58–59
Drainage pipes, 41
Drip irrigation, 153
Dwarf and miniature trees. See Fruit trees
Dwarf pyramid trees, 111

Eggplants, 184
Erosion, preventing, 149
Espaliers, 110
Fans, 111
Fences, 96, 102
Fertilizing
container gardens, 58, 64–65
hanging baskets, 78
planter boxes, 34
raised beds, 27
shrubs and trees, 70
window boxes, 84
Figs, 220–21
Fish emulsion, 65, 70
Florida weave, 94
Flower gatherers, 155–56
Flower pots. See Container gardens
Flowers. See also Bulbs; Perennials; Vines
appealing to child gardeners, 272–74
colors of, 195–97
considerations in choosing, 193–94
for containers, 200–206
for hanging baskets, 206–8
for raised beds, 22, 28
for window boxes, 208–9
fragrance of, 198–99
shape of, 197–98
sources of, 199
supports for, 117–18
texture of, 198
Flue tiles, 41
Foliage plants, 209–10
Forks, 132
Four o'clocks, 273
French intensive method, 25
Fruit bushes, sources of, 214
Fruit hedges, 113
Fruit trees. See also specific types of fruit
appropriate for child gardeners, 271
considerations in choosing, 228
dwarf and miniature, 221–222, 223–27
harvesting, 162–63
pollination of, 222
sources of, 214, 222–23, 227
training, 107–13
varieties of, 223–27
Fruits
unusual, 265–66
varieties appealing to children, 269–71
Gazania, 274

Geraniums, 273
Gloves, 127, 130
Gooseberries, 218–19, 220
Gourds, 263, 267
Grapes, 113
Greens, 176–77
Ground-level gardens
    disadvantages of, 1
    making accessible, 2–5
Growing season, extending, 27
Hands, protecting, 127
Hanging baskets, 72–78
    accessibility of, 72–73
    fertilizing, 78
    filling, 76–77
    liners for, 77
    maintaining, 78
    hangers for, 74–75
    plants for, 73–74, 206–8, 209–10
    types of, 74
    wall-mounting of, 75–76
    watering, 77
Hard water, 63
Harvesting crops, 162–63
Heirloom plants, 280
Herbs
    appropriate for child gardeners, 274–76
    for hanging baskets, 73
    for window boxes, 81
    sources of, 192
    varieties of, 192–93
Hoes, 135–36, 147–48
Hoses, 152–53. See also Watering
Hyacinths, 67–68
Indoor gardens, 283–85
Insecticides, commercial, 235–36
Insects
    beneficial, 231–32
    controlling without pesticides, 236–39
    harmful, 234
    homemade controls for, 234–35
Intensive planting, 25
Interplanting, 25, 54
Jostaberries, 219, 220
Kale, 176
Lamb's ears, 276
Leaching, 63
Leaning posts, 31
Lettuce, 175–76
Lincoln Canopy system, 112–13

Long-reach grabbers, 163–64
Marchand system, 113
Marigolds, 272–73
Melons, 101–102, 185–86
Metal containers, 43
Mints, 275–76
Mixed planting. See Companion planting; Interplanting
Moisture crystals, 58, 152
Moonflowers, 274
Mulches
    benefits of, 149
    commercial, 150–51
    for shrubs and trees, 70
    organic, 150
Multi-dibble, 24, 138
Narcissus, 67–68
Nasturtiums, 273
Natural fiber containers, 46
Nectarine trees, 223, 225, 227
Nematodes, and insect control, 234
Nuts, harvesting, 163
Okra, 187–88
Onions, 186–87, 263
Organic gardening, 230
Osmosis, 63
Pac choi, 176
Palmetter Verrier, 111
Paths and ramps, 2–5
    handrails for, 3
    slope of, 2
    surface materials of, 3–4
    width of, 2
Peach trees, 223, 225
Peanuts, 266
Pear trees, 224
Peas
    cages for, 100
    fences for, 96
    height of, 95
    short supports for, 100
    soil inoculant for, 179
    teepees for, 96–97
    towers for, 99
    trellises for, 97–98
    varieties of, 178–79, 180
Peat moss, 63
Peppers, hot, 181–82
Peppers, sweet, 181, 263, 267
Perennials

care of, 197
growing in raised beds, 28
longevity of, 196
Perlite, 56
Pesticides
potential effects of, on health, 230
pH level, of soil, 20, 21
Pick-up grabs, 157–58
Pillow pack, 45
Plant diseases, 242–45
Plant supports, 117–18
Planter boxes
choosing plants for, 35
constructing, 30–31
definition of, 29–36
designs of, 32–34
determining size of, 29–30
drainage of, 34
maintaining, 35–36
soil for, 34–35
trellises for, 114–16
Planting bag, 45
Planting boards, 24, 136, 141–42
Plastic containers, 42
Plum trees, 225
Poisonous plants, 251–53
Pole-and-post gardens, 48
Poles, 97
Popcorn, 266–67, 268–69
Potatoes. *See also* Sweet potatoes
and pest control, 238
colors of, 268
growing in containers, 44–45
in ground-level beds, 6–7
preferred soil for, 20
varieties of, 190
Pots, flower, *See* Container gardens
Pressure-treated wood, 13–14
Pruning
shrubs and trees, 71
tools for, 155–58
Pulleys, 72, 154
Pumpkins, 191, 262, 264–65, 266, 279
Pyrethrum, 235
Raccoons, 240, 241
Radishes, 267
Railing planters. *See* Window boxes
Railroad ties, 12
Raised beds, 7–29
advantages of, 8–9

choosing plants for, 22
definition of, 8
determining size of, 10–12
examples of, 15, 16
excavating, 18–19
fertilizing, 27
for children, 255
foundations for, 17
framing, 21
growing perennials in, 28
kits for, 17–18
maintaining, 27
materials for, 12–18
siting, 9–10
soil for, 20–22
trellises for, 114–16
watering, 10, 27
when to plant, 23
wide-row planting of, 23
Rakes, 135
Ramps. *See* Paths and ramps
Raspberries, 215–16
Reach, measuring, 11
Roots, crowded, 61, 71
Rotenone, 235
Row covers, 234
Scissors, 155
Scoon, 139
Seats, for gardening, 123–24
Seed dispensers, 139–40
Seed sowers, 140–41
Seed trencher, 136–37
Seeding helpers, 141
Seeds
covering, 143–44
heirloom, 280
pelleted, 142
protecting from pests, 240
seed tapes, 143, 176, 187
sources of, 170, 287–88
sowing, 24–25, 139–43
starting, 170–71
toxic, 253
Self-watering containers, 46
Sensory gardens, 259–60
Shears, 156–57
Shelves, for container gardens, 47–48
Shovels, 131
Shrubs
attractive to birds, 232–33

containers for, 53–54
fertilizing, 70
growing in containers, 68–69
pruning, 71
varieties of, for containers, 211–14
watering, 69–70
winter care of, 71
Slugs, 237–38
Snails, 23738
Soil
additives, 152
diseases, 6
for container gardens, 56–58
for planter boxes, 34–35
for raised beds, 21–22
pH level of, 20, 21
"recipes" for, 57
testing, 20–21
Soil depths, 22–23
Southern exposure, 75
Sowing seeds, 24–25
Spades, 131
Specialty gardens, 277–78
Spray wands, 153–54
Squash, 101–102, 188–90, 238, 266
Stone, for raised beds, 15–16
Stone sinks, 44
Strawberries, 217, 269–70
Strawberry towers, 99
Sunflowers, 273
Sunlight, plants' needs for, 10, 39
Sweet potatoes, 190–91
Table gardens, 256–57
Tarps, 161–62
Teepees, 96–97, 257–58
Terra cotta, 41
Terrariums, 284
Theme gardens, 277–78
Thinning plants, 25, 144–45
Three Sisters, 25
Tiered gardens, 48
Tillers, 133–35, 148
Tires, 44
Toads, 236
Tomatoes, 91–95, 171–74
alternative methods for supporting, 95
and pest control, 238
cages for, 92
determinate, 91–92, 172
disease resistant, 242

for containers, 172–74
husk, 267
indeterminate, 91–92, 172
staking, 92–93
towers for, 94
trellises for, 94–95
tying up, 93–94
very large, 264
Tools, gardening
adapting handles of, 126–27
aids for holding, 127–28
bulb planters, 145–46
caring for, 122–23
children's 129–30, 260–61
considerations in choosing, 119–20
dibbles, 137–39
for digging holes, 139
for harvesting, 162–63
for pruning, 155–58
for thinning, 144–45
for weeding, 147–49
for use in ground-level beds, 7
forks, 132
hand tools, 124–26, 128–29
hoes, 135–36, 147–48
homemade, 121, 129, 158
long-reach grabbers, 163–64
miscellaneous digging tools, 132–33
pick-up grabs, 157–58
rakes, 135
seed dispensers, 139
seed sowers, 140–41
seeding helpers, 141
sources of, 121, 289–90
spades, 131
storing, 122
support handles for, 130–31
tillers, 133–35
Topiaries, 284
Towers, 99
Toxic plants, 251–53
Transplants, setting out, 145
Trees. See also Fruit trees
attractive to birds, 232–33
fertilizing, 70
growing in containers, 53–54, 68–69
pruning, 71
varieties of, for containers, 211–14
watering, 69–70
winter care of, 71

Trees, fruit. *See* Fruit trees
Trellised plants. *See* Vertical gardening
Trellises
    for beans, cucumbers, peas, 97–98
    for container gardens, 116
    for flowering vines, 106
    for raised beds and planter boxes, 114–16
    for squash and melons, 102
    for tomatoes, 94
Trowels. *See* Tools, gardening
Turnips, 191
Vegetables. *See also* specific types of vegetables
    for container gardens, 49–52
    for hanging baskets, 73
    for raised beds, 22
    for vertical gardens, 91–101
    for window boxes, 81
    growing from kitchen foods, 284
    interplanting of, 26
    miniature, 262
    planting for color, 267
    succession planting of, 26
    unusual, 265–66
    very large, 263–64
Vermiculite, 56
Vertical Gardening, 87–118
    accessibility issues, 89–90
    advantages of, 87–88, 89
    disadvantages of, 89
    flowering and ornamental vines for, 102–7
    methods of, 88
    plans for, 90–91
    vegetables for, 91–101
Vines, flowering and ornamental
    annual, 102, 103–4
    choosing, 103
    perennial, 102, 104–6
    supports for, 106–7
    training and tying, 107
Walkers, 161
Wall-gardens, 116–17
Watermelons, 263–64, 265
Watering
    container gardens, 39–40, 62–64
    hanging baskets, 77
    methods of, 151–55
    planter boxes, 30
    plants' need for, 151–55
    raised beds, 27
    right and wrong ways of, 244

    window boxes, 83–84
    shrubs and trees, 69–70
Watering cans, 154–55
Weeding, tools for, 146–49
Wheelbarrows and carts, 158–60, 161
Wheelchair cuffs, 127
Wheelchairs, gardening from, 160
Wicker baskets, 44
Wide-row planting, 23
Window boxes, 78–84
    accessibility of, 79
    anchoring, 80
    fertilizing, 84
    filling, 83
    liners for, 80
    mixed plantings in, 82
    plants for, 81–82, 208–9
    railing (deck) planters, 81
    types of, 79–80
    watering, 83–84
Winds, prevailing, 90
Winter, preparing for, 27, 29, 71
Wood, for raised beds, 12–15
Wood preservative, non-toxic, 14
Woodchucks, 241
Wooden containers, 42–43
Worm composting, 166
Zinnias, 273

Printed in the United States
129589LV00001B/3/A